Praise for *Inside-Out Healing*

*"Richard Moss is one of the greatest teachers of our time.
He is deep, profound, and he practices what he preaches. If you
follow the techniques presented in his enlightening work, you will
be certain to find joy and vitality in the present moment."*

— **Debbie Ford,** the *New York Times* best-selling
co-author of *The Shadow Effect*

*"Those of us in the fields of body-mind transformation and spiritual
development look forward with great anticipation to a new work by
Richard Moss. Now, with* **Inside-Out Healing: Transforming Your
Life Through the Power of Presence,** *Dr. Moss has given us not
only an inspiring guide to the journey, but also a detailed navigation
system that serves as a virtual GPS to the inner world."*

— **Gay Hendricks, Ph.D.,** the *New York Times* best-selling
author of *Five Wishes* and *The Big Leap*

*"Simply put, Richard Moss is one of the most important
spiritual leaders in the world today. Why? I believe it's because
he teaches essential lessons in ways that are both accessible and
deeply transformative. He's the real thing, and I highly recommend
that you open your mind and heart to what he has to offer."*

— **James F. Twyman,** Peace Troubadour and the *New York Times*
best-selling author of *The Barn Dance*

*"Richard Moss provides a practical approach to living a fuller,
more meaningful life that is both simple and profound. He is a
living example of what he writes, and the deep insights he shares
in this wonderful book make it easy to put words into action in our
own lives.* **Inside-Out Healing** *is just what the doctor ordered!"*

— **Neale Donald Walsch,** the *New York Times* best-selling author
of *Conversations with God* and *The Mother of Invention*

Inside-Out
HEALING

Inside-Out
HEALING

Transforming Your Life
Through the Power
of Presence

Richard Moss

HAY HOUSE, INC.
Carlsbad, California • New York City
London • Sydney • Johannesburg
Vancouver • Hong Kong • New Delhi

Published and distributed in the United States by: Hay House, Inc.: www .hayhouse.com • *Published and distributed in Australia by:* Hay House Australia Pty. Ltd.: www.hayhouse.com.au • *Published and distributed in the United Kingdom by:* Hay House UK, Ltd.: www.hayhouse.co.uk • *Published and distributed in the Republic of South Africa by:* Hay House SA (Pty), Ltd.: www .hayhouse.co.za • *Distributed in Canada by:* Raincoast: www.raincoast.com • *Published in India by:* Hay House Publishers India: www.hayhouse.co.in

Editorial supervision: Jill Kramer • *Project editor:* Lisa Mitchell
Design: Nick C. Welch • *Interior illustrations:* © Richard Moss Seminars

The Mandala of Being is a registered trademark of Richard Moss Seminars.

Library of Congress Cataloging-in-Publication Data

Moss, Richard M
   Inside-out healing : transforming your life through the power of presence / Richard Moss.
      p. cm.
   ISBN 978-1-4019-2758-5 (tradepaper : alk. paper) 1. Mental healing. 2. Awareness. 3. Self-actualization (Psychology) 4. Mandala. I. Title.
   RZ400.M67 2011
   615.8'51--dc22

                                    2010026588

Tradepaper ISBN: 978-1-4019-2758-5
Digital ISBN: 978-1-4019-3083-7

14 13 12 11   5 4 3 2
1st edition, February 2011
2nd edition, July 2011

Printed in the United States of America

Dedicated to William Brugh Joy,
1939–2009

CONTENTS

FOREWORD

It is a great honor and pleasure to write this Foreword to Richard Moss's new book. *Inside-Out Healing: Transforming Your Life Through the Power of Presence* presents powerful principles, tools, and practices for staying in the present, increasing self-awareness, connecting more fully with ourselves, and transforming self-limiting patterns of thought and behavior.

As a developer, author, practitioner, and trainer in the field of NLP (Neuro-Linguistic Programming) for 35 years, I have spent my career exploring and working with techniques and methods for helping people communicate better, solve problems, and perform with both greater flexibility and excellence. NLP is about becoming aware of the structure of our thoughts, beliefs, and mental models of the world (our "neurolinguistic programs") and developing more choices to respond creatively and effectively to life's opportunities *and* challenges. My own focus in NLP has been on helping people align themselves with their deepest identity and essence.

It was this search that led me to Richard's work, which I have found to be innovative, practical, and profoundly transforming. Richard is a masterful teacher, healer, and coach, who is deeply committed to helping people be more fully themselves.

In *Inside-Out Healing*, Richard explores the "power of presence" in our lives. Our quality of presence is frequently the "difference that makes the difference" in our ability to enjoy life, heal emotional wounds, experience intimacy, and support the growth and transformation of others. Presence is associated with feelings of aliveness, connection, creativity, satisfaction, and flow. When we are not present and are disconnected from ourselves and others, we can feel empty, out of control, distant, and unavailable.

Richard likes to point out that "the distance between ourselves and others is the same as the distance between ourselves and ourselves." This implies that our relationships to others and the world around us are a mirror for our relationship with ourselves. The more we are connected to ourselves, the more deeply we are connected to others and the external world. Our relationship with ourselves, however, is frequently limited by feelings that we cannot meet, accept, hold, and welcome. This is a key area addressed by this book.

Central to Richard's approach is our capacity for awareness. True choice and lasting change become possible through the expansion of awareness. Awareness is naturally transformative in that, as Richard points out, "Whatever you can be aware of, there is something within you—beyond the object of awareness—that is being aware." In Richard's words, "We are more than anything we can say, feel, or think about ourselves." Thus, awareness helps free us from the tyranny of our own thoughts and "programming."

At the core of his practice for expanding awareness is Richard's elegant Mandala of Being, a model and tool to help individuals identify and release limiting thoughts and beliefs and connect more fully with the deeper essence of their beings. According to the Mandala, we constantly leave the present into limiting beliefs or "stories" about the past, the future, ourselves, and others. These stories keep us from experiencing and living our full potential, creating a distorted or impoverished map of the world. As Richard points out, these stories generally cover up difficult feelings that we don't know how to be with.

Working with the Mandala of Being enables us to identify where we have gone; to recognize, welcome, and hold the feelings beneath our "stories"; and to return to the present and be with whatever feeling is there from a deeper place that is centered and grounded in our bodies. The Mandala is perhaps the best and purest example of coaching at the level of beliefs and identity that I have experienced. In my view, it is a tool that every coach and therapist should be using as a key part of his or her practice.

Inside-Out Healing is well structured, well written, and practical. Richard's writing style is lucid, direct, and personal. Throughout the book, Richard provides practical examples and exercises demonstrating how principles of awareness and presence may be applied to support change in oneself and others, creating a solid bridge between knowing and doing. He illustrates his methods and techniques with clear transcripts of coaching sessions and concrete and touching case examples.

Inside-Out Healing will help you:

- Become more available and fully connected with yourself and others

- Improve both personal and professional relationships

- Be able to handle difficult situations with more elegance and ease

- Increase energy, creativity, productivity, and flow

- Build a solid foundation for healing in all areas of your life

- Expand your capacity for genuine empathy and compassion

- Experience more richness, gratitude, and fullness in your life and relationships

Inside-Out Healing is a fabulous book; a masterpiece of simplicity, authenticity, and wisdom; the fruit of a life lived in service of helping people be who they truly are. I have had the opportunity to know Richard for a number of years, and it is clear that he teaches what he lives. His work is the result of both a richly lived life and a deep caring about others.

— **Robert B. Dilts**
Santa Cruz, California

INTRODUCTION

If you or a loved one is facing a health challenge, relation-ship crisis, or any situation in which you experience emotional suffering, this book will help you understand and remedy what you unconsciously do that makes your situation more difficult. It will teach you the way to realize a timeless inner power and be restored to a sense of deeper trust in yourself. It will show you how to access the universal energy that immediately enlivens you whenever you are completely present.

As lifesaving as modern medicine can sometimes be, it does not address the true root of suffering. In many ways neither does modern psychology, because it starts from the premise that the separate self, the ego—with all of its fears and hopes—is who you really are. Where this book starts is with the extraordinary power of awareness to take you beyond ego and into presence.

More than any physical condition or outer circumstance, your well-being is ultimately determined by how present and aware you are as opposed to caught up in what your ego is constantly telling you about yourself and life. Your deeper suffering comes less from the condition of your body and more from what your ego tells you about your condition. It is the same when it comes to relationship problems: it is generally less what the other person actually does and more what you are telling yourself about his or her behavior that creates your greater unhappiness.

When you make the present moment the touchstone of your life, you will have discovered the secret of inside-out healing. In the Now you gain distance from your ego. You realize that when your ego is controlling your mind—a mode of consciousness I refer to as *egoic* mind—that is what creates most of your unhappy emotions. In the Now you awaken to an innate sense of wholeness that is independent of your circumstances.

This truth was recently demonstrated to me once again by an old friend. Although he knows that statistically he has perhaps a 1 or 2 percent chance of recovery from a rare, aggressive cancer, he has so opened himself to living in the present moment that even while in the midst of intensive chemotherapy, he is luminous with an inner light and feels, in his own words, "fabulous." My friend has chosen from the depths of his being to dive into every sensation of the chemo process, to live each moment as it is. There isn't a trace in his attitude of being a victim, and he truly means it when he says that he hasn't really felt sick despite the chemo and the cancer. Rather, for him, living deeply in what are likely to be his final days is the capstone of his life. It is as if he's holding life in his left hand and death in his right hand and there is no contradiction, no *one or the other.* There is just a state of wonderment.

This potential to embrace life so completely, even in extreme circumstances, resides in all of us. Health is not the mere absence of illness; it is the presence of something else, something indescribable that arises from within. The result of tasting this inner nectar, no matter what your situation, is to know yourself more completely and feel grateful for the life you have.

If you are facing a health crisis or any situation where your own thoughts are exacerbating your emotional suffering, you are ripe for a journey of self-discovery and awakening. Why not? Staying with your usual attitudes and behaviors will probably continue to keep you in a recurring cycle of unhappiness and stress. Truly, there is little to lose and much to gain by opening to a new possibility within you. As you do so, the richest experiences of your life can open before you.

The Most Essential Healing

Normally when we read the word *healing,* we first think of physical illness. As I wrote this book, I frequently had in mind a reader who would want to learn how to maximize the potential for his or her body to heal itself by learning to access the deeper life force that arises when one is fully present. But healing is also more than of the body; it is of the mind and of the emotions perhaps most of all.

My teaching work takes me all over the world, and for every person who is suffering from physical illness, there are many more who are suffering emotionally. Usually this is in relation to their spouses, their children, or their work. Therefore, I use examples of people dealing with physical illness as well as some whose suffering is primarily emotional.

All suffering, even physical suffering, has a mental component. Inside-out healing is about learning to free yourself of that mental component: the emotional unhappiness created by your own thinking. But this book is far more than just another text about positive thinking or how to manifest the life you want through affirmations. In fact, it isn't about positive thinking or affirmations at all; it's about presence, about learning how to live in the Now, where egoic thinking is witnessed and gives way to awareness. In other words, it's about wisdom. Inside-out healing is for everyone because it's ultimately about your relationship to yourself moment by moment.

What your illness is, why you are ill, or what you need to do to improve a troubled relationship is less important than your relationship to yourself in each moment. Change your relationship to yourself and everything else changes. As Einstein observed, you cannot solve a problem at the same level of consciousness in which the problem was created.

If suffering is the problem and that suffering primarily comes from your thinking, then you are not going to relieve your pain or solve other problems (such as fear or unhappiness) if you remain at your current level of thinking. It doesn't matter that you decide to think positively; you will keep swinging like a pendulum to the negative thoughts sooner or later.

The issue is not what you think is wrong with you or someone else; you are going to have to shift levels, to move from thinking to awareness of your thinking. This is the fundamental relationship:

the relationship of your aware self to your own thoughts, emotions, and feelings.

I have lived through challenging times myself, and I know how distressing they can be. But I know that most of my suffering dissolves when I come home to my aware self in the present moment. From this centered place, the kinds of stories the mind creates that frighten you and make you a victim cease to have power. Patterns of suffering that are self-generated become apparent, and you feel empowered to make healthy changes. With this shift of consciousness, a sense of well-being and gratitude for the life you have arises spontaneously.

I know that much is written about living in the Now, but there is frustratingly little about how to actually arrive there: how to become and remain fully present. In this book, you will be given an effective practice and a map of real value in this journey into presence. With this guidance, you will be able to experience for yourself the fullness of the present moment and how to find that place more and more consistently. You will understand where you go when you are not in the Now and what leads you away. As you learn to apply the insights and tools you will find in these pages, you may experience, as many others have, that you become almost a new person.

From Physician to Teacher

I have been trained as a physician, grounded in empirical science, and I have never lost my respect for the scientific approach. Therefore, I do not lightly make a claim for the potential of emotional and physical healing that can come about through learning to be fully present for your life. I make it based on nearly 35 years of working with tens of thousands of people—no longer in a medical office, but in retreat-like seminars that are experiential adventures in learning to come fully alive in the Now and developing the skills to continue living with presence.

My journey from traditional doctor working in emergency and hospital medicine to scientist of the mind and heart was initiated on my 30th birthday with an experience that, for want of any better word, I will call an *awakening*. For no reason I can explain, I was brought to a state of pure being, of being love, of being at one. In the weeks and months that followed, I moved between states of exceptional bliss and the darkest terror. Very gradually I taught myself how to make a space in myself for these extremes, and I learned to stay present no matter what. Little did I know that this would be the core of the work that would occupy the rest of my life.

That period changed me like a shift in the earth's tectonic plates. It opened inner doors to new levels of myself and new capabilities. Suddenly I could feel the emotions of those around me with exceptional clarity, and I could very nearly know what they were thinking in many moments. I could empathize deeply with a person's suffering in a way that made him or her feel seen and understood. I could also sense energy with my hands and softly share energy through my hands that would often take away someone's physical pain.

I felt a current of presence flowing through me and could sense how it changed with my thoughts: essentially, it grew stronger or weaker as I became more or less present. This presence influenced others by calming them and helping them become open and receptive. And as they became inducted into this presence, it became stronger in me. Because of this phenomenon, I called my first book, written in 1979, *The I That Is We*.

Shortly before this awakening, as if I somehow intuitively sensed a big change coming, I had taken an indefinite leave of absence from practicing medicine. As it turned out, I never went back. In the months that followed, I just stayed home, read spiritual classics (which suddenly I had a new appetite for), and took long walks. But very quickly a few of my old patients sought me out, and I began to meet with them in my home. We would sit together in silence, holding hands sometimes for as long as half an hour. Then we would talk. One day, a psychologist who was the therapist of one of these patients called me and said that her client had made tremendous progress and attributed it to her time with me. When she asked me what I was doing, I answered, "Just being present." The psychologist asked if I would lead a workshop about my approach for her and some of her colleagues. And so my new career began without my even trying to make it happen.

Today, I think of myself as a teacher of the soul who has a background in medicine but knows that consciousness—or more precisely, the state of awareness when you are in the Now—is the greatest of all human powers. I know that when you really understand how you lose your connection to presence and can return yourself to the Now, you will be able to be restored to well-being as predictably as a good education can teach you to master mathematics, chemistry, or physics. I know that you can more reliably bring yourself to inner peace with the work you will learn in this book than you can through taking a pill, although I'm not adverse to scientific medical achievement and the use of medications—not at all. I just know that the power of your awareness is greater still.

The retreats I lead have been and continue to be a kind of laboratory for discovering the best tools and practices for enabling people to become fully present, deeply alive, and capable of rich intimacy and love. I haven't taught this path because I had mastered it and knew it was good for others. I taught it as much for myself as for my students or clients. I needed to learn as I went along, taking one step at a time. Like any scientist, I am still learning and always will be.

What I am learning isn't about acquiring more information or having more experiences; it's about discovering the life and world that opens to you moment by moment when you are truly in the here-and-now. It's about going deeper into yourself—deeper into your body, your feelings, your suffering, your joy, and your behavior. It's about becoming more intimate with yourself, with life, and with others, moment by moment. It's about helping others live this path.

I have been teaching and writing about this subject for a long time. This book is the fruit of the last three years that I have had in particular the opportunity to refine my teaching about how to free the heart from negative emotions and master difficult feelings. All of the healing and change I have seen in thousands of people occurs when they start to really learn to be present for the kinds of feelings that are most threatening to their egos.

The Power of Presence

Presence is the greatest power any of us have. As we learn to relax into the present moment, body and soul respond. We spontaneously tap into our own intuitive wisdom and gain insight that can resolve even old and seemingly intractable emotional wounds.

Through the teaching and the exercises in this book, you will experience for yourself the difference between your natural state of presence and the stressful reality created by your thinking. This understanding—the difference between the thinking that originates in your ego and who you really are when you're truly present to life as it is—is crucial.

Medicine deals with the body, but this book deals with your consciousness. And your consciousness is your strongest means of healing your body *and* soul. When your mind and body are aligned in the present moment, you know yourself to be whole and often feel good regardless of what is going on with your body. When you learn to be present, you also open the door to an infinite source of love, which blesses you and even helps bring out the best in everyone around you.

Ultimately, you are the creator of your reality. This doesn't mean that you've caused your own illness or are solely responsible for a painful relationship; it means that moment by moment, by choosing to be fully present, you free yourself from mind-made unhappiness.

I wrote this book because I feel kinship with every person who suffers and because I know that so much human misery is unnecessary and can be relieved with the proper understanding and tools. I also wrote it because I'm concerned, as most of us are, for the future of humankind. We are so populous that the mistakes each of us makes due to ignorance of our egoic mind become amplified in ways that are so much more destructive than they were when there were fewer of us and our technologies weren't so powerful.

The Two Basic Mistakes

What are those mistakes? The first is that we tend to identify with our own thoughts, and this often creates a destructive emotional reality. Unquestioningly believing our own thoughts—or those instilled in us by family and society—frequently puts us into conflict within ourselves, with each other, and with life itself. The second basic mistake is that we are afraid of so many of our feelings, and in fleeing these feelings our egos close off much of our inner life and the wellspring for true health.

One of the key insights in this book concerns learning to differentiate emotions from feelings. Emotions are created by your thoughts, particularly unquestioned judgments about yourself or others. In contrast, feelings are an essential and intelligent way of knowing that connects you to yourself, others, and your environment in simple and, at times, profound ways.

For your ego, the emotions created by your thoughts always seem legitimate, a genuine part of your identity; but for your body, the anger, resentment, fearfulness, self-importance, or self-diminishment that your thoughts create are actually chemical poisons. The brain releases neuropeptides into your bloodstream; and your muscles tighten, your blood pressure elevates, cortisol is secreted by your adrenal glands, and insulin resistance soon follows. The simple word for this is *stress*—the kind of stress that leads to heart disease, diabetes, strokes, and probably some cancers, not to mention unhappiness.

The irony is that while the ego legitimizes emotions that can be very destructive, like resentment and hatred, it often won't let you rest in expansive feelings, like joy or love, and it instantly flees any threatening feelings, such as powerlessness. Yet learning to be open to the highest and lowest of feelings will never harm you the way destructive emotions can. Rather, making space for these feelings can bring you to a healthier relationship with what may seem like intractable situations (lifelong family conflicts, for example). It can also resolve nagging doubts as to your own worthiness. It's wise to be suspicious of your emotions and learn to free yourself from the poisonous ones, while at the same time learning to trust and make space for even the darkest of your feelings.

This book will teach you how to return to the present moment and be enlivened from a universal source. It will show you how to make better decisions from a place of inner harmony and trust. It will guide you to listen to your own intuitive wisdom and find true well-being, or at least centeredness and peace even in times of real difficulty. It will support you in honoring your genuine needs.

Sooner or later, all of us face death. For this reason, it is important to appreciate how awareness can help you in the dying process. This means asking what you really know or don't know about death. Ultimately, each of us has the opportunity to request how we want to be present in our dying process and the kind of death we would like. We may not get our wish, but it's worthwhile to state our preference and especially to be able to free ourselves from beliefs about death that weaken our capacity to be present at the end of our lives.

Embracing Change

This book is about individual healing by opening your heart to the love that is always present in the Now. It is about a way that is universal, that can be practiced by anyone who wants to become more conscious in every domain of life. All of us, the family of humankind, stand on the brink of tremendous change. We are reaching the limits of Earth's ecosystems to support life, even human life. What is being asked of us is a profound revisioning of human identity. Such revisioning is a process that happens individually, one person at a time, from the inside out. Only as you become more conscious can you also be a force that supports the collective transformation of how we organize ourselves as local communities, nations, and ultimately as a planetary society.

You may not be reading this book because you see yourself as part of a global awakening. You are probably and rightfully more concerned with what you can do to restore your own health or to heal areas of personal suffering. But if you use the methods offered to you in this book, you will be on a path of awakening; and whether you intend it or not, your presence will be supporting a higher potential for all of us.

I have lived long enough to know without any doubt that the greatest and most fulfilling adventure in life is that of becoming more conscious and building loving relationships. The only truly essential requirement is willingness. Are you willing to change yourself? Whether you're motivated by illness, unhappiness, or the quest to taste life as completely as you can, the keys are here.

You will find nothing in this book that requires the suspension of your good judgment or asks you to believe in anything other than your own power to learn about yourself. Faith in your potential to change doesn't require you to blindly believe in anything. It only asks your willingness to use the tools that you find here. They can without a doubt help you free yourself from unnecessary suffering and make you a wiser, happier person.

Connection to your true self is a state of being that is contagious. An awake, loving person creates a field of consciousness in which other people feel safe and become more loving. A frightened or angry person also creates a field, but it's one that engenders division and fear.

The simple truth is that few of us have any idea just how well we can feel and just how healthy we can be if we start to unify ourselves from within by learning to live more in the Now. This book will show you how to make your mind stronger so that the roots of your awareness will not be so easily torn from the present, and you will not fall so readily into destructive or limiting thoughts. It will teach you to trust your feelings and let them lead you to a greater capacity to love yourself and life. It puts the power in your own hands.

As you become more present, you will not only become more truly healthy, but you will also be serving the transformation of the world around you. Presence is contagious, and it is an epidemic we need.

— **Richard Moss**
Ojai, California

Author's Note: The personal examples and case histories in this book are all true. However, to protect the identities and privacy of the individuals, all of the names have been changed and certain circumstances have been modified or fictionalized.

PART I

FOUNDATIONAL UNDERSTANDINGS

As you read these first three chapters, you will learn where it is essential to focus your emphasis and attention in order to begin healing yourself from the inside out.

Sharing the benefit of my experience from working for many years with thousands of people, I will help you overcome the two basic challenges that I have recognized as most crucial to address on any healing journey.

You will see how you have been hurting yourself unnecessarily because your ego has driven your way of thinking, and you will understand what your ego really is. You will also discover that you have much more power than you realize to reduce the amount of physical and emotional suffering you experience—starting today.

Every instant of being fully present in the moment is an instant of healing. The body actually reorganizes itself in greater or lesser degrees of wholeness according to how present you are. I'll guide you in turning your attention away from your thoughts and directly into the present moment, where you'll join a limitless field of intelligence and love that is the greatest healing resource of all.

CHAPTER ONE

AWAKENING
TO THE POWER OF
PRESENT-MOMENT
AWARENESS

In this journey we are embarking on together, you hold enormous power to determine your well-being no matter what your circumstances may be. Awakening to this power and the transformation it can bring about in your life can be the greatest adventure of all. The key rests in whether you can be present with each moment of your experience or whether you're caught up in what your mind is telling you about your experience.

The deeper suffering in life is usually less a result of what is actually happening than it is a consequence of all that you tell yourself about what is happening. It is less about being sick than it is about your thoughts about being sick, for instance. It is less about your partner leaving you than it is about what you tell yourself about that separation.

It's your identification with thoughts about what you *believe* you are losing—about how life should be, what's going to happen next, whether you will have enough money, what your family needs from you, and so on—that is the real source of most unhappiness. Once you learn to step back from these thoughts and into the present moment, which is what this book is all about, things are rarely as bad as they seem. You can begin to open into wonderment and enjoy inner peace.

Of course, to have such anxious thoughts at challenging times is completely natural. But what most people don't realize is that these distressing thoughts can only be generated by the mind when awareness is not resting fully in the present moment. As we will discuss in the next chapter, the way your mind carries you away from the present moment is the activity of your ego, and if that were all that you are, there would be nothing more to do than to suffer its effects. But far more than an ego, you are an aware being—that is, you become an aware being, able to function free of the ego's limited consciousness, as soon as you are fully present.

Present-moment awareness is the greatest of all human powers and, so far, one of the least understood or consciously exercised. It is much more essential even than thinking, because it's only through this awareness that you can be conscious of your thoughts and how they limit and often hurt you.

To have an immediate taste of this awareness, stop for a moment and ask yourself, "Who or what is thinking about what I'm reading now?" If you say "Me" or "I am" in answer to that question, then who or what is aware of that I or Me that you are referring to?

The power of present-moment awareness (or, for the sake of simplicity, *presence*) means that you can be aware of your own thinking and not merely identify with it. You can feel your feelings and not define yourself because of them. Everything that you are aware of—all of your plans and dreams, your hopes and fears, your beliefs about yourself or anything else—implies the existence of something possessing that awareness but not automatically caught up in it. Said another way, there is a dimension of you that you access as soon as you are in the Now, which sets you free from mind-made suffering and allows you to create a space big enough for all of your feelings.

No one knows how it is that we human beings have come to be capable of self-awareness. Some scientists argue that awareness is a phenomenon created by the brain. Others believe the brain is a kind of profound television set that can tune in to and organize virtually infinite streams of consciousness from a universal field of intelligence. I suspect that both theories have some truth, but I am content to honor that the source or cause of awareness, and awareness itself, is a sublime mystery. In this I am entirely pragmatic: it isn't necessary to understand the source of awareness; the important thing is appreciating its power and how to use it.

Who Are You Really?

In my talks and retreats, I often ask a series of questions to help people grasp the difference between what we believe or think and what we are aware of. For example: We each have either a male or female body, but is the actual *awareness* of being male or female itself male or female? What's your guess? Obviously, the experience of being a man or a woman is very different both for biological and sociological reasons. But if all we do is argue from the position of our differences, we miss the deeper foundation of awareness that unites us at a level even more essential than our gender. Indeed, it is when we are the most present that there is the greatest energy flowing between us.

Let's take this a step further: Suppose you are told you are overweight, and your ego attacks you with judgments that you are a fat person. Is the *awareness* that you are judging yourself as fat, itself fat? Again, what is your intuitive knowing about this question? Can you see that the identity of being fat is a far more punishing state than awareness of yourself as overweight? In my observations of people who want to lead healthier lives, self-attack is much more detrimental than the state they attack themselves about. Self-attack results in a depressive stance in life that paralyzes positive action.

Finally, let's look at what you believe about time. When it comes to your memories, you are aware of something from your past, but is that *awareness* in the past? Likewise, you are always conjuring up thoughts about the future, but is the awareness of those future thoughts, itself, in the future?

When I'm posing these questions, I let people answer them for themselves. But sometimes something happens, perhaps only for a moment: they suddenly sense a space, a kind of emptiness or openness, something distinct from how they usually think about and experience themselves. This is a taste of presence.

Being aware of anything implies a mysterious distance from what you are aware of. And this distance means that there is actually a potential for a relationship with whatever you are aware of: a relationship with your thoughts, a relationship with your memories, a relationship with your emotions and feelings.

Most people are used by their thoughts, made victims by their own beliefs. They let themselves be defined by, and often victimized by, their emotions and feelings. But what you will learn in the following chapters is that you are never a victim: considering yourself as one is never more than a thought, a belief. Even when you feel like a victim, you will discover that as soon as you bring yourself into the present moment, your thinking will stop, and very quickly that feeling will be gone. You will learn to set yourself free through the power of presence.

When you step into present-moment awareness, you are always more than anything you are aware of. You are not *more* in the sense of better or superior; you are more because you can choose your relationship to your thoughts and feelings. You can choose to listen to your thoughts or not. You can watch what happens when you believe something and notice how it makes you feel, be it angry, afraid, loved, or safe. You don't have to automatically believe what you think, whether it's about yourself, your life, your illness, or anyone or anything else whatsoever, especially if it makes you unhappy or causes you to bring unhappiness to others. You can be *aware* of these thoughts. You can question them and challenge them. You can be gentle with yourself no matter what you hear yourself thinking. You can begin to find your own path to what is true and important for you.

We human beings no longer believe that the world is flat or the sun orbits the earth. You no longer need to believe ideas about yourself that come from your childhood or from an educational process that filled you with other people's ideas, but did not teach you how to think. You are an individual with the divine gift of awareness who is finding his or her way to truth. Awareness is your path to truth, to deeper insight into yourself—it is your path to love.

This awareness is the *being* in "human being" and makes possible a ceaseless relationship to all and anything you can ever know or name, yet you cannot locate awareness itself in space or time. You are not merely your body, nor are you just your thoughts or your feelings. Your authentic self is the indescribable being, which is aware of all of that. This is what makes it possible for you to consciously turn your attention toward any aspect of your experience in a fresh way at any given moment, and in so doing be capable of constantly renewing yourself. Whenever you do so, you will discover that the emotional suffering created by what you're telling yourself will diminish, and a richer feeling of connectedness will take its place.

Emotional Pollution

We are all subject to aging, genetic tendencies, environmental pollution, economic and social disruptions, and the like, which we have little power to control. Yet, moment by moment, our bodies are also responding to the additional stress of the emotional pollution created by our thinking minds.

Every thought generates some corresponding sensation in the body because body and mind are a continuum. Happy thoughts give you bursts of feeling good. But worry about the future or regrets or guilt about the past are experienced physically in the same way as your being threatened by a predator. The same fight-or-flight hormones are released. Cortisol and other stress hormones flood you, affecting your immune system, your heart, your brain . . . every cell in your body. And thoughts of this kind are not occasional: most people have hundreds and even thousands of thoughts each day that inject fear, anger, guilt, or insecurity in a steady barrage of mind-made stress.

Being physically sick in itself does not engender a sense of threat in this way. Watch a cat or dog: they can be injured or ill, yet not be confused or stressed. This kind of stress is unique to human beings—unique to thinking. Not understanding the nature of thinking and taking responsibility for it through the power of awareness is the greatest cause of human suffering. More than the suffering of actual mental or physical illness, more than dying and death itself, the suffering created by thoughts that divide us within ourselves, or between each other, creates the greatest source of human misery.

When We Are Used by Our Thinking

We human beings pride ourselves on our thinking capacity; and it is true that we are marvelous creatures who can imagine the future, invent great machines, compose wondrous music, create numinous artwork, and build majestic edifices. Yet far more than using our thinking to achieve those wonders, much of the time we are *used by* our thinking. Unquestioned and unchallenged judgments, opinions, and beliefs carry us individually and collectively (groups, corporations, religions, nations) into pride, fear, defensiveness, and aggressive behavior.

We are used by our thinking because we believe our thoughts and identify with them without asking, "Can I really know that what I'm thinking is actually true?" We are used by our thinking because it consistently puts us into opposition with our lives. We rarely say yes to life as it is; instead, we continuously tell life how it should be. We are enamored by intellect but fail to see that we use it to try to control whatever frightens us much more than we use it as a mode of consciousness for comprehending the wonders of our existence. We are used by our thinking because the fears we can imagine and the defenses we invent (with thinking) to protect ourselves too often put us into an adversarial relationship with other people, but especially with nature.

Perhaps the greatest and most regrettable proof that we are used by our thinking instead of using our amazing function of intelligent thought is that we are damaging the very biosystems upon which human and many other forms of life depend. Species are disappearing at an alarming rate. We are the source of this destruction; we know it, yet we find it difficult to change our habits—to actually change the way we think about ourselves, each other, and our world. Our thinking goes unchallenged and seems doomed to be shortsighted and short-term.

The sad fact is that we're not educated to be aware and therefore able to question the reality created by our thinking. We don't realize that we must take responsibility for our thoughts to find out if they are really true, and then set aside or at least acknowledge those that are simply opinion and bias. We don't recognize that most thoughts are ultimately judgments, and that the truth of any judgment (as we will see more fully later on) is how that judgment makes us feel.

Ultimately, the problem with thinking is not merely that you believe your thoughts, but that you build your identity—your sense of self—with them. It is identification with what you tell yourself about yourself: that you are a good person (or not), a lovable person (or not), a smart person (or not), and so on. And that becomes who you believe yourself to be.

This imagined self is the ego. The ego is not an entity, not something real like your body; it is a way of processing information that leads to a false assumption that you are a separate self. At the level of the ego, it never occurs to you that you are also that which can be aware of all those thoughts—aware of all the ways you (as an ego) interpret your perceptions and feelings. In other words, as an ego, you believe yourself to be outside and separate from life and everyone and everything else instead of part of a divine wholeness.

What is most important here isn't to focus on the broader problem of ego or thinking in general. Rather, it's vital to see how you hurt yourself unnecessarily day by day with your own thinking so that you can stop doing it. You suffer because of the thoughts you have about yourself and the situation, not because of who you really are or what the situation actually is.

I am not minimizing how weak, tired, and toxic you can feel at times of illness; possibly you have never felt worse in your life. I am not denying the sorrow, grief, and fear that often accompany a diagnosis of serious disease or injury. I am not minimizing the anguish of divorce or the pain of loss. Such times are among life's most challenging, and this is no less so for all who love you. I am saying, though, that you have far more power over the level of your suffering than you realize. You may feel unable to utilize that power right now, but as you continue reading this book, you will learn how to do so and it will change your life.

Presence Can Diminish Pain

Pain, specifically physical pain, varies moment by moment with your state of mind, or more precisely, with how present or not you are. So does your vitality. When you are caught up in the thoughts that generate fearfulness or despair, physical pain can worsen and weaken you. The moment you relax into the present and your thinking becomes quieter, the pain signal may well decrease and your vitality returns.

This can happen in an instant, and that is an instant of healing. Add up those instants of presence and decreased pain, and at the end of an hour, or a day, you will have more energy and optimism. Ten, twenty, a hundred or more of those moments each day; and you have an entirely different experience. You are more healthy than sick, at least in your state of mind. This is an immediate fruit of the path of learning to be present: to be your aware self instead of identified with your thinking—your ego. This is why the great Indian spiritual teacher Sai Baba has summarized his whole message to humanity with three words: "Watch your thoughts."

For most people, the difference between awareness and thinking is unfamiliar. We have believed that we are what our thoughts tell us we are, and the world is what our thoughts tell us it is. When we are told that we are sick and then we tell this to ourselves, we believe that we are sick. But the part of us that is aware of whatever we are telling ourselves about being sick is not in itself sick.

Letting your awareness help you step away from your thinking —which means being more present—brings you back to a healthy state of mind. Without identifying with the thoughts that compare how you currently are with how you used to be, aren't you actually okay right now? If you don't identify with thoughts that picture the future in terms of diminishing capacity, or envision yourself lacking sufficient funds for retirement, is there any real threat right now? Without thoughts that generate emotions of bitterness or hopelessness or of being a victim, this moment will hold you in peace.

When you turn your attention away from your thoughts and into the present moment, you restore yourself to a state of open receptivity to a limitless source of intelligence, a limitless field of love. You give that love and intelligence a chance to join you and transform you. Returning to a sense of wholeness in yourself is being healthy. It is also the most powerful way you have to change the future.

The ego, like a bad cell-phone connection that produces cracked, clipped noise, is constantly producing stressful mental and emotional noise that obscures the signal of this deeper intelligence. It makes you less intelligent. And it weakens your body's connection to the vibration of wholeness that is the deeper note of existence. At the level of ego, you are always more or less out of tune.

Again and again, ego makes you into who you *have* been instead of who you really *are* and *can* be. Your ego can never envision the future in a way that is new; it can only keep projecting what it has known. When you become present and gain distance from your ego's thinking, your whole being regains alignment with that larger consciousness. Now there is greater room for new possibility, including restoring physical health.

You Have More Than One Body

A receptive, open system is capable of growing and reorganizing in ways you can never anticipate, and your body as well as your consciousness is not a closed system. Who you really are is never static. Your experience of being always starts anew right now, because you are, in reality, renewing your state of consciousness and even your state of health moment by moment.[1] It is not inaccurate to say that you have more than one body or, more precisely, that your body can renew itself in every instant according to the level of consciousness you are attuned to. In one instant you can have pain, and in the next be pain free. In one state of consciousness you can be in remission, and in the next the disease process can be progressing.

What determines this difference is one of life's great mysteries. But from long observation, I can say that how fully you are present to your experience in each moment is essential. This doesn't mean that you can completely control the outcome of anything. But through presence and the quality of your attention, you have much more power than you know to find a place of healing, clarity, and trust within yourself and a new relationship to life in general.

The Feelings You Have to Face

As you learn to live in the present, the negative emotions created by your thoughts will subside, and you will also stop narcotizing yourself with positive fantasies that cause you to miss life altogether. This in itself is a major triumph. But your capacity for feeling is deeper than the world of your mind-made emotions. Feeling is a mode of consciousness that is essential to how you know yourself. We will discuss this in more depth in Chapter 8. For now though, it is enough to say that in the full range of feeling, some feelings are joyous and expansive and some are dark and difficult to stay present with.

No one has any problems with the positive feelings until they get too positive. Then many people become threatened by actually feeling very good, so they close down. They abandon their inheritance to taste the kingdom of heaven in this life. Even more problematic is that from early childhood, when you didn't have the awareness to face the dark and threatening feelings, you reflexively fled from them. In that way, you defended and maintained your fledgling ego. But now as an adult, this habit only ends up putting you in opposition to much of your experience and to the darker half of your feeling nature. The result is that you are divided within yourself.

This split is an ongoing problem. It diminishes your energy because it makes it nearly impossible for you to stay fully present as soon as there is a "negative" feeling. In my work I've found that there are two fundamental challenges to self-healing and awakening: The first is the identification with thinking and the emotional suffering that this creates. The second is the old, unconscious habit of running away from every threatening feeling and even from the truly expansive and positive ones.

The journey to inner freedom and well-being is invariably an odyssey into the kind of feelings you haven't let yourself experience for most of your life. Often they are feelings such as melancholy, helplessness, powerlessness, and emptiness that you never made room for because as soon as they were present, your ego turned them into emotions such as anger or shame. Or sometimes they are the blessed feelings of profound joy and love that your ego has turned from and caused you to become withdrawn and distrusting. In many ways, coming to genuine health is a matter of allowing yourself to be restored to the full intelligence of feeling—both high and low. As you read further, you will learn how to develop this ability.

As you come into the present and learn to make space for every feeling, a mysterious alchemy takes place. Something deep inside you responds—we can call it the soul—and you become more open to life. Connections with other people are more real, honest, and direct. You're naturally more spontaneous and playful. Simple things delight you.

To be at peace with this moment—with who and how you are, independent of circumstances—is to awaken to your full consciousness. This is something everyone can do. It is not magic, and it is more than wishful thinking or the use of positive affirmations. It is a profound and exciting work.

Right now, you can begin learning to stop the thoughts that have been hurting you. You can find a new relationship to every feeling that has threatened you. In so doing, you will discover a new relationship to yourself—to your illness, your family, your past, and your future. You can live more continually in the present and from that starting place come into conscious relationship with anything whatsoever. This is what it means to awaken to your wholeness. It is also the journey to true health.

CHAPTER TWO

UNDERSTANDING THE EGO'S GAME

Learning not to resist what is happening in your life moment by moment is something you can do in any state, healthy or not. Even if you were lying in a hospital bed, having been told that you have only weeks to live, the reality of this moment right now—without any thoughts imposed on it—could be the smile on the face of someone you love or his or her familiar voice. It could be the muted afternoon sunlight filtering through the window. It could be the repetitive beeping of the heart monitor or sounds from the television. This is the truth of the moment. Light is entering the room, relationship is happening, and other people are living their experiences. Things have a sense of intrinsic rightness when your ego does not put you into conflict with what is.

Choosing to plant yourself fully in the present moment—not in the pictures or stories created by your thoughts—is the most essential of all choices. When you are caught up in fearful thoughts and negative judgments, whatever is happening is much more difficult and painful than it would be if you could simply stay open for whatever is actually taking place. Even if you choose to affirm positive thoughts, the good feelings such thoughts engender, while welcome, are not the fullness of what any moment can bring when you can allow yourself to rest deeply in the Now.

In the present moment, you are carried by life in a way that is unavailable to your ego self, enmeshed as it is in its own stories. This is acceptance, and it is surrender. Now, surrender does not mean that you've lost the battle. It means that you've stopped fighting and instead have given yourself over to a deeper reality:

the immediacy of this moment. To your surprise, you may find that you are met and accompanied by a gentle presence.

What the ego habitually tries to avoid, this presence can welcome without reaction. In surrender you find that suddenly there is no need to be anywhere but where you are. In ego there is the habitual drive toward something other than *what is*. When you are not opposing your experience by wanting it to be different in some way, each moment is an infinite field of possibility, intelligence, and profound support.

When you are ill or life isn't going the way you want it to, it is your ego that complains, resists, gets scared or angry, and becomes strategic. But step into the present moment, which is to move away from ego and into your aware mind, and you are no longer sick, even though your body may be. You are, as an aware being, the consciousness that always exists in stillness and peace, able to observe but not become identified with the constant and noisy activity of the ego. But unless you learn to stay aware and observe your thoughts, it seems as though you and your thoughts are one. In that case, you are being hijacked by the ego, and the stories it generates inevitably compound suffering.

Making Yourself Special

When the ego is in charge, its primary mandate is to constantly confirm and reconfirm its own existence. It does this by convincing you that you are special.

For a child, feeling special is the most natural thing. Children are doted on, cared for, and played with—they receive nearly constant attention. Inevitably, children come to feel special in one of two ways: either in a positive sense because of all the love and attention they receive or; sadly, in a more negative sense because they have been poorly nurtured or have not received adequate positive attention.[1]

But the ways in which we develop our sense of specialness in childhood carry over into our adult lives. Whereas specialness, particularly in how we feel seen and loved by our parents, is very important in early life, specialness later in life becomes much more of a problem. In this discussion, I am using the terms *special* and *specialness* in a specific sense to denote the way the ego ceaselessly creates a false identity that results in a sense of overt or veiled self-importance. Of course, it is also true that we are each unique and in that sense special; however, that fact is not the point of the discussion of specialness as we will be examining it here.

When you are facing a health or emotional challenge, there are many ways in which you unconsciously make yourself special: You are special because your suffering is particularly terrible, more unbearable than that of others, or has come at the wrong time. Or maybe you are special because you can take it in stride, don't show fear or weakness, and will never bow to depressive feelings. Making yourself special in your own eyes or in the way you imagine that others see you is the main purpose and activity of the ego. Appreciating this is an essential step to freeing yourself from its limiting influence.

Ego is an essential stage of development. Before we can truly awaken as aware beings, it is necessary to first create a point of view to be conscious *from*. This is the ego, the sense of me. However, this consciousness is extremely limited, and it suffers inordinately because this point of view becomes an experience of separation.

The ego believes in *me* as completely distinct from you and everything else. It believes in *mine: my* (separate) body, *my* feelings, *my* beliefs, *my* territory, or *my* possessions. It is threatened by judgments that are contradictory to its own idealized self-image. It is threatened by any feeling it cannot explain. And it is threatened by loss of wealth or health. In short, if it identifies with and becomes attached to something, the ego will be threatened if the attachment is challenged.

In a later stage of conscious development, which is at the heart of what this book is about, you go beyond the illusion of separateness and awaken to a deeper connection to life. It is an amplification of the experience you've had many times in your life when you have become so present in what you are doing that there is no sense of you as a doer, only a sense of being.

Because there is no way to actually characterize who you really are as an aware being, your ego has to find a way for you to believe in your own separateness. The ego can't be neutral; it can't see you or this very moment as it actually is—that would be pure awareness itself. So, in one way or another, your ego has to make you stand out, make you special. It does this in one of two ways: by telling you a story about yourself that makes you either more or less than you really are.

When the ego's stories make you smaller, I call it *depressive specialness*. And when it puffs you up with a sense of superiority, I call that *grandiose specialness*.

You might presume that being superior is a better or more desirable form of specialness; but in fact, superiority cuts you off from intimacy with others, encourages denial, and leads to poor judgment in many ways. Believing that you are inferior does the same thing but in a different manner. So, no matter whether it puffs you up or shrinks you down, the ego's project of making you special isn't helping you become healthy and whole.

The Ego's Agenda

Convincing you of your specialness is the secret game of the ego, and it plays that game relentlessly. One moment you are the best, the next the worst. In one situation you believe you know best, and in another you are giving yourself away to someone else's agenda. Whether you fall into grandiose specialness or depressive specialness depends upon the context. Perhaps in your marriage you tend toward grandiose specialness: being domineering or tyrannical. But then you go to work where suddenly you take on depressive specialness: being submissive to your superiors and feeling victimized.

The ego isn't a bad thing, or even a thing at all. It is just a constantly regenerating mental construct based on unconscious identification with stories you've been telling yourself (in only slightly changed forms) since childhood. While everyone is unique, when I speak of how the ego makes you special, I am referring to the emotional quality of your sense of separateness, whether you feel superior or inferior, grandiose or depressed. Either pole strongly influences how you view yourself and react to people and situations. Grandiosity tends toward anger and impatience; depressiveness tends toward compliance and withdrawal.

The trouble is that we rarely see through and outgrow this need for specialness. Instead, we live our whole lives making ourselves feel important or unimportant, happy or unhappy (and special because of it) . . . one thought after another. We unconsciously identify with the thoughts about who we are (or aren't), and we become whatever our thoughts tell us we are.

When it comes to healing, your ego does not have your best interests at heart, to say the least. It doesn't really care whether you get well or discover true inner peace. It just needs to make sure that you always feel special in some way. So it will tell you that you can go it alone, you don't need anybody; that you deserve special care; that you have the best doctors; or that you are a fighter, a survivor against the odds. It will tell you whatever it takes to reinforce your sense of superiority and self-importance. Of course, if your ego can't get you to believe stories about yourself that make you feel superior, then it will look for ones that make you feel inferior instead. It will turn your thoughts to stories that make you feel weak and unworthy, as if you are an inconvenience, a burden on others, a failure, unattractive, incapable, or stupid.

Ego truly doesn't care that these beliefs about yourself make you inflated or unhappy. It doesn't care that most of the stories are harsh or extreme judgments. All it cares about is its own continued existence, which means having you believe that you are a superior or inferior person.

The ego is about identity—not about awareness or who you really are. And whether unhappy and ashamed, or proud and self-important, each identity is just as special as the other in its own way. It is for this reason that your ego cannot let you become fully present, for the moment you are, it recedes and there is only awareness, only being. And this scares your ego to death, because it hasn't yet understood its relationship to awareness.

"Default Settings" in Each of Us

We each have a kind of specialness set point, a tendency to default either into depressiveness or grandiosity most of the time. One segment of the population whose set point tends more toward superiority, sometimes referred to as "type A" personalities, may seem powerful, but their bodies don't appear to be very happy, because individuals in this group have a statistically higher incidence of heart disease. They are driven to keep proving their superiority, they don't let themselves slow down, and they don't know how to rest. They are always on the run and need to feel in control.

What they believe they are running toward is usually the ideal of success in terms of power and wealth. Yet this is less important to them than what they are unconsciously running *from,* which is the other side of the polarity: inferiority. The shadow of the person who believes himself to be superior is his buried feelings of inferiority. So to avoid those feelings, he keeps pushing himself, and often burnout or disease is a consequence of being so driven.

People whose specialness set point tends toward the depressive pole often don't know how to take a stand in life. They constantly undermine themselves with beliefs about their own limitations in order to prove that they are indeed special in their limitations— more wounded, needier, less worthy. Here again the shadow of the depressive tendency is the grandiosity with which they declare the world unsafe or unfair. Depressively special people are often exceptionally critical of anyone who gets attention or appears successful.

Often they believe that life owes them something. Their hidden grandiosity shows up in how they believe they should be taken care of, or in the way they blame and judge others and themselves for their plight. They believe that they are trapped, helpless, and unable to change their lives. Their sense of powerlessness, which has been built by the ego's stories, is one of the worst forms of stress. (There is also the feeling of powerlessness, which if held with awareness can be very important to psychological health, but the nature of this kind of difficult feeling and how to work with it is the subject of a later chapter.)

Either kind of specialness is a form of imbalance that creates stress, fatigue, and diminished aliveness. If you are committed to healing, waking up when your ego starts to push you into grandiose or depressive specialness gives you a chance to come back to the present and start all over again in your natural being. You are immediately restored to greater balance.

Choosing Ego or Awareness

The purpose of this book is to give you a choice between being driven by your ego or being aware of its game plan. It is a choice between the increased stress and suffering that specialness inevitably brings, and the fullness of being that arises when you are present and not in conflict with whatever is happening. Once you appreciate that your ego's sole purpose is to keep you believing in one way or another that you are special, you can begin to free yourself of its grip. In Chapter 4, you will be presented with a powerful method for learning to return to the Now that will teach you to recognize the many patterns, reactions, habits, and strategies your ego uses to confirm and reconfirm your specialness. Once you gain some distance from this fundamental ego pattern, you will recognize how exhausting it is and quickly regain vitality.

Right now you might say that you aren't special, that you don't see yourself that way, but if you are alert, you will begin to see how subtle the game of specialness can be. Anytime you hold beliefs that affirm how you are different from any other person, whether you are fully conscious of it or not, you inevitably see yourself as superior or inferior. This is specialness. Anytime you expect special treatment, cut in ahead of others awaiting their turn in a line, or become unreasonably impatient or angry, you have slipped into a grandiose identity. One good test of how unconsciously special you are is how you react to meeting someone who is famous or very wealthy, such as a movie star or the CEO of a Fortune 500 company. If anything at all changes in your bearing with such people, it is your specialness that is shifting.

Whenever you feel guilty or unimportant or undeserving, or that others' needs take priority over your own, you have chosen a depressive identity. Grandiosity might take the form of thinking: *My wife doesn't deserve to get cancer; she is such a good person,* as if disease is punishment and health is a reward. But this is really grandiosity in disguise: You or those you love merit exemption from disease. These beliefs and so many others that you will begin to recognize are all ways you might unconsciously use to affirm that you exist as an exclusive, private, separate individual. You are not just anybody—you are someone special.

As you become aware of the ego's game, it stops dominating you and you rest more consistently in your larger awareness. This larger self sees both sides of your specialness: the tendency to puff up with aggressiveness, righteousness, self-importance, or impatience with others; or the tendency to shrink into victimhood, defensiveness, shame, or helplessness. Once you are aware of both tendencies, you realize that you are more than either and don't need to identify with one or the other. In developing this awareness, a whole new dimension of yourself awakens, and a subtle presence begins to radiate from you.

When you aren't feeling well, there are many things you cannot control. But if you observe your thoughts and emotional state, you can recognize how making yourself special—big or small—is not helping you feel at peace. Everyone gets sick at some time or another. We all face challenging setbacks, and all of us die. But being like everyone else is not acceptable to the ego. It needs drama: "Oh no! Why me?" Immediately, you are a victim, and you are frightened.

But if you are aware and see this reaction, you can realize that a far more realistic, less stressful, and less special attitude is "Why not me?" Of course, the ego won't let you think that way. "Why not me?" doesn't make you special enough, doesn't make your suffering unique, and doesn't make you stand out. For the ego, you not being special is equivalent to death or nonexistence—something to be avoided at nearly all costs.

You, like everyone else, have been immersed in the belief in your own specialness since childhood. This is one reason why it isn't a simple thing to overcome and needs work and patience. But as you learn to observe your thoughts, you begin to see this specialness game operating everywhere in your life, and you can smile at it instead of being driven into grandiosity or depressiveness.

Rewarding Yourself for Being Aware

One way you can know that you are being aware rather than hijacked by your ego is that you don't beat yourself up when you find yourself moving into either kind of specialness. If you do, it is ego once again taking over and making you smaller even as you try to outgrow being trapped in its game. So resist the habitual temptation to punish yourself when you catch yourself being special. Instead, learn to smile gently at what you have seen and reward yourself for your awareness.

Rewarding yourself for your awareness is a new idea for most people. I suggest in my work that when you become aware that your ego is making you special—even if it's in a manner you generally feel ashamed of or judgmental about—say *Yes* to yourself, then *Thank you,* and finally, *Forgive me.*

The *Yes* affirms that you woke up and saw the specialness game, and the *Thank you* is a conscious bow to your aware self that woke you up. The *Forgive me* is the acknowledgment that the story you started telling yourself causes stress and unhappiness; it is an apology to yourself. When you add a smile, it is not only on your face, but it is also a feeling within your body. Try it now: let a smile bubble up from deep inside you. Don't force it; just let it come. Notice how this inner smile makes you feel—this feeling is a very tangible way to reward your awareness.

The Healing Power of Awareness

When it comes to creating the most favorable conditions for healing, it is vital to recognize that being controlled by the thoughts and emotions that arise from your sense of specialness diminishes your resonance with life's profound intelligence. It's like being tuned to a radio station that broadcasts inflammatory opinions that incite fear, anger, guilt, or confusion in you instead of being tuned to one that broadcasts messages that fill you with insight, clarity, and wisdom.

Emotionally oscillating between fear and hope or between guilt and blame is exhausting. Defending your special position is exhausting. When the ego's power to throw you around emotionally diminishes, you are restored to unobstructed resonance with a limitless and timeless field of presence. This field is always waiting and available because you are never not part of it as long as your ego doesn't tune it out. Suddenly you feel supported in ways that are unimaginable to your ego.

That is why for a person who cultivates present-moment awareness, there is much less drama around being sick. There is also less drama about dying, because it is, ultimately, an ordinary, natural occurrence. You can't be identified with your specialness and simultaneously be present, full of ease, and in flow. Genuine well-being and specialness are mutually exclusive.

But your ego simply doesn't know that it is part of a larger field of intelligence, love, and support. It believes that it is a separate entity, a world unto itself. To maintain that world, it must vigilantly keep you caught in drama and feeling self-important or undermined in some way. It must lament unwanted change and angst about the loss of the future it had been imagining. It must tell you that illness is unfair. It cannot see either illness or death as natural. It must strive heroically to get well. It does not understand that focusing on these kinds of stories creates an emotional environment that obstructs love, even when you want to share love the most. It certainly does not recognize that its own mentally generated emotional world does not help you in the healing process.

Waking Up from the Dream and the Drama

Recall a time when you woke up in the middle of the night worrying about something—perhaps a work issue or an unresolved conflict. Most likely your mind jumped from one concern to the next, as each anxious thought reminded you of something that in turn created another worry. Maybe you started thinking about an uncomfortable interaction with a family member, or you recalled the way a colleague at the office had been dismissive toward you and as a result you felt resentful. Do you remember repeating certain conversations in your mind and regretting what you said or didn't say, or rehearsing what you would say next time if you got the chance? Probably the more you thought about it, the more agitated you felt.

Or maybe you woke up and started worrying about money, about all the expenses piling up. How would you ever manage? Did this lead to thoughts about other people who were better off, or those who didn't have so many financial issues? Did the envy make you more upset; did it make you feel more helpless or angry or even more of a victim?

So there you were, tossing and turning in bed, exhausted by your own thoughts and emotions; and to top it all off, realizing that you had an especially busy day ahead, you got scared about not being able to get back to sleep. How would you get through the day after having been awake all night? And this new vicious circle of thinking continued, feeding on itself, consuming you in its reality.

If you recognize yourself in this scenario, don't feel bad. This is typical of what the ego does whenever you feel threatened or unsafe in any way, especially with the uncertainty of a health issue or if you are in the midst of major change. The ego simply does not know how to deal with challenging feelings like vulnerability and feeling out of control. When the ego is running the show, you can notice a dynamic: One thought generates an emotion that leads to another thought that generates another emotion. Round and round you go like a dog chasing its tail—well, in this case *tale*—becoming increasingly agitated and upset, even if in that moment you are otherwise actually fine, safe, and secure in your bed. Meanwhile, you never even really recognize the original feeling that triggered this mental stampede; you never actually face it and meet it with awareness.

To get you so worked up, the ego has to make you oblivious to the present moment, because the ego recedes when you are fully in the Now. So to maintain itself, your ego will yank you away from the Now—away from reality, thought by thought. If you begin to observe what your ego is doing (as we will soon discuss), you will notice that when the ego leads your awareness away from the Now moment, there are only four places it can take you: into the past, into the future, into stories about yourself, and into stories about others.

The good news is that you can get off this not-so-merry-go-round as soon as you recognize that you are not in the present. Ask yourself, "What is actually happening now?" Look around you, observe, and listen. What is the contrast between your actual situation in your immediate surroundings—the sounds, the quality of light, the colors, and so on—versus the mental and emotional world created by your thoughts? Become aware of your breathing and bodily sensations. Let yourself relax. You may be sick, but you aren't under attack, except by your own thoughts.

Recognize what your ego has done: it has yanked you out of the present, into memories and expectations. Thinking about the past has created emotions of guilt, blame, regret, or nostalgia; and thinking about an imaginary future has generated anxiety and fearfulness. You have been overtaken by debilitating mind-made emotion. This intense self-contraction is the hallmark of ego at its worst. But becoming aware that you are not in the present and realizing *I'm in the future* or *I'm in the past* is what it takes to wake up out of the dream and drama.

As you restore yourself to the present, the inner turmoil recedes because you have stemmed the tide of thoughts that had been creating and sustaining it. You are cutting through delusion. As you learn to use the power of your awareness to come back to the present moment, you become more embodied, more awake to your true self, and able to address the demands of your life with clarity.

Every time you leave the Now, you inevitably identify with a story you tell yourself, about yourself, your health, or your life. It is as though you've fallen down the rabbit hole in *Alice in Wonderland* into an imaginary universe. But unlike Alice, who knew that she was in a fantasy world, most of us are totally convinced that it *is* real.

This is crucial to understand, because blind identification with your stories will continue forever unless you recognize the pattern and expose it to the light of Now-moment awareness. You are only your authentic self when you wake up and take your rightful place as the aware being watching the whole show but no longer captured by it.

The process of awakening into greater awareness and presence is sometimes referred to as the death of the ego. In fact, many spiritual teachings talk about killing the ego. But the ego doesn't and indeed shouldn't die as you develop a high degree of presence; rather, it ceases to rule your mind and determine your experience. Thereafter, it serves awareness by providing your unique point of view, but no longer in a way that defines your identity, separates you, and makes you special. As the ego recedes and awareness prevails, your identity as a separate self becomes less dominant, and at last you really taste the fullness of being.

CHAPTER THREE

CAUSALITY AND CREATING YOUR OWN REALITY

One popular New Age premise tells you that "you create your own reality." Sadly, this is often misunderstood to mean that when you are sick, you have somehow done this to yourself. Of course there are instances in which you bear more responsibility for your illness. Perhaps you made poor lifestyle choices in the past, such as smoking or excessive drinking or drug use. But setting aside these obvious examples, most of the time you really cannot know why you have become ill. Therefore, it is important not to add insult to injury by making yourself feel guilty.

The *real* truth of this premise is that you *do* create your own reality, but *only* right now, in this present moment. You do this through the stories that you are telling yourself and identifying with. You do not create the scenery you see, only your reaction to it. You do not create the weather, but calling a day "miserable" makes *you* unhappy. Understanding that you are responsible for your own psychological and emotional reality in the present moment has everything to do with awakening to the nature of your own mind and nothing to do with creating guilt.

If you tell yourself "I (somehow) have created my disease," the immediate consequence of this belief is a feeling of shame and guilt, not increased well-being. Even if you had previously made unhealthy choices, blaming yourself for past actions does not improve your present state. The key then to maximizing your potential for healing is choosing to be fully present. In other words, let go of worrying about what caused your illness and instead enter completely into whatever your actual experience is, moment by moment.

There is a further consequence for believing that you have caused your illness: you will likely also believe that in order to find a remedy, you must first discover what you did to cause the problem. Now the pressure is on: not only do you feel guilty, but anxious as well. You are indeed creating your own reality—emotional stress— but only in this moment and only through your own thinking. Believing that you are the cause of your illness (which, by the way, makes you special) leads to much unnecessary suffering.

As we have discussed, ego is about identity and lives according to chronological time. As it observes changes over time, it assumes the notion of causality: "I was healthy and now I am sick . . . so something has *caused* this to happen." But when you are simply present and aware, you have let go of time, which means that you have also let go of ego. Things are just as they are, and you no longer identify yourself as either someone healthy or sick.

Believing in cause and effect is one way of interpreting experience. When "A" takes place, "B". results; therefore, "A" causes "B." Modern medicine and science in general rely on the premise of causality: if you can learn about and then alter the chain of events that leads to illness, you may be able to halt that illness. This approach has given us great power over many diseases. Modern medicine saves lives every day that would have been lost only decades ago.

Yet whereas the outer, objective world appears to obey the laws of causality, as you move into the present—into being—causality becomes less meaningful and completely indeterminable. It is analogous to moving closer and closer to the center of a turning wheel. Eventually you approach a point that is not moving at all.

Similarly, when you are in the Now, your mind stops thinking about you and about everything else, and you are simply *aware*. Time in a certain sense stops or slows down enough so that your sense of self is no longer that of someone on his or her way to somewhere else. You are just as you are. Your situation—or, more precisely, your state of being—is not something caused by something prior. You are not comparing your present circumstance to the past nor projecting into the future. You are no longer explaining, justifying, rationalizing, or interpreting your experience. Therefore, you are not attributing cause to what you are experiencing . . . you are just being. And in that being, you are always and already whole.

What is important is *not* how you got to where you are, but how you are present with your experience. I know one woman who is 82 years old and a constant inspiration. Her body has had diffuse metastatic breast cancer for seven years. Even so, she lives with a twinkle in her eye and a steady honesty about herself. She is a walking smile, radiating love.

She decided from the beginning when she learned of having cancer that she would not undergo chemotherapy at her late age; instead, she would let the process follow its own course. She lives a nearly normal life, hardly missing a day of gentle tai chi practice. But if she overstresses even a little, the cancer "activates" and she can suddenly be in a life-threatening crisis. Several times with her belly and lungs full with fluids, she has been on death's doorstep. But then, mysteriously she has recovered.

Maybe it's not so mysterious. She doesn't fight death; she surrenders to what is. For her, this means staying in bed and being a conscious part of the dying process if that is what will happen. She has asked herself, "What kind of death do I want?" and thought about it carefully. Her decision: "To be accepting and loving to the very end." She admitted to me, "Life may have its own plans . . . who knows how it will really go, but I have a right to express my preference." This woman's cancer seems to be held in check by her state of deep acceptance and her respectful listening to herself. For her, saying yes to life also means saying yes to death.

Reality Is Always Emerging Anew

We live in a world in which there appears to be causality, but at a more fundamental level (which is our moment-by-moment conscious relationship to our experience), the apparent "laws" of causality do not hold. Instead, there is an emergent reality, a constant dynamic of being and discovery. Take cancer, for example: it is a different disease in every person, and it is a different disease in every person *in every moment* because, as mentioned earlier, the body actually reorganizes itself in greater or lesser degrees of wholeness according to how present an individual is.

When you understand this, you can break free of the whole notion of causality: that something has made you sick, and you need to live a certain way and take specific medications in order to get well. Of course, sometimes this is partially the case, but if all you do is simply follow the doctor's orders, you will be missing the inner doctor who is a lot smarter and can be even more effective.

The other day, a good friend who suffers from chronic neck pain came to talk to me. She had arrived at a point where it was impossible to sit at her computer and work, or read or watch television; even being in bed at night made her neck worse. Over the years, she had consulted many doctors and had many studies and tests done. She knew that she had a degenerated disk. Some doctors proposed surgery; others doubted it would help. She explored the gamut of both conventional and complementary medicine treatments and approaches. Sometimes she would have a few hours of relief, sometimes a few days, but the pain kept recurring and was gradually getting worse.

As we sat together, I suggested that instead of talking about what next to try, or needing to explain her pain based on the medical studies, she could try to let her pain be the starting point for a journey into the present. I offered to try to intuitively accompany her on her journey into the pain.

As she turned her attention toward the pain, I guided her to "touch" the whole constellation of sensation in her head, neck, and shoulders very softly with an inner gaze and at the same time to extend a part of her awareness to her whole body and into the room. This latter suggestion, to also *extend* the awareness, is very important because when you *focus* on pain, it tends to become more intense unless you also keep a sense of expansiveness or spaciousness at the same time. As she felt into the pain, I suggested that she engage it as if she had never felt it before, as if it were a completely new experience.[1]

Suddenly my friend found herself spontaneously in a vision of a dense, dark-toned forest of "trees" that were made of something she could not describe, and the whole scene was underwater. She felt a strange power in this place. After a couple of moments, I sensed that she had disconnected from the present. I asked her where she had gone, and she said she was trying to make a connection between the pain and the vision. In other words, she was analyzing, which meant she had stepped back from the immediacy of the vision. Also she had let her mind pull her into the past. I coached her to come back to the image and its "strange power." I suggested she release any expectation of where this would lead, to just be present to her inner experience. A few moments later, she began to sob softly. She spoke of a feeling of warmth rising up inside of her, particularly in her chest, and the vision of the underwater forest faded away. Simultaneously, she noticed that the pain was completely gone.

In fact, the pain disappeared for nearly a week, and during that time she felt unusually well emotionally. This was not a cure, but it shows something of real importance. Her basic belief system was that if she could just pinpoint the true problem and then have the right therapy, she would recover. In effect, this put her continuously in an imagined future in which, having found the right treatment, she would once again be well. That is, she would be how she remembered herself to be in the past before the pain had started.

But she had now learned that traveling into her experience with her awareness and leaving behind both the past and the future could also lead to relief. Equally significant, it led to a better emotional balance within her. She had taken a different path, a path of intimacy with herself in the Now—one in which the cause of her problem was irrelevant and getting to a desired outcome was actually counterproductive.

It is my experience that if my friend can teach herself to take this kind of original journey of awareness—whenever pain or any kind of challenging feeling is causing her mind to move into the future or the past—she will be on a path of emotional liberation and perhaps physical healing as well.

Transmuting Symptoms Through Presence

The examples of the two women you just read about illustrate how you can address any sensation by becoming present and entering into the immediacy of your being with awareness. Although you may not be able to control many sensations, calling them symptoms of illness steals your ability to meet them originally in the Now. By being present in a fresh way with your sensations, you have much more control over how they affect you and especially where they can lead you than you may realize.

The key is learning to be aware *with* them, to *feel* your sensations and stop thinking about them. Said in another way, don't give the sensations to your ego; learn to bring awareness to them. This opens the possibility of transmuting your symptoms— letting them change into new images or insights or feelings and thereby reducing their power to limit or discourage you. Research shows that people who simply notice their actual sensations rather than labeling them as signs of illness tend to feel a greater sense of control in their lives, and this affects their longevity.[2]

I first learned how to transmute a sensation when I was rock climbing years ago. I noticed that when I thought I would fall because of the sensation of being at my physical limit, I fell. But one day I decided to observe this sensation and disconnect it from the assumption that I was about to fall. I discovered that I could cling to my place on the rock sometimes for minutes and even continue moving upward long after my mind told me I couldn't.

I took an even deeper step in meditation practice, an activity during which it was not uncommon to become sleepy and to even nod off. One day I asked myself what the experience that I'm calling "becoming sleepy" actually is. I began to carefully observe how my eyelids became heavy and my focus grew fuzzy. I noticed the way my attention was withdrawing from perceiving my breathing and other inner sensations, and that outer perceptions were becoming unfocused and nebulous. I discovered that as I precisely observed these changes of perception and stayed with how I actually felt, I soon became alert and present once again. The first and crucial step was to disengage from the mental representation—the thought *I am sleepy,* or even just the label *sleepy.*

I began cultivating a practice of disengaging the name (or story) that my ego created about any sensation or feeling and tuning in to the actual sensation or feeling. When I noticed I was telling myself "I am tired," perhaps during my lunch break or after a full day of work, I quickly released that mental representation of my state and engaged the actual sensation with awareness. I discovered that this sensation is very subtle, an almost musical dance of differing kinds of sensations: words like *dryness, vibration,* and *heaviness* only partially capture it. Also, I noticed that identifying with the thought *I am tired*—or when the sensations were stronger, telling myself "I am exhausted"—did several things. First it defined the sensations before I had actually brought awareness to them. Moreover, it made these sensations about "me" instead of just something I was aware of.

I realized that I was living from an old habit of ego: the habit of naming and identifying with what was named. Second, I noticed how my ego automatically and almost instantly created a second tier of thoughts, such as judging that I was working too hard or telling me that I needed to be more careful with my energy. Then I would immediately begin to worry about whether I would be rested enough for the next day's program, or whether I would make myself sick.

So I taught myself to be receptively present in my body and experience the nuances of the actual sensations and other feelings that were present when I had the thought *I am tired* or *I am in a rush* or *I've had enough.* I soon saw that being present for these sensations and removing any label led me into a subtly or completely new state. Often, by the time I had actually found my way to what I was really experiencing—disengaged from any mental process of naming it, explaining it, and projecting into the future—I immediately felt somewhat restored and refreshed. Even if I was indeed tired, it was now a simple sense of fatigue and actually pleasant in its naturalness.

I saw that the way I named my state and the context of other thoughts that immediately followed had the effect of making me far more tired or exhausted or anxious than I actually was. Over time I learned that this was true for any sensation or feeling, even the darkest ones (which we will discuss later). What you actually experience is usually far less problematic than the reality you create by the way you name and contextualize what you are feeling.

Transmute a Sensation Now

Today in all of my seminars, I teach this capacity to transmute sensations and feelings by bringing awareness to them. You can explore this right now if you like. Start with any sensation you are noticing in your body. Turn your attention toward it steadily and gently, and at the same time let yourself relax. Notice the way your thinking mind wants to describe this sensation—the words you are using to describe it to yourself. Let go of the words and try to experience the actual sensation(s).

Be particularly alert to how your ego may make you think that you have felt this sensation before. This is how your ego takes control and keeps your mind in the past. So recognize the assumption *I have felt this before,* and imagine that you are feeling this sensation for the very first time. Look at it like a naturalist in a tropical rain forest who has discovered a flower she has never seen before. She is studying it very carefully, but she can't name it yet. She is examining its unique characteristics: color, petal arrangement, number of branches off the stem, and so on. Look at your chosen sensation in the same way. Be focused and open at the same time, and observe what happens. Does the sensation change? Do you notice any change in your overall state of being?

Of course, it is difficult to feel good in yourself when you are in chronic pain. At the same time, pain is not only physical in origin; it is supported and intensified by your state of mind, and that is created by your thinking. Being more present changes your experience of physical pain, usually lessening it. The converse is also true: the more in the past or future you are, the more likely you are to feel increased suffering.

Your body is highly intelligent and will do its best to bring you to health in whatever way it can. But first you have to be present and disengage from your ego's stories. When it comes to health and well-being, what you really don't know is what your actual state of health could be if you didn't cut yourself off from the Now so continuously with your thinking.

I am not suggesting that it is inadvisable to try to learn the cause of your illness if that can give you a plan of action to regain your health—but I *am* counseling against seeking answers in a way that keeps your mind in the past or keeps you looking toward the future. It is not helpful to dwell on what *was* in a way that makes you resent or resist your circumstances. The only moment in which you have the ability to make new choices and the power to create greater wellness is this one.

If you pause to look from this vantage point, do you see your current healing strategy creating stress in the form of urgency, worry, or fear? Or are you relaxing into presence and discovering the greater aliveness that is always awaiting you in the Now?

Uncertainty about the future is one of the most stressful states, especially when you are in a health challenge. It is entirely natural to want to know what to do next; you want a plan, a sense of direction. But whenever you have linked your health and well-being to any healing strategy, you have done only half the work. It is good that you have a strategy, but you must also let go into the present and be nourished from this living current.

When you are not anchored in the present and experiencing your innate state of wholeness, watching for signs of improvement and waiting to see what the tests will show is often the tensest and most distressing part of the healing journey. Whether those results are your own or those of your child or other loved ones, it is understandable that you care about what they show. But until the results are in your hand, your energy field and emotional state will be far more spacious and supportive of you and everyone else if you are just living in the present.

Even bad news does not need to throw you into a fearful future. Tests are only a momentary snapshot, never the whole picture. So stay rooted in the Now—otherwise, your ego will exhaust you with thoughts that alternate back and forth between those that create fearfulness and others that create hopefulness. The simple but profound truth is that there is no sense of security or well-being outside of the present moment.

This doesn't mean that you should refrain from listening to your doctors or following their strategies or your own program of healing. What it means is that you are more than the life your ego imagines and reimagines. Your fundamental responsibility is to be here now. Who you really are is ultimately a mystery beyond statistics, and what is important—and can sometimes vastly improve the statistics—is what you are living right now.

If illness is a form of suffering that stirs you out of complacency or motivates you to learn and grow, then the gift of your illness is its potential to wake you up. Once you are awake, the gift you give yourself is the quality of attention you bring to your experience in each moment. Illness does not come along in order to change you, but consciously living the experience of it *can* and *will* change you. In the choice to start to live in the moment, a new reality is created.

With calm gentleness toward yourself, just notice: Have you been living your life reactively or receptively? Are you in the past, the future, or the present? Do you oscillate between hope and fear, or sit peacefully in deep acceptance? Are you living for others, or resting in a rich sense of connection to yourself?

No matter what you have been doing, it is never too late to make a fresh start, because you are perpetually reinventing yourself from moment to moment whether you realize it or not. The opportunity I am presenting to you in the next part of this book is to reinvent yourself consciously and with compassion. Wouldn't it be wonderful to find out just how vibrant and healthy you could be if more hours of your life were spent in a state of presence?

In the work that follows, you will begin to understand exactly how you go astray whenever you are *not* fully in the present. You will learn to trace the path that always leads you straight back to the Now. If you are ready, let's start to focus in closely on your own life to discover the avenues that will take you directly toward your fullest potential for self-healing and wholeness.

PART II

WORKING WITH THE MANDALA OF BEING

It's time to actively apply what you have learned up until now so that you can begin to heal yourself day by day. This means consciously interrupting your usual patterns of thought and waking yourself up as soon as you realize that you are telling yourself a story about the past, the future, yourself, or anyone or anything else. It means bringing your attention fully back into your body and using your five senses to notice what is actually happening right now, in its purity, without any thoughts imposed on it.

Thinking interprets and describes your experience, your body, or your feelings; but only through present-moment awareness can you know any of these directly. In the following section, I will introduce you to a process through which you can truly understand and break free from the ego's grip on your everyday experience. You will see how profoundly it affects your health and every other aspect of your life. Most important, by working with this tool, you will actually feel the contrast between living through ego-based mental activity and living in presence.

Finally, you will learn how to make space in yourself for even the darkest and most difficult feelings so that no matter what happens, your mind will be strong enough to keep you rooted in the present moment . . . where you are always safe, always loved, and already whole.

CHAPTER FOUR

HARNESSING THE POWER OF PRESENCE

Major events in life such as serious illness or injury, divorce, financial ruin, death, and the loss of those we love are intensely challenging, but they are not the worst that happens. The worst suffering often comes not from the situation itself, but from what we tell ourselves about it.

It is one thing to be unable to continue a promising athletic career due to injury. It is far worse to tell yourself that life is no longer worth living. It is one thing to learn that your beloved son has committed suicide after years of emotional struggle. The suffering is worse still if you blame and attack yourself or your spouse as having failed as a parent even though you had tried every way you knew to help him.

If you can remain rooted in the present and not let your mind carry you into these kinds of thoughts, a more complete part of you is able to meet and live whatever is happening. As a friend and student of mine said a year after her 19-year-old son had taken his life, "I have felt the most extraordinary, painful feelings and journeyed into places I still don't know how to describe. I would not wish them on anyone. But the truth is that I haven't for one moment suffered."

What allowed her to say such a thing? The years she had spent in the practice of presence.

In this practice, you wake yourself up out of any story about the past or the future, or about yourself or anyone else, as soon as such thoughts start to pull you away from the present and into painful, destructive emotions. Like waking up out of a dream, you recognize that you are telling yourself a story and it is either worse than what you are actually experiencing, or it is diminishing or distorting your experience. Rather than losing yourself in that dream, you bring your full attention back into your body and into what is actually happening in the moment. When you do so, you find yourself supported and renewed in presence.

When you are anchoring your attention in the present, you are not immune to pain, but what you feel is the genuine, unadulterated feeling that accompanies whatever is happening. Without stories, without the reality manufactured by your thinking, your actual feeling and actual experience do not divide you or cut you off from life. This mind-set does not make you special. What *is* is never worse than what you imagine it might be.

When you are embodying presence, a feeling of belonging and connectedness with everything arises spontaneously within you. Being in this state can seem precious and sacred, especially in the midst of grief when your thoughts are telling you that you should be devastated and inconsolable. However, if you are rooted in the present, such thoughts recede into the background where they are seen to be just thoughts. Your mind is less crowded and more spacious. The ego has lost its power over creating your identity and reality with its stories. You are aware that some thoughts are still coming and going, arising and falling away, but you are not feeding them with the energy of your attention.

The sensation of presence is like a subtle current of energy flowing within and around you. It might feel like a fine vibration within your very cells or just a sense of stillness and peacefulness. If you bring your attention to this subtle sensation, it amplifies. Becoming aware of your breathing and joining that awareness to the soft current of presence deepens the experience still further. Gradually, you may begin to notice that while there is a constantly changing flow of sensations and perceptions, there is also a background of well-being or sense of rightfulness. This soft place can become the foundation of your being. You will have shifted out of conflict with reality and into harmony with it.

Harmony and rightfulness do not mean that you always feel good: When my friend's son killed himself, for instance, what she experienced wasn't an easy feeling for anyone to bear. There was great heartache, but, because she did not let her thinking take her into self-attacking regret or blame, even the abysmal feelings of the loss of her son were part of a larger space of being and con-nectedness in which she felt held.

Just like the heart pumps blood, the mind still produces thoughts, but if you are fully present, you no longer need to coun-teract the frightening ones by creating positive ones. Thoughts come and go, but you are able to watch the stories emerge and dissolve before they ever have a chance to capture you. The fact is that when you are embodying presence, there is such a natural state of fullness that there is no need to seduce yourself with hope-ful thoughts. When you are simply present, you may actually find that the state created by any hopeful or positive thought pales in comparison with the fullness inherent in each moment.

Grounding yourself in the Now opens up space—a gap, in a sense—between any stimulus and your response. It is as though you have more time to choose your response to whatever may happen in your life, so you are less apt to be defensive, aggressive, irritable, fearful, or habitually reactive. You are less inclined to rush to judgment or make blind assumptions and hasty, emotionally charged decisions. Reactivity is not determined by the strength of the stimulus; rather, it is based on how far you are from your authentic self. In other words, how not-present you are.

Taking the Next Step

What I want to place before you, over and over again, is an invitation to eliminate unnecessary suffering in any circumstance by cultivating greater presence. As I have been illustrating in the previous pages, this means spending more of your life in the

Now and less time dwelling in stories about the past, the future, yourself, and anything or anyone you see as *other or not you:* other people, God, money, the environment, the world, the health-care system, your disease.

We human beings are thinking animals, but while thinking is an essential way of knowing, identification with our thoughts causes our thinking to become inferior. Once we believe our own thoughts and continue to unquestioningly assume that they are true, we are no longer thinking clearly. Actually, we are no longer thinking at all; we are simply repeating an already-programmed mental construct. We're like the software in a computer: software doesn't think—it simply organizes data according to how it has been programmed.

As essential as thinking is, there is one thing that you can never think about: the Now. That is, you can't get outside the present to make it an object of thought. This creates a fundamental dilemma: the only time that actually exists is the present moment; life is lived only in the Now. Yet nothing at all can be said about the present moment. In this sense, you cannot actually think about what is real. Your thinking is an abstract relationship to life, a mental representation; it is never anchored in something real like your body and its sensations and your true feelings. Thinking interprets and describes your body or feelings, but it does not actually let you know either directly. Only awareness does that.

Of course, thinking can be guided by reason, in which case every thought can be questioned and is understood to be hypothetical—not definitively true, and not an absolute representation of anything. But reason rarely guides thinking, and this is especially the case when you feel threatened. At such times thinking is too often anchored in your ego, with the beliefs and emotions created by your ego's project to make you separate and, in one way or another, special.

When people are unconscious of the way their ego tries to make them special, they unconsciously project their own specialness outward onto their career, their role, their nation, their religion, their ideology, and so on. When those individuals are in a position of power and influence, it can become a disaster. This is why seemingly brilliant minds can follow what appears to be a logical process and yet lead nations into war and even organized genocide. It is why the best-educated economists, mathematicians, and business managers could lead our financial system into a meltdown; or why humankind as a whole is systematically destroying the environment.

This is also why you can feel completely justified and reasonable about despising your ex-spouse and wasting thousands of dollars pursuing a divorce that will hurt him or her as much as possible, even though your judgments poison your own spirit and hurt your children (and possibly other people, too). How could you do otherwise when you are so special?

In this way, ego turns thinking (a remarkable mode of consciousness that allows you to contemplate and powerfully influence your own actions and the world around you) into an unchallenged mental reality that creates endless delusions that blind you to who you really are and the world as it actually is.

In *The Mandala of Being,* one of my earlier books, I introduced a process by which you can observe and experience firsthand the effects of the endless thoughts and stories you tell yourself. It is a simple way to understand egoic thinking and how it profoundly affects every aspect of your life experience, including your health.

In this book, my intention is to present the Mandala work in just enough detail so that you can readily grasp how to use this tool to assist your practice of presence, as well as support your own emotional and physical healing. (If you enjoy what you read in this section and would like to learn more about Mandala work, please pick up *The Mandala of Being* and/or go to my website, where there is a free e-course about working with the Mandala.)

The Mandala of Being:
A Compass for Living in the Now

Mandala is a Sanskrit word meaning "circle." It has been a universal symbol over millennia, particularly in Eastern spiritual traditions. In those traditions, mandalas are a form of sacred art—elaborate paintings that symbolically depict the journey from the world of illusion created by the ego to the realization of the timeless self at the center of us all.

The Mandala of Being is a simple way of modeling how your thinking mind operates relative to being aware in the present moment. It teaches you how to consistently live in the Now by graphically illustrating that there are only four places your thinking can carry you into when you aren't fully grounded in the present. Once you grasp the four ways you leave the Now, you simultaneously understand how to return to your aware self, which is always in the Now.

A practical tool for the practice of presence, the Mandala of Being will help you wake up and live more in awareness instead of in your head. In this way, you learn how to meet life's greatest challenges with much less suffering. And sometimes, as I have observed in my retreats, a deep experience of presence results in physical healing.[1]

Spend a few moments contemplating the following diagram. It is a representation of every single moment of your life. Notice that the arrows are pointing away from the *Now* and toward *Me, You, Past,* and *Future.* This represents where your thinking mind takes you when you are not truly present. As we progress in the work with the Mandala, you will see that what you are learning is how to turn those arrows around so that you are grounded in the present, in awareness.

The Mandala of Being: The Four Places the Mind Goes When Attention Leaves the Now

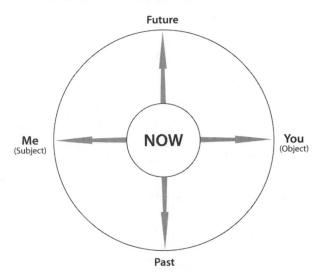

As you examine the Mandala diagram, how many Nows do you see? (Hint: This is a trick question.)

If you answered "One," look again. The Mandala of Being illustrates that there is *only* Now, but in a psychological sense, there are five different states of Now.

First and foremost, there is a particular quality of "Nowness" represented by the central Now position that is your aware self. In this central Now, you are fully embodied in the present moment. It can be likened to the state of flow or meditation. Your body is awake and ready, yet profoundly relaxed; your mind is simultaneously focused yet spacious. You are present with, and not at all in conflict with, what *is*. This state is what is meant by the expression *Being in the Now*. Relative to this, there are four other states of Now-ness:

1. The **Past** position represents when your thinking mind carries you into the past, and you identify with your thoughts about specific memories. *Past stories* will either generate a sense of pleasant reminiscence (for example, remembering something that made you proud or happy) or unpleasant reminiscence (as when you remember a situation that made you feel sad, guilty, or regretful).

2. The **Future** position represents any moment when you identify with your thoughts about the future, and as a result, your emotional state becomes determined by the nature of those thoughts. Since the future is always imaginary, these *Future stories* will either generate positive anticipation with emotions of hopefulness or eagerness, or negative anticipation with emotions of anxiety or even terror.

3. The **Me** position represents the emotional quality you experience in the present moment as a result of identifying with your judgments about yourself. As we have discussed, *Me stories* inevitably make you feel special: either grandiose or depressive.

4. And, finally, the **You** position represents what happens when you identify with your beliefs and judgments about other people or anything else you can think of: your career, the situation you are in, money, politics, God . . . the list is really endless. These stories will either elevate or diminish the person or thing you are thinking about, and as you identify with these *You stories,* you will experience emotions ranging from adoration to hate to hurt.

What the Mandala shows is that your emotional reality is not caused by something outside you. Rather, it is caused by your own thoughts: the stories you tell yourself about yourself, others, the past, and the future. These are the four ways you build a mental reality that is not actually real and in which you can create immense emotional suffering. You lose connection to your true self.

By working with the Mandala model, you will start to understand the relationship between what you are thinking and the emotions you are feeling, along with the corresponding effects you experience in your body. Here is a helpful breakdown of some of the positive and negative emotions according to each aspect of the Mandala:

Examples of Emotions Associated with the Four Positions of the Mandala of Being

Me: *Grandiose specialness:* superior, powerful, arrogant, aloof, haughty . . .
Depressive specialness: inferior, sad, inadequate, unwanted, unlovable . . .

You: *Elevating judgments:* appreciation, adoration . . .
Diminishing judgments: rage, resentment, jealousy, hate, hurt . . .

Past: *Positive reminiscence:* proud, happy, nostalgic . . .
Negative reminiscence: guilty, blame, regretful . . .

Future: *Positive expectancy:* hopeful, eager, ebullient . . .
Negative expectancy: worried, anxious, terrified . . .

By doing the work, you will have an opportunity to actually *feel* the consequences of your thoughts and stories in terms of how your body responds and the attitudes or moods your thinking creates. Soon you may find that you can correlate certain stories with the onset of muscle tension or stiffness, heaviness, contractedness, nervous agitation, changes in breathing or heart rate, stomach discomfort, or differences in your level of emotional as well as physical pain. You will also see that it is your stories about your situation—for example, about your marriage—that disturb you more than what your partner actually does (short of physical abuse, of course).

The Mandala of Being will help you understand how much the thoughts going through your head often weaken and hurt you, not to mention wounding others as well. It will give you a means of becoming aware and *waking up* right at the moment when you are being captured by a thought or story that would otherwise drag you into a stressful emotional quagmire.

Even thoughts that bring hope or pleasant reminiscences, while very welcome compared with those that frighten or depress you, do not bring as much intuitive wisdom or healing energy as when you rest in presence. Similarly, holding warm and positive thoughts of another person will not reveal the surprising depth of love or compassion that can suddenly arise when you are really present with someone and see that individual exactly as she or he is.

After a period of increasing your awareness and presence by using this practice, the process of waking up in the middle of any story that you're telling yourself will start to happen automatically. This directly affects the quality of your life and health far more than you can possibly imagine. This work will help you see what you are unconsciously doing (and what all of our minds are doing collectively) that gives rise to all the unnecessary suffering in the world.

The Now Position: Present-Moment Awareness

Discovering Focused-Spacious Awareness

The Now position at the center of the Mandala is present-moment awareness. You are resting into your natural state of being where no thought is creating an emotion in you. Your senses are alert: you are seeing and hearing whatever is happening, and you are feeling whatever is moving through you. You are aware of whatever images or thoughts are flowing through your mind, but you are not identified with any of them.

Shifting into the present moment is always a new beginning, a clean slate. Perhaps you are familiar with the children's toy that consists of a thin two-layer sketching surface on which you can draw any design, but when you lift up the top plastic sheet, everything you have created is instantly erased. Bringing yourself fully into the Now is like that toy, erasing the thoughts that are determining your emotional state. Your essential orientation becomes: *What is actually happening right now?* It is not a question you answer with another thought; it is a shift of awareness into a quality of alert receptivity in which thoughts recede and things are just as they are.

I know the concept that one must always be in the Now can be confusing. It makes it seem like you should be somewhere other than where you are. But actually, all that is being asked of you is to move from thinking to awareness. The nature of this state is difficult to describe because words make it seem paradoxical. It is a state in which you are at once focused and spacious, ready and relaxed.

In our usual or ordinary state of consciousness, we are either focused—often so focused that everything except what we are concentrating on disappears—or too spacious. That is, we lose ourselves in television or space out so that we aren't even aware of what someone is saying to us. Similarly, our bodies are often ready in the sense of being vigilant or poised for action, but not simultaneously relaxed. And when we are relaxed, we tend to drop off into dullness or drowsiness instead of being fully alert.

Generally speaking, we have been educated to train our mind to focus, not to be spacious. We become overspecialized. We learn to concentrate, to narrow our focus, but we are then unable to see the larger picture. On the other hand, when we are really present, our mind is both highly focused (every sense is vivid, colors are vibrant) and simultaneously spacious (there is a sense of being connected to a far larger reality). In our body, we are awake and poised, yet simultaneously deeply relaxed. In this state, there is a timeless sense of being at one with life and completely well in ourselves. Just as important, diving deeper into this state brings us naturally to new depths of insight and wisdom.

A way to appreciate the paradoxical yet unifying nature of "focused-spacious awareness" is to draw an analogy with the sun shining in space. Visualize the sun—its light radiating out into the galaxy and beyond limitlessly. Only a minuscule fraction falls upon the earth, moon, or other planets. In fact, even a million light-years from the sun, its light is filling every square millimeter of space, although you can only see that light when you look directly at the sun or at something it is shining upon.

The Sun Shining on Earth and into Space

Sunlight is similar in some ways to awareness. If you look for awareness, you cannot find it. What you do find is the belief that you are the one who is aware—the source of awareness—and at the same time, anything you turn your awareness toward or give your attention to is what you become aware of. For example, if I ask you to become aware of your breathing right now, you immediately will. Yet a moment before, although you were breathing, you were not aware of it. You had to turn your attention—or shine the "sunlight" of your awareness—toward your breathing to become aware of it.

Awareness is a sublime mystery; everywhere you turn your attention, you become aware of something. It gives you a seemingly limitless capacity to bring things into consciousness and grow in knowledge, yet you cannot find it—you cannot see awareness itself.

You can never make awareness itself an object of consciousness because you can never step outside of awareness to look back at it.

Of course the sun is not aware (as far as we know); it has no ego or personal identity like you and I do. It doesn't imagine that it is the earth just because its light is illuminating the earth. But this is exactly what your ego does. Your ego does not recognize itself as an aspect of a vast mind or expansive, spacious awareness. Instead, the ego identifies only with whatever it gives its attention to. It looks at an uncomfortable sensation and believes *I am uncomfortable.* Or it looks at the feeling of sadness and believes *I am sad.* Or it has the thought *I am better than she is* and feels superior. The ego has no sense that its capacity for consciousness comes from a larger mind, a limitless awareness.

Once you learn to rest in awareness, not just in ego, you can turn your attention precisely toward any sensation or feeling, but not collapse into it and identify with it. For example, take fear. If you turn your focus toward the feeling of fear and simultaneously remember that your awareness is also extending like sunlight without limit, you will be in a proper, conscious relationship to the sensation of fear. You can look directly at it while remaining expansive. You will feel the fear, but it will not be grabbed by your ego and become your identity. It will be what it is. And without the ego to create thoughts about the fear and about you, the feeling of fear is simply energy. It will flow on and become something else, just like weather flows on and is ever changing.

If you focus your attention on a powerful feeling like fear without remaining spacious, then the fear will be made worse by your stories about what might happen or what is wrong with you. Exactly the same thing happens if you turn your ego-level attention toward physical pain: the pain amplifies and is made even worse by your ego's stories about it. The ego will identify with the fear or the pain, make it about you, make it your problem, imagine a terrible future, or remember a better past. In short, your ego will make you suffer far worse than simply experiencing the sensation of fear or pain.

Practicing Focused-Spacious Awareness

Learning focused-spacious awareness takes practice . . . a lot of practice. The first step is to choose what to focus on. I suggest that you point your attention on any present-moment sensation. For example, bring your awareness to your hands, and you will notice that there is a subtle but easily noticeable sensation in them. If you then sway your arms even slightly, you will notice that as your hands move, the sensation you feel changes. You can use this subtle change of sensation as a focal point, or you could concentrate on the air moving through your nose.

Bring one of these sensations (either what you sense in your hands or in your nostrils) into the foreground of your awareness so that it becomes sharp and precise. Hold this inner gaze steadily but gently. At the same time, extend all of your senses: listen to sounds in the distance, and keep your eyes open but unfocused so that you can take in your peripheral vision. Even as you are vividly aware of your breath or hands, let your awareness also extend throughout your body and then beyond—into the room or wherever you are.

In the beginning, you may only be able to sustain this quality of attention very briefly because you have not built the muscle of this kind of awareness. But don't get discouraged; it's like any other kind of exercise in that it requires practice and your willingness. When your thoughts grab your attention and pull you away from focused spaciousness, gently return to your chosen focal point and resume practicing.

Another way to understand the practice is to work with the experience of "relaxed readiness." Imagine that your body is like a master martial artist poised at the moment before a competition begins: every sense is alert, and the whole body is ready to spring into action. Yet at the same time, the master is deeply relaxed, as serene as a contented baby.

Or here's a different image to try: See yourself in the starting blocks of a 100-yard dash just as the starter is calling out: "On your mark . . . get set . . ." But instead of saying, "Go!" he says, "Smile." A smile always brings a spontaneous quality of lightness and relaxation. And a smile together with your body fully awake and ready is—as paradoxical as this may seem—the very state in which you experience the fullness of being.

In practicing focused spaciousness or relaxed readiness, the gentleness of your attention is very important. Suppose you are practicing and notice discomfort in your body. Let go of the focus on your breathing or in your hands, and turn your inner gaze toward this disturbance. As you do so, softly bring your attention as well, as if it were a downy feather barely brushing the uncomfortable place in your body.

Do precisely the same thing if there is a strong feeling such as fear: touch it steadily with the softest attention while keeping your awareness spacious. The softer you can be with your attention, the more relaxed and spacious you will also be. It is nearly impossible to be soft and not also be spacious. The softer your attention, the less likely you will be to think about the sensation or feeling you are focusing on. And as long as you don't think, the sensation may release, and the feeling will flow onward rather than remaining stuck.

Most people understand focus because that is what they were trained to do in school, but spaciousness can be confusing. You can be spacious in the sense of extending all your senses out into your environment, but there are other dimensions of spacious. For example, consider that everywhere in the Universe, it is Now. To be present is to attend precisely to where you are, but it is also to extend at least intuitively into the Now-ness that is everywhere, into limitless vastness.

The aliveness or felt quality of every single moment of life depends on the degree to which you are simultaneously focused and spacious, ready and relaxed. Other than that, speaking of the Now is just an abstraction. There is no such thing as the Now; that is, you cannot step outside it and look back at it. So speaking of being in the Now is just another way of describing the quality of your attention. It is the quality of your attention that has everything to do with the quality of your experience.

The balance of focused-spacious awareness is a very good way to live your life far beyond meditation practice. If you begin to feel oppressed by the mundane and repetitive chores of so much of everyday life, for instance, you can simultaneously imagine the billions of other people on the planet repeating their chores each day as part of *their* everyday lives. Putting your own daily toil into the perspective of everyone's daily toil makes your own situation less personal and can help move your attitude toward acceptance.

Or if you are dwelling on your illness, you can remember that at any given moment there are millions of people who are ill, feeling more or less what you are feeling, thinking more or less similar thoughts about their fate. Again, your own illness is fully acknowledged but becomes less personal and more a part of the wholeness of life.

A balanced state of mind is also helpful in interpersonal relationships. For example, one evening recently I thought my wife was being unfairly critical of me. But before I told her what I didn't like about her comments, I did something for my own sense of well-being and for the sake of our relationship: I simultaneously brought to mind the loving and appreciative things she frequently tells me as well as the many sweet times that we share together. In other words, while I pointed to a specific instance of something I did not like, I kept in mind the larger picture of what I do cherish about her and our relationship.

The result was that I was balanced in myself, and my wife and I had an effective communication that brought us closer together. In the past I had often made the mistake of angrily reacting, and to further justify my resentment, I would recall other times when I felt wronged. But narrowing my awareness around something painful instead of holding our relationship in a larger perspective had only served to amplify my unhappiness and cause me to be more pessimistic, closed, and defensive.

The Power of Awareness

The quality of your experience in each moment is dynamic. The more balanced you are in being focused *and* spacious, ready *and* relaxed, the more fully alive and present you are. Little disturbances don't become big ones. Little fears don't become the center of your world. This is the great power of awareness: whatever you may focus on or are simply drawn toward (be it an idea, or feelings such as sorrow, fear, or love), there is always a larger space in which those specific thoughts or feelings are experienced. In this sense, who you really are as an aware being is always more than whatever you are aware of; you are always more than your stories.

Certain feelings and thoughts can seem overwhelming when you focus specifically on them. Your ego will immediately identify with them and create stories that intensify the feeling and imprison you in a narrow reality. But if you move your attention into the present and remain expansive, the feeling will not be as overwhelming; in fact, it will often transmute into presence and aliveness.

It is enlightening to realize that you can learn to consciously direct your attention in any way you choose and thereby train your mind to be both focused and spacious. As you do so, you will realize that the ego—what you mean when you think *me*—does not actually exist. *Me* itself is only a thought, a story, a very old habit of self-identification—not an actual thing. The moment you return to the Now, there is only awareness (awareness of sensations, feelings, thoughts, presence, being), not a separate me or ego. Who you really are cannot be isolated and defined; it can only be spoken about symbolically using words like *self.*

In learning this work, there isn't the expectation that you will immediately be able to step into the Now position at the center of the Mandala and instantly release worry, anger, sadness, or whatever stress you are experiencing. You certainly aren't expected to suddenly be filled with presence and bliss just because you have become more present. As with any spiritual or artistic discipline, presence is a learned skill. Sitting down to meditate or to write poetry doesn't necessarily mean that your mind will immediately become still, or that the words will flow effortlessly. With any conscious, intentional effort, there is repeated practice and also an element of mystery or grace in how you suddenly settle into a more connected, integrated state of being.

None of us will ever control this grace, but it's possible to cultivate it. So in the work I am about to describe, when I guide you to move to the Now position, it is about a choice to consciously step away from your thinking mind and bring your awareness fully into your body and into the present. It is about consciously taking charge of the quality of your attention and practicing focused spaciousness. It is about consciously bringing yourself into deep relaxation while becoming as fully alert as possible. It is inviting the timeless present to open to whatever depth it will allow to you each time you make the effort.

In navigation, it is essential to accurately know the latitude and longitude of your starting point in order to set a course for any new location. Similarly, in navigating through life, the Now becomes your starting point over and over again. This can also be seen as analogous to the way the first violinist sounds a note to which the rest of an orchestra tunes itself: the Now becomes the note that you attune to and against, as you can feel the contrast of how out of tune you become when you are identified with your Me, You, Past, and Future stories.

CHAPTER FIVE

A MAP TO EMOTIONAL CLARITY

This chapter will teach you how to work with the Mandala of Being in order to free yourself from the emotional suffering that so often accompanies a personal crisis or health challenge.

At this point, you have a choice: You can jump ahead to the next chapter and read the three examples of individuals I coach in using the Mandala self-inquiry work, or you can continue here and learn the basic steps of the practice first. But don't jump ahead just yet—at least read the next two paragraphs.

I placed this chapter ahead of the next because I believe that it will provide you with a better foundation for understanding why I guide those three people in the ways that I do. But sometimes actually seeing the process unfold (in this case, observing others using the technique) can make it easier to comprehend. So if you are someone who feels more comfortable reading examples before trying it for yourself, then do skip ahead to Chapter 6. (But be sure to return to this chapter so that you can learn how to use the Mandala for yourself.) On the other hand, if you prefer to find out more about the Mandala work and then gain additional insight by reading the case histories afterward, then continue reading through this chapter before going to the next.

Whichever option you choose, be encouraged: You are going to learn to free yourself from the kinds of stories that make you a victim or weaken you. You are also going to step away from the stories that others may want to project on you. This technique is not magic—you must do the work. But with a little practice, you will have a compass inside of you that always brings you back to center.

Getting Started

To begin, create your own Mandala. You need five cards or pieces of paper approximately five by seven inches in size. On each card, print one of these words in large letters: PAST, FUTURE, ME, YOU, and NOW. I suggest you make the word *Now* larger and bolder because it is the essential position that all of the others are relative to. Lay the labeled cards out on any open floor area as shown in the Mandala of Being diagram in the previous chapter on page 49. (You may wish to bookmark that page, as we will refer to the Mandala diagram often.)

Next, stand in the center at the Now position, orienting yourself so that the Future position is in front of you at 12 o'clock, the Past card is behind you at 6 o'clock, and Me and You are at 9 o'clock and 3 o'clock respectively. Let the radius between the Now position and the outer positions be about two feet, as if you were placing them on a clock large enough to walk around.

Your own Mandala of Being is now ready to work with. If you are not creating one at the moment, imagine that it will look like a large round board game on the floor that you can stand on and move comfortably from marker to marker.[1]

If it is a better alternative for you, instead of standing and walking around the Mandala, use a chair and move it to each position so that you can sit as you work. If you are confined to a bed or don't have enough space to work in, create a much smaller Mandala on a table or tray. Move your hand around to rest at each position as appropriate.

In this practice, you'll be revisiting a situation in which you became emotionally stressed or reactive and using the Mandala model to learn where your ego took you and what you were telling yourself that created your state of "contraction." The premise of this work is that once you become aware of how the stories you tell yourself do this to you, you won't have to get caught in such a state again.

Recognizing When You Are Contracted

To appreciate what I mean by *contraction*, first connect to a memory when you felt filled by life, utterly peaceful and joyful. Or think about a time when you could regard even challenging circumstances with calmness and see many possibilities for improving the situation. Can you recall the expansive sensation in your body, the feeling of well-being, and the vividness of your senses? What kind of thoughts were going through your mind, if any? As you relish this memory of when you were simply present and working with your circumstances instead of fighting against them, note that this is actually your natural way of being.

Now, for contrast, bring to mind a situation when you were short-tempered, impatient, or emotionally insatiable—nothing could satisfy you, nothing was right or good enough, and people easily got on your nerves. Can you remember how you felt? Perhaps you sensed that you were tightly wound or on edge. Were you ready to flee or attack, or did you feel so numb that nothing registered?

When you are contracted, you may not recognize it at first or even have any idea what is causing it. For example, a woman I was working with was totally oblivious to what was really happening to her at the closing session of one of the seminars I conducted. She was just starting to fall in love with a man who was also in the program, and he had left that morning while she was staying on for a few more days. She knew that she felt off-kilter emotionally because certain others in the group were annoying her immensely, and she nearly bit their heads off for no reason at all.

She recognized that she was contracted and could even describe feeling like a little kid flopping her legs on the floor in front of her with a sort of resigned sigh, a "fed-upness." Yet all the while she had absolutely no clue that she was upset about her new love's recent departure; in fact, she was not even aware of thinking much about him. Later I told her that I sensed her contraction was about this man leaving, which she immediately recognized as spot-on, and could hardly believe she had not seen it herself.

Her state of contraction was like wearing blinders. She was irritable and uncomfortable in her own skin and acting out, but she was unable to connect to or identify the root cause. It was especially distressing to her because it happened despite her having the recognition that she was indeed contracted, which shows just how blind one can be in this state.

When you are contracted, like the word suggests, you have become psychologically smaller: you don't have access to your own sense of fairness; your wiser self is submerged. Yet you do not understand what it is that you are subconsciously telling yourself, which is causing this state.

Ordinarily, we are happy when these moods pass and don't want to go back and revisit them. But once we are on the path of consciousness and self-healing, every time we become contracted, it is an invitation to find out what we were consciously and also subconsciously telling ourselves. In other words, it is an opportunity to grow in self-understanding. Therefore, instead of feeling ashamed of becoming contracted or wanting to forget about it and bury it in the past, we actually become enthusiastic to see what new understanding and clarity we can arrive at about ourselves.

♺ ♺

Each time you use the Mandala work, the first step is to always begin at the central position labeled Now because, like a sailor, you cannot navigate to a new destination unless you know where you are starting from. (Of course, the only true place one can ever start from is the Now.)

Once you are centered at the Now position and experience your natural state free of thought-generated unhappiness, you can bring the specific episode in which you became emotionally contracted into mind. Then begin to look for the stories you were telling yourself that created that contraction. As you do so, you will move from the center (Now) position to the position on the Mandala where it seems each story most belongs. Some stories will pertain primarily to the Past position, some will concern the Future, and some will be about yourself (Me) or other people and things (You).

In this work, the crucial touchstone is your quality of being when you are standing in the Now position in focused-spacious awareness. That state is then consciously compared to how you are when you are identified with one of your stories at any of the outer four positions. The skills for experiencing this contrast are clearly described in the discussion that follows.

When you experience the energetic shift and palpable sensation of calm or relief as you repeatedly set your stories aside and return to the Now, your body begins to recognize what presence feels like, and then that state becomes increasingly easier to inhabit. As you work with the Mandala and return yourself over and over to the Now position, you join a vast field of awareness, an unlimited source of vital energy and intuitive wisdom that will bring you new insight and restore you to well-being.

Working with the Mandala of Being

I strongly recommend that as you start working with the Mandala, you write down your stories in simple sentences before you begin. I also recommend that you say or read each story aloud and actually speak out loud during the whole process, even if you are working alone. Hearing your own voice makes the learning much more immediate than just thinking your way through it. I also encourage you to actually move around the Mandala in whatever way you are able. (We learn more effectively when we involve our bodies rather than just relying on our thinking alone.)

When you are ready, choose a location that is private and quiet, and ensure that you will not be interrupted. Turn off any phones and set aside enough time to give yourself the gift of unhurried self-exploration that will assist with your healing.

As you read the following steps that describe the Mandala process, please don't worry if at first you don't fully understand it. When you get to the actual examples of people working with the Mandala in the next chapter, I suggest that you read them through and then return to this section and reread it. Then you will be ready to begin to do your own inside-out healing.

Let's get started.

Step #1: Define the Issue You Want to Work On

For the purpose of doing the Mandala work, I use the word *issue* in a very specific sense: an issue is *a situation* in which you become emotionally contracted, or what I refer to as being "muddy." Perhaps you have heard a variation of the phrase "letting your mud settle." For me, it describes returning to your natural state of being, unclouded by the churning of emotions. Being muddy can mean feeling scared, guilty, angry, or resentful; it can mean that you're becoming temperamental, getting into an argument, losing confidence (or being overconfident), becoming despondent, or attacking yourself.

Being muddy encompasses just about any state when you are agitated or stressed and lose connection to the natural clarity of your awake, spacious awareness. The circumstances in which this might occur are nearly limitless. Perhaps the greatest muddiness (and suffering) occurs in interpersonal relationships where there is judgment and conflict, but health problems can certainly make you muddy, too.

The important thing in choosing an issue to work on is to clearly define it. For example, one of my clients has emphysema that limits her ability to walk or climb stairs. On a particular day she underestimated the time it would take for her to arrive at an appointment, and as a result, she pushed herself too hard. This precipitated a full attack of shortness of breath that required her to use an inhaler and spend a half hour getting her breath under control. While resting and waiting for her breathing to settle down, she fell into feelings of shame and despair.

Initially the issue my client wanted to work on in the Mandala process was having emphysema, but having emphysema is not an issue—it is a fact of her life. With a little coaching from me, she defined the issue specifically in this way: "Rushing to an appointment, I became short of breath and felt despair." Now we could work on the stories about herself and her health that created her negative feelings.

How you name the issue you want to work on using this technique is significant. Remember that an issue should be defined concretely in a way that links the specific situation to the state of contraction.

Here is another example of an issue that could be readily worked with using the Mandala process: "The argument with my boyfriend yesterday at lunch." Stated in this way, you could now look for the Me, You, Past, and Future stories that you were consciously or subconsciously identified with that caused the argument. But suppose you jumped to an analysis of yourself and defined the issue as this instead: "I give my power away too easily." With this generalization about your behavior, you think you understand what you do that caused the argument. In fact, the belief "I give my power away too easily" is just one Me story, at most a piece of what might have provoked the argument. In my experience, it is much harder to do the work when the inquiry process begins with a story or generalization about yourself or others and is not grounded in a specific situation.

Although it happens to everyone—sometimes quite frequently —it is not your natural state of being to be muddy. It is not just "human nature," something that you have to simply accept and live with. Muddiness is created by your ego, which is only *an aspect of* human nature. To become contracted, or muddy, you have to tell yourself stories that generate defensive, reactive, depressive, or aggressive emotions and behavior. All of the Mandala work is predicated on the acceptance of this basic truth: *It is not what others do or the situation itself that causes you to contract and become muddy; it is the stories you tell yourself about all of that.*

So take a thoughtful look at your life and notice when you were feeling contracted recently. Write down the situation and what happened to be sure you have formulated it as specifically and clearly in your mind as you can. This notation can be brief, but it should state the basic problem or issue that is (or was) disturbing you. You can use the Muddy Me Worksheet in the Appendix to help you. I call it "Muddy Me" because I think this way of describing oneself adds a bit of humor. The work is serious, but it's good to smile a little about it. Learning to let your mud settle is an excellent metaphor for the Mandala work because it speaks directly to how emotionally churned up your stories can make you feel and how by returning to the Now you are restored to calm and clarity.

Step #2: Center in the Now

Once you have clearly described the issue, the next step is to center yourself in the Now. (For a refresher on how to do this, reread the section on focused-spacious awareness in the previous chapter.) I recommend that you actually step into your Mandala and stand over the Now marker as you bring yourself into focused-spacious awareness. Once you feel yourself present in your body, ready and relaxed, you have created your reference point for how it feels when you are fully aware and not caught up in your thoughts.

As the Mandala shows, when you are not really present in the timeless Now, there are only four other places you can go: into a Now emotionally determined by identification with stories about yourself (Me) or others (You), or into a Now emotionally created by your Past or Future stories. Keep in mind that how you experience the present moment is always powerfully influenced by what you are telling yourself.

Often it may seem that the reaction that precipitated your muddiness came on in a flash; that you were not thinking. You might believe that your reaction was spontaneous and therefore entirely natural, not something created by your ego. But trust me; there are always a whole host of stories that you have been telling yourself for a long time so that you no longer have to consciously think them in order to be influenced by them. These long-ago internalized stories are the subconscious foundation of whatever reaction occurred. The work is to learn to recognize both the conscious and subconscious stories. It is a process I call "unpackaging," unwrapping the specific stories hidden within a muddy state and making them conscious in order to free yourself from their influence.

Step #3: Unpackage the Specific Stories

Even if you found yourself muddy (angry or fearful) so fast that you don't think there are any stories behind it, take a few moments and pose this question: "What must I have been telling myself about myself, others, the past, and the future in order to have become so muddy?" Another version of this question is: "What was I believing [about myself, others, the past, or the future] in order to have become so disturbed?" Then, to get started discovering your stories, sense which of the four outer positions on the Mandala you feel drawn toward first and move there.

For instance, if you recognize that you did go into the future and became scared, step to the Future marker and look to see what you were telling yourself about the future. If you use the Muddy Me Worksheet, you will see that for each of the four positions there are a series of statements. These are meant to help stimulate your discovery of your stories. If these statements are helpful for you in finding your stories, that is good; but they are not the only way you can frame your stories, so do not feel limited to what the worksheet offers.

Keeping the issue in mind, move around the Mandala to the different positions and examine what you were telling yourself when you became muddy. In the Me position, look for what you were telling yourself about yourself. In the You position, look for your judgments about the situation or a specific person. In the Past position, look for what memories come to you as you keep the issue in mind. What stories do you tell yourself about those memories?

One at a time, unpackage the stories you were telling yourself. Sometimes you may not be aware of them for all four positions; this is not important. Simply do your best to recognize as many of the stories as possible, and write them down as well as speaking them out loud.

Sometimes a particular story may seem to belong in more than one position, and it takes a little experience to know which position is the appropriate one for each story. For instance, suppose you are upset in a relationship and you tell yourself, "I feel sad that my boyfriend doesn't care about me." At first glance you might think this is a Me story because it starts out as a description of how *you* feel. So, working with the Mandala, you might move to the Me position. However, saying "I feel sad" is actually reporting your emotional state, which presumably is a true description of how you feel: a factual statement and not a story at all. On the other hand, the emotion of sadness is the result of the belief "My boyfriend doesn't care about me."

Therefore, if I were coaching you, I would suggest that your belief is the actual story and that you should move into the You position. It is a You story because it is *your* judgment of your boyfriend's attitude toward *you*. Believing it makes you sad, but it doesn't make the story true.

Generally, you can tell if a story is a Past or Future one by the tense of the verb. For example, the belief "My father abandoned us when I was nine years old" is a story about your father, and you might want to call it a You story. But it is actually an old interpretation of your father's behavior, so I would call it a Past story.

Always being correct about where a story belongs is not important. Just recognizing that you are in fact telling yourself stories is really what you want to grasp. So do not worry if it isn't obvious at first where a story belongs on the Mandala. With practice you will gain clarity as to how to recognize the kind of story you are telling yourself, and soon you will easily know which position to move to on the Mandala.

Remember that the more simply you state the story, the easier it will be for you to work with it. For instance, a story could be stated as: "My parents treat me like a hypochondriac," or "My father doesn't acknowledge how sick I really am." These are straightforward You stories because the first one is your judgment about how your parents treat you, and the second is your judgment of your father's behavior. Another story might be: "I'll never really feel good again." This is a simple Future story because it is how you imagine yourself in the future.

Avoid long complex statements such as: "I feel that my wife doesn't care about how much money she spends; therefore, I have to keep working more than I want to even though I am ill." In this example, there are really three separate stories: "My wife doesn't care about how much money she spends," "I have to keep working more than I want to," and "I am ill." Also, notice how the story starts with the words *I feel that*. Actually, this is not a feeling at all but a thought—specifically, a judgment of your wife's behavior that you are disguising as a feeling.

It is not uncommon to disguise judgments as feelings, but there is a distinct difference. Feelings are facts. If I ask you, "How do you feel?" and you say, "There is a heaviness in my chest," I do not consider that statement a story. It is a description of your state, presumably an accurate one. But if you answer, "I feel things should be different," that is a judgment and therefore a story.

Step #4: Consciously Experience What Each Story Creates in You

Now that you have unpackaged the stories, it is time to consciously experience what identifying with each one creates in you. As the Mandala shows, there is only Now, but your state of being and how each moment is experienced depends on what you are telling yourself.

Suppose the issue is your dissatisfaction with your marriage, and at the Me position you saw that you were telling yourself this story: "I have thrown away 20 years of my life in a bad relationship." Stand at the Me position, speak your story aloud, and begin to explore it with an open mind and willing heart. Look inside and ask yourself: "When I believe this story and I'm identified with it, how does it make me feel? What happens to my energy? What emotions are present? What physical sensations does it create in me? What images, if any, does this story call forth?" Let yourself fully experience what each specific story creates in you when you identify with it.

Even if it is quite painful to embody a particular story, such as the one just mentioned, don't be afraid. This is a precise **awareness experiment:** you are intentionally embodying the psycho-physiological (mental and physical) effect of a specific story. This is conscious work in contrast to being reflexively hijacked by the story, which is what happened when you reactively became upset and muddy. I call this work of conscious identification with a story that creates distress "tasting the poison."

Of course, not every story creates unhappiness; some can make you quite excited, eager, or even sexually aroused. You are human and have the freedom to indulge your fantasies. Sometimes it is relaxing and healthy to do so. But if you are repeatedly captured by what is otherwise a pleasant story or fantasy that pulls you to the past or the future, the emotional state created by that story blinds you to this moment, to what *is*. I call consciously experiencing these hypnotically pleasing stories "tasting the narcotic."

Step #5: Create Contrast with the Story

When you have truly tasted—embodied—how the story makes you feel, return to the center of the Mandala. As you take this step, prepare to be leaving the Now created by identification with the story and moving to a new Now. This time, once you are standing in the Now position, explore a new awareness experiment: imagine yourself in exactly the same situation in which you became muddy, but *without* that particular story.

For example, one of the stories that my client John worked on with me was about how he became easily tired and short-tempered at his job. When he unpackaged his stories, one of them was a Me story: "I am wasting my life in a career I don't like." So he moved to the Me position in the Mandala and felt how tired, depressed, and resentful that story made him. Then I asked John to step back to the Now marker and visualize himself at work facing the usual challenges, but this time the depressive Me story never entered his mind. He was quiet for a while and then said that he felt more spacious, relaxed, and even more confident about himself. He described imagining himself at work with more patience and with a sense of trust that this stage of his career was just a stepping-stone to new possibilities.

This **second awareness experiment**—imagining that in exactly the same situation a specific story never entered your mind—utilizes the skill of "active imagination," a powerful tool for any kind of inner work. In using this tool, you don't try to impose what images will come or what you think you should feel or how things should look. You don't automatically assume that you will feel relieved or better. Instead, you surrender the process to your unconscious mind and let it take you to how you would be without the story. You relax and don't rush to some expected outcome. You allow your unconscious mind to present you with a new experience of yourself. You observe whatever spontaneous imagery may arise and let yourself fully taste and embody whatever quality of feeling comes. What is this state like? How do you truly feel?

Your intellect may argue with this process, saying, for example, "This is not real. The story I told myself is what I was actually thinking in those circumstances. Now you are changing the circumstances." And that is precisely the case; you are changing the circumstances *of your thinking* in order to create a contrast in which you are making the story you were telling yourself *relative* to another possibility. What the intellect doesn't understand is that the original story is also just an invention of the ego and in that sense just as relative. The ego is choosing its particular version of a story not because it is intrinsic to the situation, but because it is the ego's habit of interpreting any situation through the lens of depressive or grandiose specialness. But until you create a contrast, you cannot be conscious of the relativity of the original story.

In doing this new experiment, just as you did when you were feeling what the story created in you, take enough time to actually feel how different you would be in the same situation if the story never entered your mind. Don't just think of how you would probably feel—actually let yourself feel it.

Ordinarily, you simply identify with your stories and are immediately caught in the emotional reality they create. You implicitly believe that the story is true and is the only reality. (This is how most of us experience our stories.) By doing this experiment, you are not denying the story or trying to let it go or refute it. You are simply using your imagination to actively create a new scenario, a potential for a different Now. The important thing is to really feel how you would be without the story, and to stay with this feeling. Stay in your body and notice what happens to your energy, your posture, and your breathing as you imagine yourself in an entirely different scenario, one in which the story never captured you.

♨ ♨

This is where the magic happens. There is a basic Law of Consciousness: To be conscious of something, there needs to be contrast with something else. I like to say that "consciousness loves contrast."

Put simply, you cannot be aware of something without contrast. In the contrast between the felt sense of who you are when you are identified with a story and who you are in the Now position imagining yourself without the story, you are experiencing two distinct versions of yourself. More precisely, you are experiencing two distinct Now moments, two distinct states of being. In this contrast, you have the potential to awaken to the new beingness available to you in every moment.

In this embodied experience of two different states, you are essentially two different people: one is your ego that has been creating your emotional reality through each story it tells you; and the other is a new and unknown you, born when that ego-generated story is not present. It is actually being "born again." To be clear, I do not mean in the traditional religious sense that would have you identify yourself with a new belief system. No, this is being born again in an existential sense; this is a new you, albeit a glimpse of someone you have not known consciously before.

In experiencing this contrast, you suddenly have the potential for a whole new relationship to yourself. You are opening to a wider and healthier emotional possibility. This is wisdom and it happens spontaneously. I have seen this intuitive wisdom emerge countless times in working with a great many people. It arises naturally through the contrast between an old mind-made (story-created) ego state and the immediacy and clarity of who you experience yourself to be in the Now.

Step #6: Re-experience the Original Story

Once you have thoroughly embodied how you feel as you stand on the Now marker imagining yourself without the story, you can explore a **third awareness experiment:** *Slowly* return to the position where you first explored how the story made you feel and try that same story on again. That is, once again experiment with identifying with the original story, but this time remember how you felt in the Now position a few moments ago when you imagined yourself without it. To reinforce this memory, when you step back to the position that corresponds to the story, turn and face toward the center of the Mandala.

Returning to the example of John, who was tired and irritable at work, you saw that when he actively imagined himself without the depressing story ("I am wasting my life in a career I don't like"), he felt more spacious and experienced a sense of confidence in himself and trust that new opportunities would come his way. Once I was sure that he had thoroughly tasted this new state of being, I invited him to make the third awareness experiment: to once again try on the original depressive Me story, but to do so while remembering how he had felt moments before when standing in the Now position without the story.

Immediately, he said that he didn't want to. When I asked him why, his response was that to identify with that story again would be stupid; it would be like intentionally striking his thumb with a hammer, even though he knew exactly how much pain that would cause him. He had no desire to do so.

The quality of inner listening when you conduct this third experiment is to sense whether the story has the same power or immediacy as it had when you first consciously identified with it. If you sense that its power over you has changed, how has it changed? Then ask yourself if you now have a new understanding or insight about the story, or about the whole muddy episode.

Whenever you arrive at this step—experiencing the contrast between who you are with and without the story—spend a few minutes really considering the veracity of each story. This is crucial because (as we will discuss in a moment) most of the stories you tell yourself are not really true. But as important as it can be to recognize that a story you are telling yourself is not true, it is equally important to clearly see which part of yourself the story *was* true for. In other words, a part of you believed the story to be true, or it wouldn't have identified with it.

For instance, in the case of John's story, "I am wasting my life in a career I don't like," when I asked which part of him had believed that story, he intuitively saw that it was primarily his depressiveness that believed it. But as he thought about it, he also began to realize that it was his grandiosity that made him feel that he was above that job and therefore wasting his life. This was a key leap of insight for him, because he had not seen that while he often put himself in a victim position, he was also unconsciously holding on to a sense of grandiosity.

When you judge yourself or others, a part of you believes that those judgments are true. I will tell you a secret, though: there is no way to know if a judgment is true, but there is a truth to every judgment. That truth is what that judgment makes you feel. If I were telling myself that I was wasting my life in my career, I would feel quite depressed and angry with myself—just as John did. If I did not know enough to offer myself a contrast so that I could see what this judgment was creating in me and instead simply assumed it was true, I would be poisoning myself with my own thinking and blaming myself or my career.

When you defend a belief, presuming it to be true, what you are really defending is how the belief makes you feel—the identity it helps you support, whether grandiose or depressive. Whether any belief is ultimately true is very difficult and often impossible to know, especially when it involves your subjective opinion. But even with things that are seemingly objective—such as trees, genes, viruses, and so on—what we believe about these things is hard to call true.

The whole project of science is to try to use reason and empirical data to determine if an assertion is true. But as those in the medical profession well know, a lot of what we learn in medicine is not true; often, it proves to be outright wrong. It just takes us some time, and often a lot of unnecessary suffering, to figure out what information is false or what is true enough that it is worth continuing to rely on.

By letting yourself actually feel what happens when you are identified with a story, you are feeling the personal truth of that story. But that is not real truth; it is the delusion created by identification with the story. As you examine it more closely, see if it holds up as really true or begins to sound like it could be a fiction created in your own mind. Even if you insist that it is true, look at what that belief is doing to you in terms of the stress it creates. Then you can ask yourself, "What part of me believes this is true?" See if you can recognize in what way it makes you special. Is it your grandiose or depressive self for which the story seems true?

Remember that your ego doesn't care whether you are miserable —it only cares that it remains the part of you that is calling the shots. It keeps you in a dream, and while it may promise you happiness (perhaps by telling you that once you find the right career everything will be better), until you see the ego as the contraction that it is, wherever you go it will find some way to make you dissatisfied once again.

Spending even a few minutes free from any stress-producing story is deeply healing for the body and soul. The soul has a hard time shining out through fearfulness, guilt, resentment, jealousy, and hurt. Realize that you always have a choice whether to hang on to a story, change it, or let it go because your true self is the deeper consciousness behind any story. Once you become aware of how a story makes you feel, you can decide for yourself which choice best supports you on your healing journey.

Step #7: Reframe the Story

Often by the time you have felt the contrast between the Now with a particular story and the Now without that story, you will have gained enough insight not to let yourself remain identified with the story. If you hear your ego trying to hijack you by telling you that same story again, you know exactly where that story leads (emotionally). Therefore, you don't have to be tricked into following it. You can choose to stay present and spacious and taste the Now moment as a constantly renewed and reborn self. This is real freedom and transformation; it is usually as far as you need to go. But sometimes it can prove helpful and lead to even deeper insight to allow yourself to explore what happens when you embody alternative ways of framing the story.

This is advanced work. I am including it now because not only can it help guide you to a deeper realization of pure awareness, but it is also a good practice for clearing the webs of delusion that can be so hurtful in interpersonal relationships. And it is precisely with the pain of interpersonal conflict that this discussion continues.

Let's look deeper at this step, using my client Carl as an example. Carl has had an argument with his partner, Janet, and he is using the Mandala to gain insight into how he became muddy with resentment toward her. In working with the Mandala, he realizes that one of his stories about his partner is: "Janet doesn't trust me, and she never has." Standing in the You position, Carl recognizes that this You story creates shame and anger in him. He then explores standing in the Now position and imagines being with Janet *without* that story; and in doing so, he begins to feel somewhat lighter and more relaxed. Then returning to the You position and tasting the story for a second time, he at first thinks that this story comes from his depressive side.

But on further reflection, Carl realizes it is a story that feels true to his grandiose side: of course, everything would be fine if Janet trusted him. "Nothing grandiose about that!" he mutters sarcastically. This additional insight helps him feel more caring and be more empathetic toward Janet. But Carl still senses a lingering taste of contraction around this story of his partner's distrust of him. So I invite him to take a further step and suggest that he work with the opposite story: "Janet trusts me, and she always has."

Concepts always exist as pairs of opposites: *up* and *down*, *good* and *bad*, *left* and *right*, *yes* and *no*, *does* and *doesn't*, and so on. In telling himself the story "Janet doesn't trust me, and she never has," the opposite, "Janet trusts me, and she always has," is automatically presumed even if it is not consciously thought. Therefore, by asking Carl to spend some time identifying with the opposite story, I am calling him toward a more complete embrace of his consciousness. Said in another way, the second version of the story is a shadow of the first version.

While standing in the You position and identifying with the opposite story (that Janet does trust him and always has), Carl feels that it creates warmth and a sense of openness in him. He likes feeling this way.

The next step is for my client to move to the Now position and imagine that this (opposite) story has also never entered his mind, but he finds this difficult to do. He recognizes that it is far easier for him to imagine himself without the first painful version of the story than to imagine that the second pleasant version never entered his mind.

Recognizing Carl's dilemma, I ask him to imagine that he is holding the first story ("Janet doesn't trust me, and she never has") in his left hand and remember the shame and resentment that story creates in him. At the same time, I ask him to imagine holding the opposite story ("Janet trusts me, and she always has") in his right hand and experience the warmth and openness this story creates. I ask him to shift his attention back and forth between the two stories and the two different emotional states. Then using the image of each story being a dove sitting in each hand, I guide him to visualize letting them both fly away at the same time. A moment later, I ask my client how he felt as he observed them fly off. He describes a sense of stillness and space, a sense of just being. He feels clear and at peace.

The purpose of this fourth and **final awareness experiment** of releasing both stories at the same time is to experience what is there without either story. However briefly, you taste your natural state of freedom when you are simply aware and not identified with either version of the story. This is the ancient wisdom of "Neither this nor that," which is a foundational understanding of many contemplative religious traditions. In attempting to free the mind from illusion, a contemplative—a person who is trying to realize Freedom or Truth—knows that he or she must go beyond the pairs of opposites. For a moment, this is what Carl has experienced: his simple essential being. It is a moment of no thought, of pure awareness. It is a taste of the authentic self.

But the work is not finished. There are several other ways to reframe Carl's original You story: "Janet doesn't trust me, and she never has." One is reversing the story so it becomes a Me story: "I [Carl] don't trust Janet, and I never have." And the next is the opposite Me story: "I [Carl] trust Janet, and I always have."

These new ways of reframing the original story come from understanding the interconnected and thus interchangeable nature of the Me and You poles of the Mandala. Instead of a You story about how Carl believes Janet judges him, the story is reframed as a Me story: how Carl judges Janet.[2]

As before, I guide my client to identify with and embody the story that he has now reframed as "I don't trust Janet, and I never have." Immediately, Carl senses that this is actually truer for him than believing Janet doesn't trust him. This story makes him feel sad and brings him to, in his words, "that abysmal place I know so well." Taking the next step in the process, Carl returns to the Now position and imagines himself without this story. Gradually, he feels some relaxation, but it is hard for him to shake a sense of heaviness. When he steps back to the Me position and tries the story on again, he feels the weight of his own feelings of distrust. He recognizes this way of thinking as an old habit he has used to push away people who get close to him.

Carl's mood changes completely when he works with the opposite story: "I trust Janet, and I always have." This story creates a sense of well-being, and Carl tells me that his heart feels open. When he steps back into the Now position and imagines that this story never entered his mind, he again feels as though he doesn't want to release the happier version.

As with the other stories, I ask him to hold both of these stories and then alternate left and right, feeling what each one creates. I then guide him to release them simultaneously. He says, "Well, I knew what was coming—but actually, there is a sense of a different kind of space."

"Different how?" I ask him.

Carl is quiet but then responds, "I'm not sure. . . . We really do screw around with our heads, don't we?"

"So you are beginning to understand that?"

"Oh yes," he replies.

The deepest moment for Carl came next when he reframed the original story by taking Janet out entirely and placing himself as both the subject and object. The stories then became "I don't trust myself, and I never have" and the opposite "I trust myself, and I always have."

This way of reframing is often the most powerful because so many of our judgments of others are projections of the unconscious ways we judge ourselves. When Carl stands in the Me position and lets himself feel what the story "I don't trust myself, and I never have" creates, he describes a really dark place: "It is total shame, total self-rejection—the dark place of self-hatred that I often get pulled into."

"Try to step to the Now position and imagine that this story never entered your mind," I suggest.

Carl steps to the center of the Mandala and is quiet for a long time. "It's lifting a little," he tells me. "I can feel more space." Spontaneously, he imagines that he is speaking to Janet, telling her, "I am so sorry. I put so much on you, but it's my stuff." Then with a laugh at the irony, he points to the Me position and assures me, "I'm not going back there—at least not to that story. Let's do the other one."

"Perfect," I respond.

Carl steps to the Me position and speaks out loud: "I trust myself, and I always have." Immediately his eyes begin to water. "I feel pardoned, as if a great sin has been lifted from my shoulders," he reports. "There is heat in my chest—a feeling of sweet warmth."

"Enjoy it," I offer. "Let your body restore itself in something that is just as valid a belief about yourself and one that is far more generous and gentle. Being gentle with yourself is not something you have had much practice with."

"True," Carl responds. "But damn, I know that you're going to ask me to walk back to the Now marker and imagine that even this story never entered my mind. Can't I stay here?"

"You can, if you want to, but I suggest that you don't worry about imagining yourself without this last story, and do one last exploration." I guide Carl to slowly step back to the Now position and take the story "I don't trust myself, and I never have" in his left hand and the opposite "I do trust myself, and I always have" in his right. Once again, I ask him to let himself engage first one story and then the other—to feel the shame and self-rejection as he shifted his weight to the left side and the pardon and sweet warmth as he shifted his weight to the right side. I again use the image of two doves; this time a black one in his left hand and a white one in his right hand.

"Just keep going side to side, from one story to the other. Speak each story aloud, and let yourself fully feel what each creates in you. Don't rush. Look at how each is part of two different emotional realities, two different psychologies—each created simply and only by your thinking.

"Now let them both fly away and just remain present." After a short pause, I ask Carl to describe what he is experiencing.

Immediately, he says, "Pinpoint awareness. There is everything and nothing. I am solid and I am space."

Once again, Carl has seen beyond the veil of this or that and has a taste of pure awareness.

After a minute I acknowledge him for doing a challenging piece of work and ask him what insight he has gained. He responds that he has never before seen so clearly how much emotion and false identity hides in almost any judgment he makes of himself or anyone else. He recognizes that from one thought to the next he is either hiding in depressiveness when he is really being grandiose, or being grandiose to disguise depressiveness. He says that he sees that if he really looks at all the alternative ways of reframing a story, he can't believe any story. After these reflections, he vows to apologize to Janet because she has had to deal with so much of his unconsciousness. It is clear that he means what he is saying.

From Ego to Awareness

If you want to free yourself from the power of your own judgments, take a good look at all of the ways those judgments can be reframed. In doing so, you view aspects of yourself that you might not otherwise appreciate. You expose your shadow and quickly see how much you are projecting, sometimes on others and sometimes on yourself.

Once you understand that every story can be reframed in several ways and that each reframed story has an opposite, the only path to freedom is to see and feel the reality that each one creates and rest in the awareness that acknowledges both and is neither. If you choose one version, the other hides somewhere in your life and someday rears its head. Each version is a different you—a different psychology, a different way of viewing the world. And none of those ways, even though some feel better than others, sees accurately or honestly.

In our culture we are constantly told to choose the positive over the negative. But everything is always both, starting with our body. We cannot flex a muscle without stretching another. It is the dance of positively and negatively charged ions that makes it possible for nerves to conduct their signals. Psychologically it is the same: we cannot make something important without something else being ignored or remaining unseen.

To taste a moment of pure awareness and know yourself as neither the happy nor unhappy person, as neither the weak nor strong person, this is freedom; it is the birthplace of wisdom . . . a place where you can be surprised by love and life's beauty. It is a place of awakening where any psychological wound can heal.

If this last section has seemed confusing or challenging, don't be discouraged. Realize that when you hear yourself making a judgment of yourself, your life, or anyone or anything else, you can play with discovering all of the ways in which you can reframe that story. The key is not to just do this with your thinking, but to take enough time to feel who you are with each version of the story. It is in feeling them—in actually embodying each version— that you can discover the space that is always there between the stories.

Learning the Mandala takes time because it is about going beyond ego to awareness. If at this point you do not yet fully grasp the concept or feel confident that you can use the Mandala on your own, don't worry. The particular steps that I have laid out in this chapter require practice and time to be comfortably understood. To help you gain greater understanding, in the next chapter, you can follow along as I guide three people in using the Mandala of Being to face their health challenges.

CHAPTER SIX

WITNESSING THREE HEALING JOURNEYS

In this chapter, I'd like you to join me as I facilitate Joseph, Virginia, and Marie-Claire, all of whom volunteered to work on a troubling issue during one of my seminars using the Mandala of Being. Each one of them was dealing with a different health challenge.

To gain a clearer sense of how to work with the Mandala, I suggest that you pay careful attention to the following three dialogues as if you were one of the people in the circle listening as I converse with my volunteers on their respective issues and guide them through the process. You will learn a great deal from seeing how others have transformed themselves by embracing this powerful method.

Joseph's Dialogue

RICHARD [R]: Hello Joseph. In working with the Mandala, it is very important to clearly describe the issue that is troubling you. What is it that you want to work on?

JOSEPH [J]: I have metastatic liver cancer. I went through two rounds of chemotherapy, which I finished in the winter. It was terrible. I was so sick; I wanted to die. Now I feel much better, but two weeks ago I had a new scan, and my doctor told me that there are new tumors, so the cancer is spreading.

[*Joseph is silent for several moments.*]

R: [*repeating Joseph's statements with empathy*] You have liver cancer, and going through chemotherapy was very difficult. You felt very sick. Now you have learned that the cancer is still spreading. I can certainly appreciate that this is difficult news to receive. But what you have told me so far are medical facts about your circumstances, and there is little I can do to help you in that regard. On the other hand, medical facts in themselves are never the whole picture, and facts alone don't necessarily have to distress you. It's what you think about those facts that causes your greater distress. Can you be more specific about what is troubling you?

J: It's about feeling that I should do something . . . something more. But I don't know what or even if I want to anymore.

R: Now I can really begin to understand what is troubling you: you believe there is something more that you should be doing.

J: Yes, that's it exactly.

R: Can you say a little more about this—perhaps a few specifics about your circumstances?

J: I have a new family; my wife and I got married two years ago. She is much younger than I am, and we have a young daughter from her previous marriage. My wife is constantly on the Internet researching cancer treatments. A few months ago, she wanted me to go to Brazil and see a healer, but I was too sick to travel; actually, I didn't have a desire to do so. Then it was a clinic in China. Now she has found something in Italy that she feels might be good for me, and she wants me to go there . . . but I don't want to.

And there are other friends who keep proposing ideas for treatments that they think I should investigate. But the more they tell me these things, the more angry and despondent I feel. I should be doing something, but I'm not. It makes my wife angry, and I just get depressed.

R: Okay, now I have a much clearer sense of what you are struggling with. Can we call this issue: "I should be doing something more"?

J: Yes, I should be doing something to heal myself, but I'm not.

R: [speaking slowly] "I should be doing something to heal myself, but I'm not." Does that encapsulate the issue?

J: Yes.

R: Good. I think this is something that the Mandala work may help you become clearer about. Shall we start?

J: Yes.

[*Prior to this conversation, the Mandala had been laid out on the floor in front of where Joseph is sitting.*]

R: The first step in this work is to move to the center of the Mandala and give yourself a chance to become as fully present and embodied in this moment as you can. So go ahead and step into the center.

[*Joseph stands up and steps to the Now position.*]

R: I know you are aware that you are standing in front of me and a group of people. Try to put the group out of your mind, and let this work be completely for you. It is entirely understandable that you may feel uncomfortable being so exposed. Acknowledge to yourself whatever you are feeling, and don't resist it.

Imagine that you are in a big space, bigger than this room, so that you are not crowding any feeling tightly inside you. Wherever you sense any tension, turn your inner gaze toward it and touch it very lightly, as if you were softly caressing that sensation with a feather. At the same time, be present in your whole body and relax as best you can. Take your time. Focus on any tension or discomfort, and touch it very gently. Also, keep softening everywhere else in your body.

[*Richard is quiet for about 20 seconds.*]

R: Joseph, let your awareness stay in your body, but at the same time extend yourself into the room and beyond it. Can you hear the birds chirping outside? Can you hear the low rumble of the city coming through the open windows? Softly touch whatever you are feeling in your body while also sensing that your awareness is expansive and open, surpassing your body, this room, and even the city.

In this moment, and in all moments, it is Now everywhere. A part of your being extends into that limitless Now and encompasses all that, although it is at an intuitive level. It is a kind of vastness, a stillness, a silence. It is a way of listening . . . almost like you are asking a question and are receptive but without ever expecting an answer.

[*Richard is silent again for about 30 seconds.*]

R: I can hear that the situation has been very troubling for you, Joseph. But for the moment, see if you can set the issue aside and just be here. Gently bring your attention to your breathing. Don't change your breathing; just let it do what it wants to . . . follow the exhalation to the very end, and notice the precise moment when the next breath begins.

[*Richard observes Joseph carefully and is quiet for another half minute or so.*]

R: Can you tell me how you are in yourself?

J: I feel quieter.

R: Good. [*short pause*] Bend your elbows so that your hands are in front of you. Go ahead and bring your attention into your hands. Don't be a spectator observing from somewhere in your head—actually bring your awareness into your hands. . . . Can you sense the subtle sensation in your hands?

J: Yes.

R: What is it like?

J: They're warm. There is a sense of tingling. My fingers feel a little thicker.

R: Good. You can feel warmth and tingling in your hands, and your fingers even feel a little thicker. [*short pause*] Now become aware of the space around and between your hands. With very subtle movements, compress the space between your hands and notice how the sensation changes. . . . What are you sensing?

J: It's as if there's sort of a cloud between my hands.

R: That's good. Keep observing that cloud sensation for a few moments longer. See if you can bring the sensation into stronger focus, but also stay in your whole body and continue to notice your sense of the room and the sounds from outside. Gently refine your focus, but also stay open to a larger space.

[*Richard is silent for about 30 seconds.*]

R: How do you feel in yourself now?

J: Very calm . . . warm. My mind is quiet. I can't remember it being this quiet. My breathing feels like it's caressing me.

R: That's excellent. This is your (and everyone's) natural state of being when you are not caught up in your thinking—when your mind is gathered and, paradoxically, also extending into a larger space. I want you to feel this for a few moments longer. Really let your body, your cells, know this peacefulness.

[*There is a 20-second pause.*]

R: Okay . . . now are you ready to work?

J: Yes.

R: I want you to bring the issue back into your consciousness: "I should be doing something to heal myself, but I'm not." Repeat it out loud to yourself.

[*Joseph repeats the statement aloud.*]

R: Visualize yourself with your wife. She is suggesting different things for you to investigate, and you're thinking, *I should be doing something to heal myself, but I'm not.*

What is happening?

J: [*after a brief silence*] Well, the peace is gone.

R: The peace is gone . . . I'm not surprised.

J: I'm getting the same feeling of confusion, and my stomach is like a hard lump. What's the use?

R: So you are feeling confused, and your stomach is a hard lump. You say to yourself, "What's the use?" Of course, telling yourself that you should be doing something and then not knowing what action to take—or even if you want to take action—has to be very stressful.

J: It is. I want something that can do the job as best as possible. But as soon as I—

R: Hold on, Joseph—you're getting ahead of yourself. "I want something that can do the job as best as possible" is another story. What I suggest you do is just hold the feeling of the issue in your awareness and look around the Mandala. Which position do you feel drawn toward? Stories about yourself? About someone else?

[*Joseph is uncertain for a few moments and then steps to the Me position.*]

R: Good. You want to look at the things you are telling yourself about yourself. Well, you have told yourself several already, including the issue itself: "I should be doing something to heal myself, but I'm not." And also what you just said: "I want something that can do the job as best as possible." Do you understand that those are stories about yourself? They are about what you believe you should be doing or what you should want.

J: I can see that.

R: Okay, I've written those down. As you stand in the Me position and hold the issue in your awareness, are there any other stories about yourself that come to mind?

[Joseph is thoughtful for a few seconds.]

J: I don't want to just wait and be passive. I need to do something soon . . . *now.* I must make a choice.

R: Well, that is quite a collection of Me stories. Let me repeat them all back to you *[recites the statements in an empathetic tone]*: "I should be doing something to heal myself, but I'm not." "I want something that can do the job as best as possible." "I don't want to just wait and be passive." "I need to do something soon . . . *now.*" "I must make a choice."

Before we work on a specific story, look around the Mandala again. Is there another position you want to explore to see what stories you are telling yourself there? You mentioned that your wife has been researching possible treatments for you. What do you tell yourself about that?

J: I know that it's her way of showing love, but I wish she wasn't so determined. She's so intense when she gets the bit between her teeth. She's Middle Eastern and they—

R: One moment, please. Just so you can learn to differentiate among the types of stories and understand the Mandala work better, leave the Me position, and walk over to the You position.

[Joseph walks to the You position.]

R: Good. By walking to the You position, I am asking you to realize that now you are looking to see what it is that you have been thinking about your wife or anyone else in the context of this issue: "I should be doing something to heal myself, but I'm not." For example, you just said that you know that your wife's online research for possible treatments is her way of showing you love. That is what I call a You story. You are telling yourself some-thing about your wife.

J: I know that it's her way of showing love, but it puts me under so much pressure.

R: Yes, it puts you under a lot of pressure. You started to say something just before I asked you to move positions . . . something about your wife being Middle Eastern.

J: She is hot-blooded. She comes from a very liberated family— I mean very pragmatic, not religious. She is outspoken and practi-cal. Once she decides something, she doesn't slow down and will spend hours at the computer researching.

R: So you tell yourself that she is "hot-blooded" and "very pragmatic." What does that mean to you?

J: She's pushing me. And the more she pushes, the less I feel like doing anything. It's too much pressure. She should let me make my own decisions about my health.

R: Excellent, Joseph. Those are two more stories: "She's push-ing me" and "She should let me make my own decisions about my health."

J: Yes.

R: Okay, I think we have more than enough of the stories you're telling yourself that are contributing to your stress and un-happiness. Before we go further, move back to the Now position in the center of the Mandala. It is essential to take a few moments and come back to the sense of calm you were feeling before.

[*Joseph moves to the center, and Richard guides him once again to relax into focused-spacious awareness. After a few minutes, Joseph sig-nals that he feels ready to continue.*]

R: Do you have an intuitive sense of where you want to begin? The Me stories or the You stories?

[*Joseph looks around and then turns toward the Me position.*]

R: You're looking at the Me position. Is it okay to go ahead and move there?

[*Joseph nods and moves to the Me position.*]

R: So remember that everything we are going to do now is in the context of this issue: [*with emphasis*] "I should be doing something to heal myself, but I'm not." You have metastatic liver cancer, and you have recently learned that there are new tumors. You are telling yourself several things: "I should be doing something to heal myself . . . I want something that can do the job as best as possible . . . I don't want to be passive . . . I need to do something now . . . I must make a choice." Is there any one of these stories in particular that you want to start with?

J: I'm beginning to see that they are all sort of similar. I guess it really comes down to the fact that I should be doing something to heal myself. But I just don't—

R: Hold on. Don't jump away from the chosen story to the next thought that enters your mind. This is what so many of us keep doing. It's why people keep spinning in circles, one story after another, and cannot find their center. This is how your ego keeps you from coming into the Now where true healing can happen. It's really important to slow down your thinking and inquire into one story at a time so that you can see what each one does to you.

All right, let's work with the story "I should do something to heal myself." [*brief pause*] Joseph, please repeat the story out loud to yourself a few times.

[*Joseph says the story softly two times.*]

R: Now, stay in your body so that you can feel what happens inside. What I want you to do is let yourself consciously feel what this story creates in you when you are identified with it, as you have been over these past weeks. How do you feel?

J: [*in an agitated voice*] I keep feeling that I need to do something.

R: Yes, you just said that you keep feeling that you need to do something, but can you see that that statement is itself just another thought—a belief really? It isn't a feeling. What does believing "I should do something to heal myself" create in you? Stay in your body. *Feel.* You have learned that the cancer is still growing. Your wife wants you to try alternative therapies. You are telling yourself that you should do something to heal yourself. What does that create?

J: Pressure . . . I feel pressure.

R: You feel pressure. Is that just a memory of feeling it, or can you really feel it right now?

J: No, I feel it. And it makes me angry . . . but also heavy. I feel heavy and dark inside.

R: Where do you feel heavy and dark? Can you show me?

[*Joseph puts his hands over the center of his chest.*]

R: Good. Let yourself feel this as completely as you can. This is a conscious experiment, and it's not meant to hurt you. It is to help you understand what telling yourself the story "I should do something to heal myself" and unconsciously identifying with it (which is what you have been doing) is causing in you. Pressure, anger, heaviness, and darkness in your chest, around your heart . . .

J: Yes, and I feel like such a failure . . . that I'm disappointing everyone.

R: You feel like "such a failure," but I'm not sure that failure is a feeling; I think it is a judgment about yourself, a story. And so is "I'm disappointing everyone." It is also a judgment, not an actual feeling. Stay with just what the story we are working on creates in you: "I should do something to heal myself." Can you sense what is really there underneath that story that made your mind go to the stories of failure and disappointing others?

[*Joseph is quiet for a while.*]

J: Helplessness. I feel so inadequate and depressed. I hear this voice saying, "I don't care. It's no use."

R: And that voice makes you feel . . .

J: *Despair.* That's the darkness—it's despair.

R: You are really feeling despair now?

J: Yes, it is a heaviness, so heavy. My body just wants to fall down.

R: I know that it's hard to consciously stay with this, but let yourself feel it for a few moments longer. Don't turn from the feeling at all, but recall what we did before: let your awareness extend into your whole body and out into the room and beyond.

[*Joseph begins to cry. Richard remains silent for about 30 seconds.*]

R: That's good, Joseph. You are letting yourself feel what the story "I should do something to heal myself" creates in you. I think you have allowed that deeply. Now I want you to prepare to move back to the center of the Mandala, to the Now position. Move slowly when I tell you to, and understand that this movement represents a shift of your state of consciousness. You are moving from identification with the story back into the Now. [*short pause*] Okay, go ahead and slowly move to the center.

[*Joseph takes slow, small steps back to the Now position at the center of the Mandala.*]

R: Now I invite you to do a simple thought experiment. You are still in the same context: new tumors were found, and your wife and others are urging you to try other treatments. But as you stand in the Now position, I want you to imagine that it never enters your mind to tell yourself: "I should do something to heal myself."

Go ahead and visualize this, Joseph. Perhaps you are with your wife, and she is showing you something on her computer about the clinic in Italy. You are paying attention to what she is saying, but it *never* enters your mind to think *I should do something to heal myself.* [*Richard emphasizes each word.*] It's not trying to let that story go—it's just imagining that you never thought it. Stay in your body, take your time, and feel how you are if you never thought that story.

[*Joseph is silent for a while, but then his arms move a little away from his sides and his palms turn slightly forward.*]

R: What's happening?

J: It can't really be that simple.

R: What are you experiencing?

J: I suddenly feel so free. The heaviness disappeared almost instantly.

R: Actually, it *is* that simple, but before we go into any analysis, stay with what you're feeling. When you say that "the heaviness has disappeared," you're expressing your experience in the negative—that is, in terms of what has left. Gently look inside. What is actually there?

J: [*taking his time*] Yes, it is warm, clear—a sense of being upright.

R: Upright?

J: Yes. I feel connected to myself, to my life . . . and also to my death. I'm not afraid in this moment.

R: I'm glad that you aren't afraid. Stay with your sense of feeling upright: of connection to yourself, of warmth, of being clear. Let your whole body share in those feelings, right down to your cells and molecules. This is very important. You have been bathing yourself in very difficult feelings with that story, so now it's wise to give your whole being a chance to experience another state.

[*There is about 30 seconds of silence.*]

R: I sense that you're thinking once again, Joseph. How are you in yourself?

J: I started to move back to needing to do something.

R: Yes, it can be hard to trust feeling good—it's not the familiar habit. But come back once again to visualizing yourself with your wife as she shows you her research findings. Remember that the thought *I should do something to heal myself* never enters your mind.

[*Joseph is still for a moment, and then he reaches his arms out as if he were hugging someone.*]

R: May I ask what you are doing and what you are feeling?

J: [*almost shouting*] Love! I'm taking my wife into my arms and hugging her. I'm telling her that I love her, and I'm thanking her for caring so much about me.

R: Beautiful. Let that image keep living in you and really let yourself feel what you're feeling.

[*Joseph is visibly moved and is actually hugging himself. There is a brief pause.*]

R: Okay, you are feeling a whole different possibility, and it is truly lovely to be with you. But from my experience, I have learned that it is important for you to once again engage the story "I should do something to heal myself" because it is likely that it will come back into your mind, and I think you can have more insight about it.

So I am asking you to once again prepare yourself for a shift of consciousness. I want you to slowly walk back to the Me position—*slowly* so that you are signaling to yourself that this is a conscious change of state—and take on the story "I should do something to heal myself." Repeat it out loud, but this time stand at the Me position facing toward the center, the Now position. As you consciously reidentify with the story, remember the state you were in these past minutes while you were in the center of the Mandala.

J: Do I really have to? [*Joseph laughs nervously.*]

R: Our stories are only thoughts, and if you remain afraid of a thought, it will capture you again.

[*Joseph moves slowly to the Me position and faces the center; then he repeats the story out loud.*]

R: Take your time to feel this story again and notice if there is a change—*any* difference between how you experience yourself now and how you experienced yourself the first time you stood in the Me position.

[*Joseph is quiet for a few seconds.*]

J: I can feel where the heaviness wants to take me, and if I let it, I can sense that it's coming back, but it's much weaker. It feels like a dream . . . and it's stupid.

R: It's weaker . . . it feels like a dream. Why are you calling it stupid?

J: I can see that this is just a story, and I don't have to live that story.

[*Richard repeats Joseph's statement.*]

J: Yes, it's *my* life.

R: Can you explain what you really mean by "it's my life"?

J: I have been pushing away my wife's love because I felt I had to do something, but now I know that I don't have to do anything—

R: Do "anything" . . . what are you referring to specifically?

J: I don't have to do anything to heal myself. But I see very clearly that from now on, I want to tell her how much I love her every time she shows me a new therapy. And I'm willing to keep an open mind. If she shows me something that I sense is worth investigating, then I'll look into it. I can trust my own intuition.

R: Good. You can trust your own intuition. Can you give me an example of how you know that?

[*Joseph is silent for a moment.*]

J: Well, when I saw the e-mail about this seminar, I immediately knew that I wanted to attend, even though it said nothing about physical healing.

R: So your story about not wanting to be passive . . . ?

J: I thought I was being passive because I couldn't push myself to travel and try all those things out. But I am *not* passive—I came here.

R: Yes, you certainly did. [*brief pause*] Joseph, I'm looking at the other Me stories, and it seems to me that you have essentially dealt with those as you worked on the key story. Also, what you just said about your wife indicates that we don't really need to address the You stories: "She's pushing me" and "She should let me make my own decisions about my health."

J: She isn't pushing me . . . I can see that now. *I* have been pushing me.

R: Yes, that is the truer insight: you have been pushing yourself, which has caused you a lot of unhappiness.

J: And it has also hurt our love. But right now all I want to do is hug my wife and thank her.

R: I'm very happy for you, Joseph. And while I'm not so sure that it has hurt your love, telling yourself that story probably isn't the best thing for either of you.

[*Joseph laughs and nods his head.*]

R: Thank you for being so vulnerable in front of all of us.

J: Thank *you*. I haven't felt this well for a long time.

Virginia's Dialogue

RICHARD [R]: I am pleased to meet you, Virginia. I have your note that describes your health challenge. Clearly, you have been having a very difficult time. You understand that this work isn't going to address your physical diagnosis—

VIRGINIA [V]: There isn't one, and that's part of the problem. All the doctors I've seen have their own ideas, but even after countless tests, no one has really defined the problem or recommended a treatment that has been helpful.

R: Thank you. I appreciate how frustrating it must be to have seen so many doctors and had so many tests and *still* not know what you're dealing with. But the point I was about to make is that it really isn't necessary—or even relevant in the context of our work—to concern ourselves with your diagnosis, and certainly not with any treatment protocol.

What I can help you become more aware of is what you may be doing to make things more difficult through the stories that you're telling yourself about your condition. Is that clear?

V: Yes. I've wanted to meet you because I've followed your work for many years, and I believe that you're a true physician. So many doctors act as though—

R: Hold on. Excuse me for stopping you, but I'm sure we will get to your beliefs about doctors as we do the Mandala work. I guess I will take your remark about me being a "true physician" as an indication that you have come with a lot of expectations— positive ones—but I hope you won't find yourself disappointed. I always say that when someone has such high regard, it's only downhill from there. [*Virginia laughs.*]

As you've heard me say, the first key to using the Mandala to support emotional well-being is to clearly define the issue you want to inquire about. Can you tell us what the issue is?

V: I gave spiritual counseling for many years, which was my work and service and, of course, I was deep into my own mystical journey. I was an activist, locally and globally, working with visionary leaders to help spread the message of conscious evolution. But I gradually became almost immobilized by mercury poisoning due to dental amalgams. I took care of that more than ten years ago, but my health has continued to deteriorate. I experience frequent "brain fog," and I have no physical or mental energy. Nor do I have the clarity to write like I once did. All of my systems have been compromised.

I've held on to the faith that there was deeper meaning to this "initiation by fire"—a gift to be shared with others perhaps. But I've been unable to find anyone in the health-care field (conventional or alternative) who could help me regain some energy and clarity for creative work. I'm pretty disillusioned with doctors.

I'm unable to travel except for the shortest trips—like this one—and only if I have help. And I hate to inconvenience other people every time I need to go somewhere. I even have difficulty talking on the phone. I've often felt that I was preparing to leave this body, but at other times I hear the message that my work isn't finished and I still have more to contribute. It's like a roller coaster.

R: Thank you. That is a clear summary of what you have been living and some of the very real challenges you face. So how do you encapsulate what the issue is that we will work on?

V: The real issue is that I'm not well. I can't do my work. What's the meaning of my life if I can't do creative work and be of service to others?

R: Okay. Now it's becoming clearer. You are not well—that is a fact. Next is that you can't do your work. What that belief means is that you are referring to what you did in the past: the work you find yourself no longer able to do. For the moment, I'll treat this as a fact, as you have . . . you can't do your work—at least your previous work.

Of course, perhaps your work has changed to something new, and you can't see what that might be yet because you're looking to the past. But if we frame the last thing you said not as a question, but as a statement, maybe that would succinctly define the issue. [*speaking slowly*] "My life has no meaning if I can't do creative work and be of service to others." Does that speak to what you are really unhappy about?

V: My life has meaning; everyone's life has meaning. Not being well is the problem. [*Virginia is clearly uncomfortable.*]

R: I'm not saying that your life has no meaning—of course it does. I simply reframed what you said as a statement, instead of a question. Many times when we say something by making it a question instead of a statement, it is a way of distancing ourselves from what we really believe.

It's a way that the ego deflects you from seeing what you're really telling yourself that is making you unhappy. It is a fact that you aren't well, and I certainly don't want to diminish how much this has affected your life. But in listening to you, it seems the central issue is that you are telling yourself that your life only has meaning if you can be creative and serve others. If so, that must be quite an unhappy dilemma to be in: to be sick and feel unable to contribute in the way you wish to.

V: It is. Let me get this straight: you are suggesting that the problem is *not* that I'm sick, but that I keep looking to the past and wanting to be the way I used to be . . . is that correct?

R: Exactly.

V: I haven't thought of it in that way. I guess I really am in the past a lot. But you're right—what really hurts is that I don't feel that my life has meaning if I can't write and be of service. It's pretty obvious now, but I hadn't seen it so clearly. So that's the issue?

R: Well, it's a place to start. Actually, I think there is another level to this issue, but maybe we'll get to it later. Okay, so if you agree, we can call the issue what you just said: "I don't feel that my life has meaning if I can't write and be of service."

V: Yes.

R: Good. We're almost there. When you say "I don't feel that," what follows is *not* a feeling; it's a thought, a story you're telling yourself. A feeling is something you can say in one or very few words, such as *tired, sad,* and so on. That's assuming it's something you can describe—some feelings aren't describable.

But what you said is a story, not a feeling. It is very important to recognize when you are telling yourself a story disguised as a feeling, instead of describing what you actually feel. When you're telling yourself a story, you're in your head. When you're describing what you're feeling, then you're in your body. [*brief pause*]

V: I see . . .

R: So shall we say the issue we'll work on is that you believe: "My life doesn't have meaning if I can't write and be of service?"

V: Yes. I really feel useless, and I'm so fed up with the medical establishment.

R: Well, "fed up" might be termed a feeling, I guess. Do you mean frustrated?

V: I do . . . very frustrated and discouraged.

R: Okay, I hear how frustrated and discouraged you feel about not being helped by your doctors. But when you say you "feel useless," I think that once again you are disguising a belief about yourself as a feeling. Aren't you really saying, "I'm useless because I'm sick and can't be of service"?

V: [*Virginia is clearly irritated.*] I'm not useless.

R: I don't believe that you are, but it *is* what you said: "I really feel useless." You didn't say despondent or sad; those are feelings. "Useless" isn't a feeling. Isn't it really a judgment you are making of yourself?

V: Okay. I see what you mean.

R: It sounds like a version of the issue: "My life doesn't have meaning if I can't write and be of service." But it's even more negative. Which story feels like the real issue?

V: I suppose they are different ways of saying almost the same thing, but for me, it is more about not having a sense of meaning than it is about being useless.

R: I think it's time to go deeper into the Mandala work.

V: Okay.

[*As in the previous dialogue, the Mandala is already set up on the floor near to where Virginia is sitting. She now stands.*]

R: Take a look at this diagram that I call the Mandala of Being. How many Nows do you see?

V: [*after a brief pause*] One.

R: That's what most people say. And if you mean the card with the word *Now* on it, yes, there is only one. But what the Mandala is actually showing you is that there are infinite Nows, but they fall into five basic categories. The Now in the center is embodied awareness: it is when you are present and your mind is quiet so that your thoughts aren't determining how you feel or distorting how you experience yourself and your situation. The other categories of Now are what happens to you emotionally and how you feel in your body when your mind is in the past or the future, or in stories about yourself or others.

That is what we are going to look at in a moment. I want to help you uncover the stories you are telling yourself that are creating this issue: Past stories, Future stories, and so on. Can you see that?

V: Yes. Although I've read your book, I'm understanding everything better now as you explain it.

R: Good. Well, since you've read my book, then you know that I always start at the center of the Mandala. It's essential to have a "felt-sense" of who you are in presence—who you are when you are in your body, focused, and spacious—and there are no thoughts pulling you away. So go ahead and step into the center of the Mandala.

[*Virginia steps into the center. At this point, Richard guides her to become wide awake and yet relaxed, to experience being both focused and open to a large space. This is similar to the work already described with Joseph. If you wish to review the process of coming into embodied awareness, reread that section in the dialogue with Joseph.*]

R: Virginia, now you seem ready to begin working on the issue: [*speaking slowly*] "My life doesn't have meaning if I can't write and be of service." Bring this issue into your awareness, and say it out loud to yourself. Recall the larger context of all of the trips to doctors, your deteriorating health over more than a decade, and your loss of certain capacities.

[*Virginia is silent. Then she begins to cry, and tears roll down her face.*]

R: I can see that you're crying. Just be with yourself in any way you need to. We aren't in a hurry. When you feel ready to go on, let me know.

[*Virginia is quiet for about a minute.*]

V: It's been a long struggle. . . . I'm okay to continue.

R: Yes, it has been a long struggle. Let's see if some of that struggle can be released. Now I am going to ask you to consider a question in the context of this issue. Ask yourself, "What have I been telling myself about me, others [for example, your doctors], my past, or how I envision my future that is creating this issue?"

And once again, the issue is "My life doesn't have meaning if I can't write and be of service."

State that question softly to yourself, but say it out loud. Remember that it's vital to hear yourself audibly—not to just think this question or your answers. When you hear yourself, you are able to be more objective than if you just think something. So ask the question and then begin to look around the Mandala to see where you're drawn.

[*Virginia murmurs the question to herself and is quiet. She looks around the Mandala.*]

V: I'm not sure where to start.

R: Would you like my help?

V: Yes.

R: I could hear a lot of irritation in your voice when you spoke about the health-care field. What have you been telling yourself about the doctors or others you've gone to for help? Do you want to examine those stories?

V: Okay.

R: In that case, in a moment, take a step to the You position. This is where you inquire into what you have been telling yourself about other people or about many other things, but right now we'll focus on your doctors. This change of position—moving from the Now to the You marker—signifies that you are leaving the timeless Now (your true center) and moving to who you become emotionally and psychologically when you are telling yourself stories about your doctors. Be aware that you are inviting a change of state and move slowly.

[*Virginia walks slowly to the You position.*]

R: When you described your situation, you said that you've been unable to find anyone in the health-care field who could help you regain enough energy and clarity to resume your creative work.

V: Yes, I've been to everyone: internists, endocrinologists, naturopaths, energy healers, meditation teachers . . . you name it, I've done it.

R: I can truly appreciate that when you are sick—especially when you don't know what is wrong with you—you urgently want to find an explanation. So in that quest, and even today, what have you been telling yourself about those doctors and healers?

V: I know they try to do their best, but they really don't know how to help me.

R: Okay. So there is a story—actually two: "They try to do their best" and "They really don't know how to help me." Are there others? Look into your memory. What else have you been thinking about your doctors?

V: [*seemingly hesitant*] I think that's it.

R: With these stories, you are a lot more accepting than it sounded earlier when we were talking about it. But let's see what happens. So take the first story: "They try to do their best." When you tell yourself that, what does it create in you? How do you feel?

V: I—I feel fine, but . . .

R: But what?

V: You know . . . they shouldn't hold out so much hope when they can't really help me. [*Virginia sounds angry.*]

R: So you don't really feel fine.

V: No, I guess not. It takes so much time to go to all these appointments, and I still don't have any answers.

R: I can imagine how disappointed you've felt, but let me guide you back to what you said a moment ago. It's a perfect example of a You story: "They shouldn't hold out so much hope when they can't really help me." When you're identified with that story, and it sounds as though you have been, what does it create in you?

[*Virginia tilts her head and looks upward.*]

R: I see that you're gazing upward, which makes me think that you're reaching into your memory. Look down into your body. How does this story make you feel? Who are you when you believe "They shouldn't hold out so much hope when they can't really help me"?

[*Virginia closes her eyes and seems to be turning inward.*]

V: I feel angry . . . actually, *very* angry. How can they call themselves healers? They are *not* true healers!

R: So that story makes you very angry. Don't go into the additional story that they aren't true healers—at least not yet. Letting your thinking take you into another judgment prevents you from doing the work on the first story. And you will keep jumping to new stories and never actually work on any.

This is what people are doing all the time. In fact, it's why most people are lost in their thoughts and drown in the emotions their thoughts create. So stay with the first story, which you said makes you very angry. *Feel that.* Stay in your body. It's very important for you to "taste" what that story about your doctors creates in you.

[*There is silence for about 30 seconds.*]

R: What's happening, Virginia?

V: I can feel the anger and something else—a sense of shame. Why can't anyone help me? Something must be wrong with me.

R: So now you're talking about yourself. You are standing in the You position, and the other side of that continuum is the Me position. What you have just done—or actually, said—is create a new story about yourself.

This happens all the time: we are talking about someone else, but we are really talking about ourselves or *about* someone else *from* a part of ourselves and don't realize it. But it always swings to the other side, from the You story to the Me story, or vice versa. [*articulating each word*] "Something must be wrong with me."

V: Yes, I see it and really feel it. It's shame.

R: Shame—yes, that is a very difficult feeling. But I think you're getting a little ahead of yourself. Before we move to the Me position and work on "Something must be wrong with me" (if we do work on it), for now stay with the story "They shouldn't hold out so much hope." Feel the anger. Feel the shame, too, if it's there. Is there anything else?

V: I feel tired. In the last few minutes, I've gotten very tired.

R: I'm not surprised. Anger is ultimately fatiguing and even a small taste of shame is exhausting. But remember, this is an inquiry into what happens when you tell yourself a story like the one we're examining. Feeling tired means that you're experiencing one of the effects directly and quite immediately. But suppose you didn't tell yourself that specific story. [*Richard pauses briefly.*] You've done good work letting yourself feel the anger and shame.

But now I want you to get ready to move back to the center of the Mandala—the Now position. Be aware that you're inviting a change of state, so move slowly and consciously.

[*Virginia moves to the center.*]

R: I invite you to do a thought experiment; actually, it's an *awareness* experiment. You know the state when you're identified with the story "They shouldn't hold out so much hope when they can't really help me": you feel angry, ashamed, and very tired. You have consciously tasted it just minutes ago.

Virginia, what I want you to do while you stand in the Now position—still in the context of all the doctor visits and your deteriorating health—is to imagine that that story never enters your mind. You never think it. There you are with your doctors on your search for an answer and maybe an effective treatment. You experience no improvements, but you don't say to yourself, "They shouldn't hold out so much hope when they can't really help me."

Take your time, and stay in your body. Find out what your body knows if you don't tell yourself that story.

[*About 15 seconds of silence passes.*]

V: I feel . . . more *space*. The tiredness is lifting.

R: That's good. Keep attuning to what your body knows without that story.

V: I'm breathing easier. Earlier, my chest felt collapsed, and it seemed hard to breathe.

R: Yes. Stay with the sense of more space, of the tiredness lifting, and that it's easier to breathe. Give your whole being a chance to live something other than what that story was creating.

V: It feels much better, but . . .

R: I had a sense that "but" was coming. But *what?*

V: I want to be able to write and give spiritual counseling like I used to do. It helped people, and I had such a sense of purpose.

R: I know you want to be able to write and work with people again. But as you're saying those things, what's happening in you? What is your body experiencing?

[*Virginia is quiet for a few seconds.*]

V: The tiredness is back—it's even worse, I think. And I feel hopeless. I . . . I don't want to say this, but . . . I hate myself.

R: First, good work. I could see you turn inward and listen to your body. You are really learning something. And your body is speaking to you. When you tell yourself that you want to write and work with people, you become even more tired and feel hopeless. And the anger—maybe the same anger you had toward your doctors turns against you. You hear yourself thinking that you hate yourself. That must be very painful.

V: It is. If no one can help me, how am I going to fulfill my potential as a healer and guide?

R: Do you remember my discussion of Me stories, and how when you unconsciously identify with your stories about yourself they make you special either in a grandiose or depressive sense?

[*Virginia is silent for a moment.*]

V: What are you saying?

[*Richard watches Virginia carefully for about 30 seconds without saying a word.*]

R: I think you know what I'm saying. I have a sense that you've already made a jump of understanding, a new insight, but maybe you don't want to look at it.

V: But does that mean I have to give up wanting to be creative and do spiritual counseling?

R: You don't have to give up anything, Virginia, but your body is telling you what your energy is like—what your Now is like. You're fighting against yourself, insisting that you be the self you remember, not opening to who you are presently. . . . But that isn't what you saw—your insight. At least that isn't what I sense you realized.

[*Virginia is quiet for a few seconds.*]

V: It's grandiosity, isn't it? I made myself special as a counselor and because I was writing and teaching about conscious evolution. But I loved speaking at the conferences, and I loved the people I was hanging out with.

R: You're allowed to love your life and enjoy the work you do, but for whatever reason, things have changed. You mentioned earlier that you could see that you spend a lot of time in the past. But you didn't see your own grandiosity.

V: No, I didn't. Or maybe I did a little, but . . .

R: It is never an easy part of oneself to acknowledge. But right from the beginning when you started speaking, I wondered what part of you says that your doctors aren't true healers. Are you implying that an ordinary doctor might not be able to heal you, but a "true healer" could?

What part of you speaks of being on a "mystical journey" and has framed your illness as an "initiation by fire"? Who can't be sick just like other people can be sick? What part of you would rather believe she is living an initiation that gives special mystical meaning to her sickness? I'm not saying this to hurt you, but so that you—so that both of us—can understand why the heart of your suffering is not that you're ill but that you're telling yourself that your life doesn't have meaning if you can't write and be of service. Which part of you is punishing yourself because it judges your life as not meaningful?

V: The grandiose part. [*pauses briefly*] It's pride, isn't it? [*sighs*] I've read about spiritual pride for years, but I didn't see it in myself.

R: Perhaps it's pride, but that is a defense.

V: A defense? A defense against what?

R: Well, consider the story you mentioned earlier: "Something must be wrong with me." I think it's time for us to look at that.

V: Okay. [*Virginia looks apprehensive.*]

R: It is a Me story. So go ahead and leave the Now position and walk over to the Me position. Remember to move slowly because this indicates that you are leaving your true center, which is only lived when you are in the Now. You are moving to the state that is created when you identify with the story that there's something wrong with you.

[*Virginia moves slowly and stands at the Me position.*]

R: Speak the story out loud and watch inside. What does it create in you?

[*Virginia recites the story and then becomes quiet.*]

V: [*angrily*] I'm *not* comfortable with this.

R: [*speaking calmly*] What do you mean by that? What is "this"?

V: I mean that I'm not comfortable saying "Something must be wrong with me." I'm ill, and I'm tired all the time. I can't work. Something is wrong with my body, even if no one has been able to diagnose me.

R: Of course something is wrong with your body. I don't believe that this is in your head. But being uncomfortable with examining the story (which you yourself said) sounds like pride again. Virginia, when you first said this story, you said you felt shame.

V: Yes, I did.

R: I can hear that you're uncomfortable with the belief "Something must be wrong with me." But becoming angry is another defense. You felt shame before, and my intuition tells me that it wasn't because you are ill. It was because of something else. What was it?

V: Yes, at times I've felt like a victim, and I don't like to feel that way.

R: Okay, but right now I think you are in your head. I don't think being sick or sometimes feeling like a victim is what you meant when you said, "Something must be wrong with me." I think you were referring to something else altogether. Look inside. *Feel.* What is it?

[*Virginia is quiet for about 20 seconds.*]

V: There's a sense of shame, but it's not because I've been ill. I just don't like feeling sick.

R: No one likes feeling sick, but that isn't what we're getting at here. Stay in your body. . . . Tell me about the sense of shame you feel.

V: It isn't shame about feeling sick. It's about . . .

[*Virginia falls silent. She is clearly looking deep into herself.*]

V: It's about being . . . me. [*She starts to cry.*]

R: [*pauses before speaking*] "Shame about being me"—okay, I can hear that. But I want to make a suggestion: I don't think that what you're genuinely feeling is what you're calling "shame about being me." That is the story you are putting on the feeling—or, more accurately, your ego is putting that spin on whatever this feeling actually is.

For your ego, letting you feel shame about being you is a way to keep you in depressive specialness instead of grandiosity, but it's still specialness, still ego. . . . So now it's time to inquire directly into this feeling. To do so, because it's work that can only be done in the present moment, please move back to the Now position on the Mandala.

[*Virginia takes a step to the Now position.*]

R: Virginia, stay in your body. Don't listen to any thought about the feeling. Look right at this feeling you called "shame about being me" and don't put any words on it. What is this feeling in itself? [*Richard is quiet for about 15 seconds.*] Turn your inner gaze directly toward what you're sensing inside you, what you called "shame at being me." Focus on the feeling itself. Very gently, touch whatever this feeling is in you, but also be steady. Don't let your inner gaze drift away into any thoughts. [*short pause*] At the same time, sense your whole body and expand beyond it—sense how your aware-ness, like sunlight, shines outward without limit.

[*After about 20 seconds, Virginia balls up her fists and begins to tremble. A deep groan comes from her.*]

R: Good. Stay with your experience. Keep touching it ever so softly with your attention, one breath at a time. If you can, try to relax. Open your hands, and let your whole body be soft. Can you show me where you are feeling this? Is it localized anywhere in particular in your body?

[*Virginia opens her hands and tentatively places them over her upper belly, then moves them up to her chest over her heart. Her hands slowly move up and down between her belly and chest.*]

R: Good work. Keep your inner gaze on your chest and upper belly, but invite the rest of your body to relax, to become as soft as possible. Make as much space as you can around this feeling. [*short pause*] Can you describe what you're feeling?

[*Virginia is silent for about ten seconds.*]

V: It's like darkness. I've failed . . . somehow I've failed.

[*She begins to sob.*]

R: Wait. You said, "I've failed," but that is *not* a feeling. It's an-other thought, another self-judgment. Your ego wants to keep you feeling depressive so it stays in control. Don't let your ego seduce you into believing that you know what you're feeling. You don't really know yet what this is, do you? Not really. This feeling is not "I've failed."

V: You're right—I don't know what this is.

R: But it's familiar.

V: Yes!

R: Keep looking carefully at this familiar feeling. Touch it very softly with your attention, and imagine that it's a distressed baby. You are holding it with total attention and tenderness. But also remember to stay spacious—extend your awareness into the feeling and into the room. Can you hear the sound of the room? Can you hear the air blowing through the ducts? Let all your senses work. Be spacious, but don't turn your gaze away from the feeling. [*Richard is silent for about 15 seconds.*]

Now, you said that "it's like darkness." That, too, is a story, but it is less subjective—less about you. Try to gently gaze into that sense of darkness. It is a deep ache, but stay expansive and fill the room and beyond. . . .

[*A pause for about 15 seconds.*]

R: What's happening, Virginia?

V: It's getting lighter. I feel warmth spreading through my chest, and it's flowing down into my belly. It's very strange . . . I feel well, *really* well.

R: Look more carefully into what you mean when you say that it feels strange.

V: It's just that a few minutes ago, I felt absolutely terrible—like there was no reason to keep living—and now that feeling is completely gone. But it's more than gone. I feel so much space in me, and I feel light—not in the sense of weight, although that too as I think about it. . . . The *light* is like sunlight.

R: Yes, stay with this new feeling: space, lightness, warmth. You feel well. Let your cells bathe in "feeling well"; let your whole being know this state.

V: This is a miracle!

R: Just stay with how well you feel, and we can talk about it more in a moment.

[*Virginia stands quietly for about a minute.*]

R: A moment ago when you described how you were feeling, you said it was as if you didn't have a reason to live.

V: What?

R: You said, "I felt absolutely terrible—like there was no reason to keep living." Before that, you also mentioned that you failed. However, neither of those descriptions is a feeling—both are stories. I want you to understand that whatever this feeling is or was, you don't really know how to describe it or name it directly. You had to resort to a simile; that is, you had to say that it is *like* something: "It's like darkness. . . . Somehow I've failed."

This tells me something, and it is what I suspected from the moment we began the work. The key here isn't really the stories about your doctors or even the issue that your life is meaningless if you can't write and serve others. It is this dark feeling, but you also said that it's familiar. Can you go into your memory and recall the feeling?

V: I think so . . . but it isn't strong now.

R: I understand that it isn't strong now; do you know why that is?

V: No. I guess like most feelings, they come and go.

R: Feelings do come and go. They keep flowing as long as you don't link them to a story, and few are really terrible until you join a negative story to them, such as "I've failed," or "It's not worth living." I believe that whatever you were feeling transmuted into a sense of inner light and well-being because you turned your awareness toward it and gave it direct conscious attention without collapsing into it. You relaxed and stayed spacious.

Your ego kept creating stories, which is what it has done all your life. And if I didn't stop you, you would have identified not with the actual feeling but with your stories about the feeling. Then you would have been caught in real suffering, as you have been caught many times before.

So look inside, Virginia. How long can you remember feeling this almost unnameable feeling? I mean the one that was so terrible a few minutes ago? The one that you said made you feel ashamed of being you?

[*Virginia is quiet for a few moments.*]

V: All my life.

R: When you were in college?

V: Yes.

R: When you were a teenager going through puberty?

V: Yes.

R: When you were a child?

V: Yes. I sense that I've known this feeling throughout my life.

R: I believe you have. But until today, you've never used your awareness to be present for the feeling itself. Instead, you believed the stories your ego made up about the feeling, and that created a deep sense of shame about yourself. How could you profess to be a spiritual counselor when deep down you had this terrible feeling?

Perhaps you turned toward spirituality and consciousness work because of that feeling—trying to avoid it, to find the light in another way. You never realized that the feeling you've been running from is also the light. [*brief pause*] Is any of this making sense to you?

V: Yes, a great deal of sense. I've always had this feeling—that something is wrong with me—but now I see that it's a *story* about the feeling.

R: Yes, and when the doctors and healers hadn't been able to help you, it only confirmed what you've been subconsciously telling yourself most of your life: "Something must be wrong with me." Although it suited your ego's desire for your grandiose specialness to be a spiritual counselor, it never changed or healed that inner feeling. No compensatory behavior can resolve that because those feelings don't originate in your ego. You can't will them away. At best you can temporarily bury them, but they always resurface in time.

I call these kinds of feelings *untamed* or *abysmal,* and there is no healing them in the usual sense . . . but there is much we can gain from them when we learn to hold them with conscious awareness, focused-spacious awareness, in the Now. And that is what you just did, Virginia.

[*Virginia is silent for a while.*]

V: Thank you very much. You've helped me understand something that has been haunting me all my life. Now I feel like maybe I *can* get better. But even if I don't, I can see that I don't want to keep living in the past. I don't know what my work will be, but I know that I have the power to stop making myself miserable by grasping for my same grandiose patterns.

R: I love how you're seeing yourself. And you know, I don't know whether or not your body will recover, but I have no doubt that you *are* doing profound service if every time you feel this feeling returning, you can make a space big enough for it that your heart doesn't close. You said yourself that you've heard a message that your work isn't over yet.

V: Yes . . . it's what has kept me going.

R: I think the deepest service that any of us can do is to make space for the disowned and dark feelings so that they don't get projected into our lives as illness, self-negation, power trips, or one of the many other ways we try to compensate for them. Virginia, thank you very much for being so open.

V: Thank *you,* Richard!

Marie-Claire's Dialogue

RICHARD [R]: Welcome, Marie-Claire. What would you like to work on?

MARIE-CLAIRE [M-C]: I have tinnitus in both ears. I've had it for many years, and several doctors have told me that there's nothing I can do about it.

R: What is it like?

M-C: Sometimes it's a ringing in my ears, and sometimes it's more like paper crackling.

R: Do you experience it all the time?

M-C: Yes, but sometimes it gets worse.

R: So given that you have tinnitus, what specifically is bothering you about it that you would like to address today?

M-C: Well, I recently retired. I used to teach literature at a university. My lifelong interest has been studying the lives of female saints, and I've been focusing on an exceptional French woman who went to Australia in her early 30s, which was about 80 years ago. She has been dead for a long time, but one of the women she influenced has sent me her diaries, as well as newspaper clippings and the journals of some of the other people who worked with her. I've been studying her diaries and was asked by a university in Australia to write a book about her life. I'm very excited. I've never written a book before, although I've edited several over the years.

R: That sounds like a fascinating project. Tell me, though, how does it relate to your problem with tinnitus?

M-C: The issue is that whenever I sit down to write, the tinnitus becomes much worse. It totally distracts me, and I can't work.

R: When you try to write, the tinnitus gets worse.

M-C: Yes, that's correct.

R: So how would you define the issue you want to work on?

M-C: [*speaking decisively*] My tinnitus is keeping me from writing.

R: Okay, so the issue is that your tinnitus is keeping you from writing. Is this the way we should state what you want to work on?

M-C: Yes.

R: That's fine. Let's get started, so go ahead and step into the center of the Mandala.

[*Marie-Claire steps into the center and stands over the Now position.*]

R: There are different depths to what we mean by being present, or in the Now. When you stand in the center of the Mandala as you are doing, this represents a conscious decision to come into your body and bring your attention to a fine focus, while at the same time keeping your overall awareness expansive and spacious.

Don't reject any thoughts that come and go in your mind—just bring your attention to your breathing. I suggest that you focus on each exhalation. Follow each breath out and become aware of the precise moment when the next in breath begins. . . . One breath at a time, bring that moment into precise focus.

[Marie-Claire closes her eyes and becomes very still. At this point, Richard continues to guide her to become wide awake and yet also relaxed. Remember that you can reread the dialogue with Joseph at the beginning of the chapter if you wish to review the process of coming into present-moment awareness.]

R: So, Marie-Claire, how are you?

M-C: I feel calm. My mind is quiet.

R: Good. I want you to take a few more moments to feel calm and have a quiet mind. It's important for you to have direct experience of who you are and how you are when your awareness is both focused and spacious. *[brief silence]*

Now let's begin. Bring the issue into your awareness, and repeat it to yourself out loud: "My tinnitus is keeping me from writing."

[Marie-Claire repeats the issue out loud.]

R: Okay. Look around at the Mandala. Where do you feel drawn to go?

[She looks around and steps into the You position.]

R: You've stepped to the You position. What are some of your You stories?

M-C. About the tinnitus?

R: Why not. You stepped to the You position, so your beliefs about the tinnitus would fall into that category. By the way, you said *the* tinnitus, instead of *my* tinnitus. Why is it impersonal this time?

M-C: I'm not sure. I want to talk about the tinnitus, not about me.

R: Fine. So what are your stories about the tinnitus?

M-C: *[with rapid-fire delivery]* It's terrible. It keeps me from writing. It's stealing the pleasure of being alive. I don't want it.

R: Let's start with the first statement: "It's terrible." Instead of saying *it,* can you be more specific and say, "The tinnitus is terrible"?

M-C: Yes.

R: Okay. Now look inside, staying in your body so that you can be in touch with what you feel. What does telling yourself "The tinnitus is terrible" create in you?

[*Marie-Claire is quiet for a few seconds.*]

M-C: Anger.

R: Good—stay with feeling angry. Is there anything else?

M-C: I'm frustrated and sick and tired. . . .

R: Are you remembering feeling this way (which is just thinking), or are you actually feeling those feelings?

M-C: I'm feeling it right now.

R: Very good. Consciously stay with those feelings for a little longer. This is what the judgment ("The tinnitus is terrible") makes you feel. We don't know what the tinnitus itself makes you feel, but we do know what that story about the tinnitus creates in you.

So now prepare yourself to experience a shift. To do so, I want you to slowly step back to the Now position.

[*Marie-Claire takes a quick step to the Now position.*]

R: That wasn't exactly slow, but we'll continue on. The next step is to do a thought experiment. Visualize yourself sitting at your computer, preparing to write about this exceptional woman. Your ears are ringing and crackling, but it never enters your mind to think: *The tinnitus is terrible.* Stay in your body, and tell me how you feel.

[*She is quiet for about ten seconds.*]

M-C: I'm fine. It is . . . just a sound. I can hear it like I hear any other sound.

R: The tinnitus is just a sound like any other sound. Can you be more specific about feeling fine?

M-C: The anger is gone, and I actually feel ready to work. In fact, I feel *happy.*

R: Good, Marie-Claire, I'm glad for you. So now it's important to step back to the You position and try the story on again.

M-C: I don't have to. *I'm fine.* It isn't a problem anymore.

R: Okay. Do you want to look at any other stories—perhaps Future stories?

M-C: No. I really feel fine—it's a miracle. Thank you very much!

[Marie-Claire walks to Richard and gives him a hug and then takes her seat.]

I want to comment on this last dialogue. At the time, I was uncertain (frankly, I was skeptical) whether Marie-Claire had made a true shift—because it was so abrupt—or if she just wanted to stop the process. But I decided not to ask her about this, and instead just trusted her. As it turns out, from her point of view, it *was* a miracle.

In that brief instant, she felt a shift and absolutely knew that she was fine. From that day forward, she never let the tinnitus get in her way. While the tinnitus continued, it ceased being a problem in her life, and she was able to complete her book. That was in 2004, and since then she has also completed a second book.

Experiencing Grace Through the Mandala

The Mandala work that frees you from the suffering created by your own beliefs involves a combination of effort and grace. You have to make the effort to discover your stories and consciously allow the emotions and feelings those stories create in you to be fully experienced. Then you have to make the effort to explore the contrast between who you are when identified with those stories and who you are in the Now when your thinking mind is silent and you rest in an alert and spacious awareness. This ready yet relaxed state of being is not a conceptual experience, a mental identity created by your ideas about you. This is an embodied state of being; it is the felt-sense of you right now independent of any thought.

It is by experiencing the contrast between these two states of being—identification with your stories or resting in the Now—that your life opens to grace. Grace comes to join you in the form of spontaneous insight and sometimes deep release into a state of clarity and peace of mind. This new understanding arises, I believe, from your own intuitive wisdom.

Such wisdom is available to everyone, but it cannot be listened to until you stop polluting yourself with stories that cloud your ability to dive deep within yourself. By tuning in to your authentic self, you will find that you are able to release yourself more fully into your life and can accept whatever is happening. As my friend who has aggressive cancer (whom I spoke of at the beginning of the book) said to me: "I am fully aware of the statistics that say I have maybe a 2 percent chance of recovery. But because I am not fighting anything anymore and am even excited to embrace everything that is happening—the tests, the chemotherapy, all of it—I have never felt more alive and fabulous."

Truly, to reach a state of such acceptance and openness is grace, but it is not an accident. Grace comes after you make a sincere and intelligent effort to be who you really are right now and *not* who your thinking mind says you are.

As you become liberated from the drama of your stories, you can let go and allow every story to be explored, every feeling to be felt, every moment to be just the way it is. That is your work, your responsibility. But the actual movement whereby you come back home to yourself is ultimately a matter of grace: the spontaneous shifting of something deeper inside.

If your mind didn't hurt you, how would you live your experience of illness, health crisis, or surgery—even dying? How would you live the experience of being laid off from work or of divorce? By realizing that your true story starts now—perpetually, in each breath of life—you come to see that you can start all over in any moment. It's never too late.

The effort required of you is to take responsibility for whatever you are doing to yourself and to others because of the waywardness of your mind; that is, the lack of focus and discipline of your thinking. This is not about judging or chastising yourself for the way you have routinely been letting so many of your thoughts and stories go unquestioned. Rather, it is about accepting the sweet obligation of consciousness: now that you are gaining greater awareness of what you are doing, it is time to begin anew. With the aid of the Mandala, you can intentionally distance yourself from all of the stories that you have been telling yourself and find out what it is like to simply be present with whatever you are feeling right now.

Shedding Your Stories

The primary reason why few of us learn to live in the Now is that to do so, we have to evolve beyond ego. But ego by its very nature is the product of identification with beliefs, assumptions, and judgments—in short, identification with thinking. And thinking only stops when you are in the Now. Until we step beyond ego to presence, our very identities depend on remaining in the past or future or identifying with Me and You stories.

Likewise, from early childhood, it is in the present moment that we encounter the most difficult feelings: those that are threatening either because they are too wonderful or too dark. And our egos have been fleeing both aspects all of our lives. But once a conscious life is chosen, living in the Now becomes where we have an opportunity to learn to hold any feeling with focused-spacious awareness.

Ask yourself, "What is it that my parents couldn't love, accept, or embrace? What was it that made my mother unhappy? What couldn't she claim in her life because of cultural forces or her own fears? What caused my father to hide his feelings or to work or drink too much?" Inevitably, it was a feeling that they didn't know how to hold without closing their hearts. It is likely that in your own life you will find yourself challenged to open your heart to what they could not.

By closely examining your stories, you can choose a new relationship to yourself. And as you do so, you are healing what your parents could not heal in themselves—whether or not they are still living. In this sense, you are "reparenting" yourself.

You can be as imaginative and creative as you want in choosing a relationship to any feeling or story. You can be grateful to your familiar old stories, thanking them for the personality they have built in you. When you are ready, you can finally stop making yourself special with these stories and open yourself to the exquisite vulnerability that is initially present when you no longer use them as your defense against a deeper aliveness. Eventually, the vulnerability gives way to humility and joy. Just a short step beyond the ego's contracted dynamics is the true holy land.

It may at first seem unwise to allow yourself to become more vulnerable. After all, that is what our culture teaches: deny difficult feelings, keep up a positive front, and pretend that you are okay. But the blessing of this vulnerability is how it opens your heart. Suddenly you can feel, enjoy, and appreciate *everything* more, including tastes and smells, the quality of light, the sounds of people's voices, and so on. You know that things are as they are.

It becomes okay and even life-giving not to have to understand everything. You can look at yourself and at life and say, "I don't know" without that being equivalent to defeat or weakness. In fact, it is liberating. There is nothing to run from and everything to open to.

This acceptance of yourself and your situation expands your ability to listen from the heart, empathize, and relate with a fine sensitivity to everyone around you. When you touch the present moment with such tender receptivity, you find that your life right now is gracious toward you.

ঌ ঌ ঌ

CHAPTER SEVEN

Waking Up to Embodied Awareness

"The Emperor's New Clothes" is an allegory about how easy it is—indeed, how common it is—to live in a dream and oftentimes not even realize it. In the well-known tale, it takes a little boy who hasn't been "hypnotized" by society to shout out the truth: that even though everyone is proclaiming that the Emperor is wearing fine new garments, he is in fact naked. The young boy's view of reality is a wake-up call for us all, reminding us to stop living in a waking dream.

The Emperor is a metaphor for the ego, the level of consciousness that generally rules the show and determines what we believe is reality. This "level of mind" is one of the greatest accomplishments of evolution. It gives us the power of self-reflection as well as the capacity to imagine the future, which has made human beings the dominant species on the planet. Yet nothing stifles the deeper life of the soul more than the egoic mind (when ego is in full control).

Without that inner life, we can never really be emotionally healthy or experience a sense of genuine fulfillment. Our psychic roots remain in shallow soil dominated by narrow self-interest, fear, and control; and we don't have access to the generative forces of our souls. Keep in mind that soul sickness and physical sickness go together. Once there is room for the soul to live, however, even if we are physically ill, we can still be in touch with an enlivening sense of well-being.

In the issues we examined in the dialogues of the previous chapter, my volunteers Joseph, Virginia, and Marie-Claire were all living in a kind of dream fabricated by their egoic minds. They were adding to their own suffering with their Past, Future, Me, and You stories. In order to awaken from their dreams, they needed to be able to feel what their stories created and contrast that with how they felt in themselves when standing in the center of the Mandala.

So how can *you* wake yourself up? The answer is really quite simple: examine your thoughts so that you can identify any stories. For example, you might realize: "I'm telling myself a Me story—one that is making me depressively special," or "I'm telling myself a Future story, which is making me worry."

The reason it is so important to *feel* what each story creates—and not just *think* something like *This is a Past story or a You story*—is that when you actually feel the consequence of believing the story and then feel the Now in which you are in focused-spacious awareness (ready and relaxed), you will start to change your behavior.

No one who consciously experiences how painful it is to grab a hot frying-pan handle will intentionally do it again and again. Likewise, when you realize how often you emotionally poison yourself with stories that create guilt, jealousy, resentment, or fear, you will want to stop doing that to yourself. And when you understand that dwelling in pleasant reminiscences can also be a way of avoiding life, why would you choose to go there too often rather than rest in the fullness of yourself in the present moment?

I know of no better way of waking yourself up than to really understand the price you pay for letting your ego pull all of your strings like a marionette. For that reason, I think it is vital at this point to recapitulate the nature of emotional reality created at each of the four positions of the Mandala. It is not in your best interest to repeatedly make yourself muddy, so whenever you find yourself in emotional turmoil, remember to ask: "What am I telling myself about Me, You [that is, other people], the Past, or the Future that is making me so muddy?"

Of course, to do this work presupposes that you have accepted that it is not what others do to you but what you do to yourself with your own thoughts that is the real issue. While you have no power to control what others do, you do have power to wake up in the middle of a story that you are telling yourself before it sends you into anger, guilt, or worry. The story stops, and you start anew in the Now with its infinite possibilities.

Reviewing the <u>Past</u> Position

If you look carefully at what happens when your mind is in the past and you are no longer rooted in the Now, you will see that certain emotions are inevitably present. Guilt, blame, regret, sorrow, and loss are the typical emotions that accompany your stories about unhappy memories. If the memory is a pleasant one, reminiscing about it will create positive emotions of happiness or contentment, or perhaps the futile but intoxicating longing of nostalgia. In terms of the effect on how you feel right now, it is important to realize that the issue is not the specific memory itself; it is the story you are telling yourself about it in this moment.

How often have you spoken of a memory from your childhood or adolescence, perhaps something like, "My father abandoned us," using many of the same words you used 20 or even 50 years ago? How often do you close your heart to your spouse because you are telling yourself the same story today as you have told yourself countless times in the past about what he or she did 2, 5, or 30 years ago? When you do so, without questioning the story, you create the same emotional reality—the same psychology —today that you created all those years ago.

Can you recognize that you are telling yourself and others the same old stories year after year about events you recall from the past? Do you see that you are making the same interpretations, reinforcing the same old judgments about an event that is long past?

This is how your ego perpetually re-creates a past version of you, and with it comes the same old suffering or escape. It is how your long-established pattern of specialness (for example, the identity of being the *abandoned* son or daughter) is experienced over and over again.

What would happen if you were to look at your memories from the fresh perspective of the new, aware person you are each day as you learn and evolve in your consciousness? What if you could hold the memory spaciously so that you could view it through the eyes of the other people involved, with a broader appreciation of the circumstances and conditions in which the events occurred?

Note that you create the same old feelings of guilt with judgmental thoughts that continue judging you in the same way today as you judged yourself yesterday, a month ago, or many years ago. You re-create the pain of being betrayed with a constellation of thoughts about how you should have been treated and how someone should have behaved. It isn't a question of whether or not betrayal actually happened; you have to keep repeating those thoughts in order to continue feeling outrage, self-righteousness, victimhood, or guilt.

Likewise, you cannot reminisce about something wonderful without calling forth an image from the past and thinking about it. And as pleasant as this nostalgia can make you feel, what is actually happening is that the immediacy of the present moment has faded away and is displaced by the fond memory. This is not always inappropriate, but it is still an avoidance of life in the present moment. The present situation is most likely either being ignored or subtly being deemed *less than*.

As long as you are identified with something wonderful in the past, you may also believe that life isn't as good right now, or this person isn't as right for you as that person of your memories was. Telling yourself Past stories, even happy ones, can blind you to seeing who you are with and what is happening *right now*. You are looking at the present moment—if you see it at all—through an old lens, even if it is a rose-colored one.

In terms of how thoughts create predictable emotions, the egoic mind is more like a computer than actual consciousness: it is absolutely certain what emotion you are going to feel depending on the thoughts that you tell yourself.

After you have worked on several issues, you will begin to see that there is a basic system of stories that repeats again and again.

There may be many seemingly different situations in which you make yourself muddy, but once you begin to unpackage the stories you are telling yourself, you will realize that they often have a similar quality. This is because the author of your stories is either your grandiose specialness or your depressive specialness.

Depressive specialness will look at the past and selectively remember whatever tends to make you feel guilty, ashamed, or sad—regardless of if the issue concerns your health, your career, or a relationship. Grandiose specialness will look at the past and tend to recall only situations in which you were successful, important, and a winner; or it will be dismissive of the past in general, avoiding any memory that might undermine its grandiose stance. Remember that your ego has a selective memory: it recalls whatever supports its particular quality of specialness and ignores any memory that might undermine the identity it has chosen.

You have been telling yourself some version of the same kinds of Past stories (and all the others as well) over and over again for most of your life. They are the very foundation of your ego, your belief in your separateness and specialness.

By practicing the Mandala work, you learn to take one story at a time and experience precisely what that story creates in you, which is different from unconscious identification with it. As your self-observation becomes more astute, you will recognize one of these familiar Past stories as soon as it begins to enter your mind. Instead of letting it lead you into muddiness, you can choose to return your awareness to the present moment—to your deeper self. You are waking up.

Reviewing the Future Position

The future is inherently uncertain; that is, the thinking mind can only anticipate and imagine it. Since it doesn't know what actually will be, it has to create either fearful or hopeful stories. It has to imagine a possibility that is either better or worse than however it judges the present situation or remembers the past. This is why when you imagine the future, some thoughts inevitably induce worry, anxiety, or fear; yet others evoke positive feelings and happy expectancy.

Fear is provoked through imaginings such as: "Something could go wrong with my surgery, and I could be worse off than before," or "My partner may get fed up with my being sick and leave me." Positive expectancy arises from thoughts that make things look better or hopeful: "The surgery will be just what I need," or "My partner will stand by me no matter what."

When your mind goes into the future, it will automatically oscillate between fearfulness and hopefulness. The more identified you are with the fearful story, the more you will begin to grasp for a hopeful one. And the more you try to hold on to a hopeful story, the more likely you will swing back to a fearful one. The cycle does not stop until you bring yourself into the Now.

Of course, it is valid and intelligent to anticipate and plan for the future. It is necessary for human survival, and it is one of life's great satisfactions to envision something and bring it into existence. But when you identify with your future thoughts and they become more real to you than the experience of your life right now, then you have lost your anchor in reality. You are disconnected from your true self. Then you can make yourself miserable because you haven't arrived where you want to be, instead of enjoying just being.

Obviously, hopefulness feels a lot better than fearfulness. But the real source of a positive, hopeful attitude is not that you tell yourself happy stories or wait expectantly for a good outcome, it is that you live each moment accepting *what is.*

Letting go of hope does not mean that you fall into hopelessness; rather, it means that you have let go of the future and are in a state of acceptance. This does not indicate that you have stopped working toward beneficial change; you simply know that your sense of self isn't determined by getting there. The positive attitude many people demonstrate in the face of truly challenging circumstances does not come from their thinking—it wells up from within them from the timeless source that is presence itself.

Entering the Now more completely places your Future stories in perspective. You don't have to refute the stories, push them away, or let them go. Simply moving into the Now and experiencing the contrast in your body brings insight. Your own intuitive wisdom allows you to realize that these stories are future images you are using to help chart your course in life, but they should not be confused with living life. Or you understand that these Future stories are destructive fictions and that, moment by moment, you have a very real option: return to the Now and let your sense of being be renewed. In presence, there is a deeper equanimity than can ever be achieved by clinging to false hope. That's because when you are genuinely present, feelings of belonging, connectedness, trust, forgiveness, compassion, and gratitude are naturally there; you don't have to conjure them with stories.

Whereas the shadow of the fearful stories is a false or ungrounded sense of hopefulness, and the shadow of the hopeful stories is anxiety and fear, the states you experience when you rest deeply in the present have no shadow. The spontaneous experience of joy, trust, love, compassion, or forgiveness are natural states of being. They are *not* thought generated or temporary emotional excitations that require being continuously regenerated by a stream of stories or that will automatically switch to their opposites.

Reviewing the Me Position

The Me position can be the most difficult to understand because, to our egos, the thoughts we have about ourselves have always been who we believe we really are—and it's been this way since we were about five years old. Who is angry? *Me.* Who has cancer? *I do.*

Of course, your body may have cancer, but the part of you that is aware of this and of all of your thoughts about it . . . does *that* part of you (your aware self) have cancer? For most people, the inability to differentiate thinking from awareness is the great ignorance, the great sleep. Only after you have cultivated Now-moment awareness can you begin to observe the stories that you are telling yourself about yourself as they arise in your mind and know that these stories are not who you really are.

Perhaps the easiest way to notice that you are telling yourself a Me story is to become aware whenever you hear yourself saying or thinking anything that begins with a declaration, for example: "I am," "I am not," "I should," "I shouldn't," "I need," "I don't need," "I can't," "I always," and "I never." When you recognize these assertions, get cautious. Wonder about which *you* speaks in this way. See if you can step back and avert the emotional trouble that you are about to get into.[1]

Thoughts such as: *I am not free to enjoy myself like other people, since my life revolves around my health issues; I can't relax until I have paid back my debt and gotten ahead with my finances; My reputation rides on whether or not this business plan works; I know what's best;* and *You should listen to me* are all Me stories. And if they were yours, each would have consequences in terms of your emotional state and sense of stress.

Every time you realize that you're telling yourself a Me story, try to figure out how it makes you special. For instance, if you tell yourself one of the Me stories from the previous paragraph (such as, "I know what's best"), ask yourself, "In what way does this make me special?" Don't just think about an answer and comment to yourself, "My credentials are better." Remember to take a complete step and actually experience how your body is answering that question. Can you sense a feeling of aggressiveness, impatience, irritability, or frustration? Those emotions are pretty reliable signals that you are caught in grandiosity. On the other hand, do you feel squashed, weak, confused, or inadequate? Those sentiments are a pretty good indication that you are defaulting into depressiveness.

If you find it hard to recognize what you feel, look at the images your mind creates. Do they show you succeeding, winning, dominating, or being the savior? Or do they show you as left out, losing, ignored, or unappreciated?

Perhaps you are wondering, "If I am not the thoughts I tell myself about me that make me special, then who am I?" That of course is one of the great questions—one that is essential to a path of awakening. But you don't need to attempt to answer that question here, as the answer would only be another thought, another story. What is more important is to realize who you are *not:* you are not your stories about you because the fact of being aware of such a story means (as we've seen) that you are more than that story.

One of the most astonishing and gratifying experiences in life is to wake yourself up and consciously step back from your Me posture into focused-spacious presence. Suddenly your whole bearing changes; your body language changes; the whole significance of the situation changes as if someone had flipped a switch. Where before there might have been conflict or distrust, now there is space for connection and reconciliation. You actually feel your heart open.

Although we discussed this earlier, it is good to be reminded not to punish yourself for what you see, but to reward yourself for seeing. In other words, when you catch a depressive story, for instance, don't judge yourself for it. If you do, you have allowed your inner critic to return you to depressive specialness once again; you have let your inner seeing be co-opted by ego. Instead, congratulate yourself for recognizing it. Acknowledge that you indeed woke up as you heard yourself reciting that old depressive or grandiose Me story. And say "Thank you," to honor the part of you that woke you up so that you could become aware of the story.

Dwell long enough on your accomplishment and reinforce it with an inner smile. Give yourself a brief bath in self-appreciation. Cultivate a sense of humor about how persistent your ego can be. At the very least, reward your aware self by connecting to your body and extending your senses so that you fully taste the present moment.

Lost in a Me World

"Me" is not one thing; it is a hoard of things. Within the domain of what I call *Me World,* there is a whole host of inner voices or subpersonalities. They cause you to objectify yourself by telling you who you are (or aren't) and how you should (or shouldn't) act. These subpersonalities (this is a broad but no way complete sampling) include the *critic;* the *pusher;* the *pleaser;* the *perfectionist;* the *fixer;* the *bully;* the *flake;* and, one of my favorites, the self-appointed *psychoanalyst.* Each of these inner voices brings forth a different Me story.

The critic can be brutal: "I'm a failure," or "I don't take care of myself, and that's why I am ill now." The pusher is unrelenting and aggressive: "I can't stop now," or "There is more that must get done." The pleaser won't let you say no or take care of yourself first instead of others: "I have to make so-and-so happy," or "I have to take care of my mother." The perfectionist tells you: "It isn't good enough," or "I could have done it better." The fixer says: "I need to meditate more," or "I need to exercise more." The bully enjoys intimidation: "I'll make you pay," or "I'll crush them if they get in my way." The flake promotes apathy: "It doesn't matter," or "I'm not going to bother with those things." Finally, the psychoanalyst continuously diagnoses you and likes to label others as well: "I am neurotic," or "He's such a narcissist."

These inner voices have different agendas that reflect different values, needs, and even worldviews. Some were probably impressed upon you by your parents, teachers, or other significant people as you grew up. Some come from cultural and religious ideals, and others likely stem from your own innate character.

Regardless which subpersonalities are in play and the various ways that they predispose your inner dialogue, like most crowds where everyone has a different opinion and agenda, they inevitably create inner conflict. For example, while the pleaser urges you to be accommodating of your supervisor, the pusher tells you to go over his head to the boss. It is worthwhile trying to discern which of the inner voices authored a particular story, but it is simpler to appreciate that invariably, at the end of each battle between these different inner voices, your ego will temporarily land you in one of two places: grandiose or depressive specialness.

I say "temporarily" because as you become conscious of Me stories, you will see that in certain situations you tend toward depressiveness and in others grandiosity. Think about this now: Do you tend to be grandiose in discussions of politics or in your criticism of your spouse? Do you become depressive when faced with difficult decisions or when money is tight?

One of my students, Cleo, felt abandoned when she learned that her sister needed more time to prepare for school examinations and cancelled a holiday weekend they had planned to share together. Cleo told herself, "My sister doesn't really care for me as much as I care for her," a thought that made her feel rejected and hurt. But then Cleo also became very critical and angry at her sister. That side told her: "I've always given my sister so much; she owes me. She should study some other time, not when I have time off from work. She's depriving me of seeing my nephews." Cleo even fantasized breaking off the relationship with her sister indefinitely.

Working with the Mandala, Cleo was able to quickly recognize her depressive specialness, the side that told her stories that generated her emotions of abandonment and rejection. But she had trouble seeing that becoming critical and angry and threatening to break off relations with her sister was her grandiose side in action.

This is very typical: depressiveness and grandiosity shadow each other, and it is rarely too long before one side replaces the other. Yet, most people tend to only see one side of their behavior: generally, the side that feels slighted and not the one that does the slighting.

Waking up is making a basic decision: do you want to remain identified with a story—a thought whose origin you don't even really know—or do you want to experience yourself being present, awake, and clear in the Now?

Reviewing the <u>You</u> Position

The You position of the Mandala represents what happens when your egoic mind has become identified with thoughts—generally, judgments—about anything you consider outside or other than yourself. You stories run a wide gamut, including all of your judgments about family members, friends, work associates, politicians, health-care professionals, counselors, lawyers . . . virtually anyone. You stories can also be about your circumstances, the treatments you are receiving, the medications you are taking, the health-care system, your own body, your illness, your work, politics, religious beliefs, money, and thousands of other things. One way or another, You stories either elevate or diminish whomever or whatever you are judging.

Everyone has a ceaseless flow of such thoughts; there are limitless things to think about. But it is not *thinking* itself that is the problem; it is that you become identified with your thoughts. Then defending your ideas or the ideas you have been educated or encultured to believe becomes about defending your identity, a far more serious project. Your thinking is no longer clear when you subconsciously believe that in arguing for your beliefs, you are defending your very sense of self. Now disagreement isn't just about differing perspectives, it is about survival. You have lost your ground in reality. As soon as that happens, your stories will powerfully affect your emotional state, making you angry, hurt, jealous, frustrated, resentful, superior, intolerant, and possibly even violent. You will have lost contact with a larger, more complete *you*.

When you step to the You position of the Mandala, you are admitting that it is the stories you are telling yourself about your situation or about someone else that create the unnecessary and greater suffering—not the words or actions of others. This does not mean that you are accepting or excusing untenable situations or abusive behavior from others; nor does it mean that you have become indifferent to injustice because you stop telling yourself stories about actual cases of injustice. Instead, in stopping your own stories in such instances, you will clearly see the healthy choices you need to make for yourself and what the best approach is to righting the injustice.

Comparing Me and You Stories

It is impossible to accurately evaluate yourself through thinking because Me stories inevitably make you bigger or smaller in some way. In the same way, You stories also magnify or diminish the thing you are thinking about and especially other people.

Some stories make people more important, significant, or powerful; and others make them unimportant, insignificant, or an object of scorn. You can elevate someone to the heights of adoration or submerge him or her in the depths of bigotry and hatred. You can go from the throes of infatuation to cold rejection in hours (even minutes) and believe that it is because of the other person. But most of the time, it is the stories that you tell yourself. Just as Me stories blind you to your true self, You stories blind you to truly seeing others.

The closest you can come to genuinely experiencing another as the "other" that he or she really is—and not just as a projection out of your depressive or grandiose psychology—is when you are in the Now, focused and spacious, ready and relaxed. When you are really present, you will often be surprised by how much appreciation and love you will spontaneously experience, even for someone quite different from you.

It is not romantic or sentimental love, nor is it love encumbered by attachment or expectation of becoming something more personal. It is unconditional love, which is not of the ego. It is a quality of love that comes unbidden, and it feels like grace. To behold the beingness of another in this way is truly a blessing, as it is when you are seen by another in a similar way.

But as soon as the ego takes over love, it will start telling stories that elevate the other person, perhaps turning him or her into your "soul mate." As the ego imagines its vision of your future together, the intoxicating pictures it spins promise eternal happiness. But life is complicated; the field of daily necessity is not romantic and takes so much attention and time. Soon people stop making the effort for meeting in the present where the deeper, spontaneous love was first discovered and where it can be renewed. Then the tide turns—and instead of amplifying the desirable qualities in the other through its stories, the ego begins to amplify the qualities that it finds undesirable. Love and trust give way to reservations and fears.

Put simply: you fall in love and build a relationship because of the stories you tell yourself, and you fall out of love and tear the relationship apart in just the same way. If you find yourself at the point of divorce, consider how many stories it took to come to that point. What if you had been able to discard many of those stories?

Mature love can begin only after you have challenged your relationship-poisoning stories and have taken responsibility to set them aside and meet your partner nakedly in the present. Unlike falling in love—which was a blessing received without any conscious effort or practice—*rebuilding* love is an emotional risk and takes significant conscious effort.

As we will discuss in the next chapter, for love to thrive, not only must you stop identifying with your stories, but you must make space in yourself for the darker feelings as well. Then you see that love is not a story; rather, it is a blessing that arises when you let yourself become naked and open in the Now.

The Mandala as a Compass

As you work with the Mandala, you will see the emotional and physiological consequences that follow when your mind believes your stories, and you will strengthen your capacity to remain in the present. A mind that runs from position to position on the Mandala, untethered to the Now, is like a boat with no anchor that can be thrown around wildly by every wave or gust of wind.

In this state, let's say that you were to receive a message from your doctor's office asking that you call them back. You are instantly thrown into complete turmoil. Stories about what this could mean rush into your mind at a furious pace, and you are at their mercy. Stress hormones are immediately released throughout your body.

On the other hand, a mind more practiced at returning to the present might temporarily flood itself with worrisome thoughts, but would soon recognize them as thoughts and find a place of calm much more quickly. Through the practice of waking yourself up out of your stories and back to the present, your mind becomes stronger, like a muscle being exercised repetitively. You start to rest effortlessly in presence. Simple things fulfill you. You no longer need to find something to keep you busy or distracted, like having a TV on much of the time or spending many long hours on the Internet.

Navigating your life with a compass like the Mandala of Being causes you to turn the arrows of your attention around, away from your stories about you or illness, or about others and the world around you, and back to your embodied self. You will eventually become aware of a gentle presence, a sense of rightness about yourself and life. Acknowledging this presence—even though you cannot logically understand your experience—makes you want to rest there more, because deep within yourself you innately recognize it as *home*. Something is awakening inside you.

The more you use the Mandala, the more it becomes abundantly clear that there are only four places you have ever gone (or will ever go) when you are not fully present in the Now. It shows you where you are—that is, where your thinking has carried you to—and then guides you back home. Embodying awareness in this manner brings your mind to quietness and peace.

Gradually, living more in embodied awareness, your conscious mind stops stifling your soul. Each of us has access to a deeper intelligence, and you can begin to uncover yours in this way. Anything that you have become identified with—even a story you have been telling yourself all your life—may be ready to shed itself like a snake's skin and reveal your true self. This is awakening from the inside out.

CHAPTER EIGHT

EMBRACING YOUR DARK FEELINGS

If you pay close attention when you are experiencing feelings of expansiveness, you will see that this has not come about as a result of thinking. I am referring to feelings such as oneness, fulfillment, peace, clarity, connectedness, belonging, forgiveness, compassion, gratitude, joy, and love. Each of these is like a spontaneous gift that seems to be telling you that somehow you are in harmony with yourself, with others, and with life in a broader sense.

The fact that these elevating feelings arise spontaneously, independent of thought, is more than just my own personal observation. For decades, I have been guiding meditations in which people report all the feelings mentioned above as I invite them to become fully alert and simultaneously relaxed. I never mention any of these feelings, nor do I suggest that they will feel anything positive. It is simply an exercise in developing a focused-spacious awareness. However, the quieter their minds become, the more present they are, and the stronger these feelings manifest.

Granted, certain ways of thinking, such as considering and acknowledging someone else's concerns and circumstances, can lead to a sense of empathy and even compassion. And telling yourself that someone didn't really mean to hurt you might bring about a feeling of forgiveness. But in my experience, the deepest and most complete states of compassion or forgiveness, as well as the other expansive feelings, arise quite spontaneously when your stories stop in the Now and you see in a new way.

But they are not the only feelings that we experience. A living being capable of expansive, elevating feelings also experiences what I call the *dark feelings,* those that span a range from mildly disturbing to profoundly threatening. The milder and more manageable dark feelings include a vague sense that something isn't quite right—a sense of aloneness, emptiness, heaviness, or foreboding. Most of us experience these fairly regularly. It is like a turn in the weather, a darkening of the skies, but not yet a real storm. We don't feel well, but it's not hard to distract ourselves by reading, watching TV, being active, or just staying busy. But when we are overcome by the darkest feelings such as powerlessness, helplessness, or dread, there can be a sense that our very identity is being threatened. As we enter the domain of what I call the *abysmal,* all of the ego's pretenses are stripped away and we feel defenseless, naked, and raw.

Why Don't We All Live in the Now?

If you ever wonder why, particularly in contemporary society, few people really learn to trust living in the Now, it is because their ego won't let them. It runs away into stories in the midst of the abysmal feelings. The survival value that being really present offered our early ancestors (who were constantly alert to the wilds of nature) no longer pertains to the vast majority today.

For us, survival is fleeing any threatening feeling while always relying on intellect to organize for the future. Of course, as we have seen, this leaves us living in a world of thinking and emotion. It is why modern people are generally more stressed and unhappy than people from simpler cultures who live much closer to nature.

In our modern society, we place an emphasis on love and joy and supremely value rationality and reasonableness. But in the natural balance of opposites, the more we elevate the light feelings and a need for order, the more we become fascinated by the dark ones and disorder. Perhaps this is why Hollywood has made a fortune on film noir, horror, and chaotic violence. It seems that the very emphasis on love and happiness spawns the craving for the horrific and macabre. But while millions of people watch these scary films, vicariously titillated by faux darkness, few individuals can actually face real dark feelings when they are present as inevitably they will be.

Embracing the Dark and the Light

The dark feelings are not evil or wrong—in fact, they are entirely natural. Indeed, I believe that they are not only unavoidable, but meeting them consciously is indispensable to becoming a complete person. There cannot be transcendent bliss without abysmal wretchedness. Although these feelings come and go naturally like weather, there are times when you are much more prone to experiencing the abysmal side of your feeling nature.

In general this is whenever your ego feels deeply threatened, as in times of illness, divorce, loss of loved ones, financial misfortune, loss of employment, or whenever you are undergoing inordinate stress. Likewise, strong contrasts or big changes (such as moving to a new home, starting a new job or changing careers, or retiring) destabilize the ego and have the capacity to provoke the darker feelings. Just as when you are rested and calm you are likely to find yourself spontaneously experiencing joy or gratitude, so too when you are depleted by treatments like radiation and chemotherapy, don't get enough sleep at night, or are emotionally taxed, the dark feelings tend to surface.

The abysmal feelings can also be pronounced at times that can be likened to spiritual emergence or spiritual awakening, a subject I have written about extensively in several of my earlier books.[1] And dreams are also a frequent means for bringing forth the dark feelings. It is as if the psyche knows when you are out of balance, living too self-assured, unconsciously imagining that you are in control of your life. Then along comes a deeply disturbing dream or a nightmare to show you that you are really just a child standing before forces far greater than your ego will ever let you acknowledge.

However, it is the dark feelings, if you can meet them with awareness, that have the greatest potential to transform you—indeed, to deepen your capacity for love and joy. But dark feelings are so threatening that your ego steps in to defend itself almost instantly. It does so by making you identify with these upsetting feelings: they become *your* feelings and then something is wrong, often *very* wrong with *you.*

In the blink of an eye, the ego has carried you away from awareness and the immediacy of what you are actually feeling into grandiose or depressive specialness and all the emotions that accompany those patterns of self-identification. You become locked in a destructive cycle of negative thinking that creates anger, guilt, blame, hopelessness, and other negative emotions. In this way, emotions are often defenses against real feeling, especially against the darker feelings.

⅗⅗

What I am calling *feeling* is a mode of consciousness, quite distinct from *thinking,* through which you experience yourself in an immediate, embodied way. You are able to perceive information at several essential levels, which are expressed on the following chart along with some examples:

"Categories" of Feelings

Sensations: hot, cold, rough, soft . . .

Felt-Sense: well, unsafe, fatigued . . .

Essential Feelings: joy, love, aloneness, dread . . .

Emotions: guilt, envy, worry, happiness . . .

At the most basic level there is *sensation:* Is it soft, hard, rough, smooth, hot, cold . . . and so on? At a much more profound level, but still closely related to sensation, is the consciousness of your own being, your *felt-sense* of self. How do you feel? "I feel fine," or "I feel tired," for instance.

Another major category of what you know through feeling (distinct from sensation) includes what I am calling *essential feelings,* such as expansive ones like joy and love or darker ones like aloneness and dread, which we just discussed. Essential feelings, despite being so familiar, are also in a certain sense mysterious in that they come from a deeper level than the egoic mind. This means—and it is a crucial distinction for our work—that essential feelings arise independent of thinking.

This distinction between feelings that arise with and without thinking leads us, finally, to the fourth category: *emotions*, such as guilt or envy. Emotional states are generated when the feeling mode of consciousness is merged with thinking, as expressed in this diagram:

Emotions Result from the Amalgamation of Thinking and Feeling

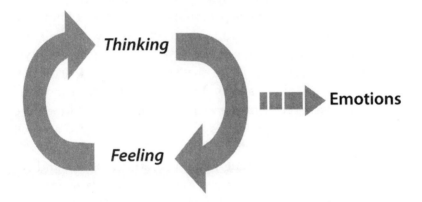

Throughout this book, I have consistently referred to states that we feel (such as resentment, jealousy, guilt, and worry, to mention but a few) as *emotions* and not as *feelings* because they are created specifically by thoughts. For most people, the distinction between feeling and emotion is a new understanding. But as we shall see, without this distinction, it is harder to learn how to explore the depths of presence.

Your Feeling Nature

The feeling mode of consciousness is highly intelligent, although it is a very different kind of intelligence than thinking. It is a bodily knowing that tells you whether you are in flow or resistance, in harmony or conflict. Through empathy you can sometimes intuit other people's feelings or emotions and sense whether or not they are being genuine. Sometimes feeling speaks to you through what are called "gut feelings," which give you that felt-sense of whether or not you are safe in your surroundings or if something is or isn't right for you. You don't have any logical reason or rationale for what you know—you just *feel* it. In this way, certain aspects of feeling are kindred with intuition.

Feeling is never abstract—meaning that what you know through feeling, you know directly and immediately. You may not always understand what you are feeling, but you know that you are feeling something. To be fully in touch with your feeling nature, you need to be present, as the only information you ever get through feeling is about the Now. The experience of this knowing can be as mundane as the sense of hunger or recognizing that you are angry. But even the realization of sublime states of oneness and transcendence is primarily experienced as a felt-state of being.

Feeling, when it is not caught up in emotions, is fluid and ever changing. Moment by moment it flows through you, bringing new information about yourself and your connection to the larger environment. In some people, the feeling nature can be very highly developed, but less so in others. The essential difference between having a highly developed feeling nature or not is really a matter of presence: the more present you are, the more accurate and complete your "felt-experience" of yourself and the world is.

It is through feeling that you appreciate beauty and are moved by great ideas. Even symbols don't come alive until you actually feel them. Mere intellectual understanding is sterile; it is like looking at a grape instead of tasting it. It is through feeling that you are touched by music and art. And it is only through feeling that the deliciousness of love, the tenderness of compassion, or the misery of suffering have any tangible reality.

Your capacity for feeling spans a broad continuum from simple well-being to vague uneasiness, from joy to dread, and from the heights of the most blissful to the depths of the most abysmal (as illustrated in the diagram below). These feelings never lie to you or misinform you, although it is not always possible to readily name or describe exactly what you are feeling or what it is informing you of. Emotions, on the other hand, are easy to name, and you know exactly how they *feel*.

The Continuum of Feeling

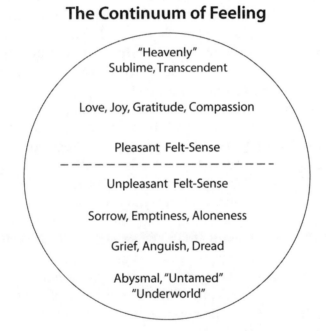

"Heavenly"
Sublime, Transcendent

Love, Joy, Gratitude, Compassion

Pleasant Felt-Sense

- - - - - - - - - - - - - - -

Unpleasant Felt-Sense

Sorrow, Emptiness, Aloneness

Grief, Anguish, Dread

Abysmal, "Untamed"
"Underworld"

There is nothing inscrutable about jealousy or worry. But with many feelings, recognizing what you are actually feeling is not so simple. To do so, you have to learn to be patient and steady with focused-spacious awareness. It is important not to try to label your feelings or define them too quickly. Then, with practice, even the inexplicable feelings can open you to new vistas, leading beyond your egoic identity into new depths of being.

The fundamental difference between feeling and emotion is, once again, that *feeling arises spontaneously without thinking, while emotions are highly specific feelings that are always linked to thoughts.* Oftentimes you may not be aware of the underlying thought that is creating an emotion unless you make the connection through a self-discovery process such as the Mandala of Being or some other form of inner work. With careful observation, you will be able to separate essential feelings from emotions.

All feeling comes and goes in an ever-flowing manner because we are living beings embedded in and interpenetrating a vast and mysterious network of life and consciousness. We act on that network with how we are present—with the quality of our attention (not to mention our actual behaviors)—and that network acts on us. Feeling is a way of recognizing that interaction; through it, we interface and exchange information with the environment in a way that is immediate and nonrational.

For example, one of the beauties of interacting with animals—let's say riding a horse—is that the horse is highly attuned to your feeling state. Certain emotions, particularly anger or anxiety, make the horse uncomfortable and uncooperative, but as soon as you relax, the horse becomes responsive. Likewise, its feeling state actually influences yours. Together, you can work as a unit.

Emotions also come and go but not because you are interfacing with and responding to the larger reality. They specifically arise according to what your conscious mind is thinking and telling you. You have a thought that makes you jealous, but then jealousy quickly becomes anger, anger becomes fear, fear becomes hurt, and hurt becomes desperation, which then becomes anger again. This is because each emotion triggers a new thought that in turn triggers another emotion. Round and round you go, like a dog chasing its tail, and the basic pattern of suffering and contraction continues until the thinking stops.

Most often the train of thought is interrupted simply because you distract yourself and become involved with doing something else. Maybe you have to focus on your work, or you get on the

Internet or turn on the television. While you are thus occupied, it's like pushing the PAUSE button; the thoughts that were keeping the emotional maelstrom going stop, and the emotions quickly subside. But as soon as the distraction is gone, if the same thinking restarts, then the same emotions take over once again.

Stories Create Emotions

Emotions, despite how crazy they can make you, are quite rational and predictable. They can be directly linked to whichever of the four directions of the Mandala of Being your thinking mind carries you into. Notice that in the following diagram (on the next page), the large arrows are pointing away from the center (the Now), and much smaller arrows are pointing back to the center. This represents that when the ego is in control, you have very little contact with presence. In other words, you are identified with your thoughts and are in your head, not your body, which is why emotions can so readily take over. By learning to inquire into your stories (as we have explored in the Mandala work), you are changing the direction of your attention, turning it back to the Now, and restoring yourself to presence. Doing so immediately frees you from getting lost in emotional reactions.

The Mandala of Emotional Reality

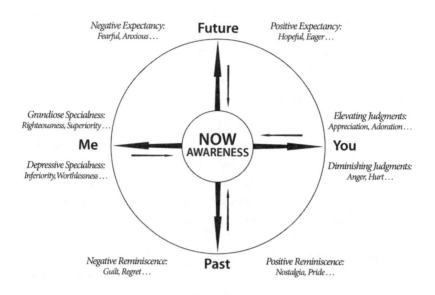

Negative Expectancy:
Fearful, Anxious...

Future

Positive Expectancy:
Hopeful, Eager...

Grandiose Specialness:
Righteousness, Superiority...

Me

Depressive Specialness:
Inferiority, Worthlessness...

NOW AWARENESS

Elevating Judgments:
Appreciation, Adoration...

You

Diminishing Judgments:
Anger, Hurt...

Negative Reminiscence:
Guilt, Regret...

Past

Positive Reminiscence:
Nostalgia, Pride...

As we have explored, Past stories create guilt, shame, regret, and loss. But also reminiscing about positive memories can invoke a range of pleasant emotions such as nostalgia, happiness, and pride. Future stories (or images) generate anxiety, worry, and fearfulness when the stories or images are threatening; or hopefulness and ebullience or eagerness when they are desirable and pleasing.

Emotions created by You stories include anger, resentment, bitterness, envy, jealousy, hatred, and hurt; in addition to respect, appreciation, infatuation, and even adoration. Finally, the emotions created by Me stories include the whole range of grandiose feelings like superiority, righteousness, impatience, smugness, and pomposity; as well as those of depressive specialness such as inferiority, self-loathing, inadequacy, and worthlessness. (If you wish, review the chart titled "Examples of Emotions Associated with the Four Positions of the Mandala of Being" on page 51.)

Some of these emotions are very specific to where your mind is. For example, guilt is always the result of a Past story, while resentment is always the result of a You story. But other emotions can belong to more than one direction: you can feel *demoralized* by a Me story ("I can't do this") or a Future story ("This will never work").

As I have said, the important thing is not to be exactly sure of which position on the Mandala a specific emotion corresponds to, but to grasp that emotions are states created by your thinking. They don't just happen to you, and other people don't cause them. You have to tell yourself a specific story.

Emotional Fatigue

There are also physiological conditions you might not ordinarily consider emotional—such as being drained, exhausted, rushed, or overwhelmed—that are caused by specific ways of thinking that drive habitual, energy-depleting behaviors. There is, of course, a normal, healthy kind of tiredness at the end of a full and active day. The way you know whether your fatigue is normal is that you can fall asleep easily and wake up feeling rested. Burnout or depletion, on the other hand, does not come from a hard day's work, but from battering yourself all day long with stories that create resentment, resistance, anxiety, or reactivity.

This mind-made emotional suffering so depletes your nervous system that it then becomes difficult to sleep. In turn, this creates a disastrous negative-feedback loop where the more exhausted you are, the more prone to negative thinking and emotions you become. Until you can bring yourself into the Now and stop the stories, you will continue to be the victim of your own mind.

It's also important to note that there are many times when the distinction between an emotion and a feeling may be unclear. For example, I intentionally did not list grief as an emotion because I believe that the feeling of grief is a *true feeling*. It is also true that simple grief is relatively rare, since most people tell themselves stories that complicate this feeling with guilt or anger, or they amplify it with other stories.

But if you can remain silent and spacious with the feeling of grief (whatever the loss is), you may discover that pure grief actually involves more than a feeling of absence. It can also bring recognition of timeless connection and a sense of acceptance with parting and loss. There can be an expansive quality in grief as well as pain; it can stop your thinking mind and, in so doing, sometimes lead you to wonderment in the midst of suffering.

Feelings Are Intelligent—Emotions Are Not

As mentioned earlier, it is the ambiguous nature of many feelings that distinguish them from emotions. Emotions like guilt and resentment are unambiguous; we all know what these emotions *feel* like. But grief (as we just saw) and many other feelings are not so easy to describe because they are multifaceted, more nuanced, and constantly in flux.

Rather than worrying about an exact distinction between feeling and emotion, what is vital to realize is that while feeling is an essential and intelligent way of knowing, emotions are feelings that have lost their intelligence. That is, emotions are stupid or, more accurately, stupefying, precisely because they always give you the same information or lead you into similar patterns of reaction and behavior. Resentment gives only further resentment, which might also cause you to be spiteful or withholding. Jealousy always produces more jealousy, which may cause you to behave manipulatively or even violently. Until you break the link between the story you are telling yourself and the emotion that the story creates, you will remain trapped in some immature emotional-behavioral loop.

Remember that emotion is the feeling nature of the ego. It is feeling that has lost its interface with the larger reality and relates instead only to the egoic mind. Since emotions are triggered by stories that when inquired into almost always prove to be untrue—that is, not based on what is actually happening—emotions are in a certain sense not sane. They are thought-generated sensations that distort or blind you to where you actually are and what is actually happening. And the irony is that when emotions become truly extreme (such as in deep self-loathing, rage, and hate), it is almost invariably because your ego is trying to protect you from an underlying feeling, almost always a very dark feeling.

The Darkest Feelings

Feeling arises from a preverbal level of being, earlier and more fundamental than the egoic mind. In this sense, feeling is essentially nonrational or "extrarational." To allow yourself to fully feel means, to one degree or another, to let go of egoic control and just *be*. When what you feel is elevating, like joy and love, this is not much of a problem (although as we shall discuss later, the most sublime feelings can also threaten the ego). But when the dark feelings overtake you, they threaten your ego. The darker the feeling, the more threatening it is, and the more difficult it becomes to relax and let yourself be.

I refer to these feelings as *dark* not only because they are disturbing, but more specifically (as we have seen), because you cannot easily describe them. It is not that you cannot describe them to someone else; it is that you cannot describe what you are feeling even to yourself. And when your ego is experiencing something it cannot name and thereby comprehend, it feels like it is being invaded and overcome. This is part of why these feelings are so disturbing.

Actually, it is impossible to accurately name the dark feelings, so inevitably you have to resort to the use of metaphors like referring to the feeling as "demonic" or "hellish." Or you have to use similes such as "It is *like* my life is draining away," "It is *as if* no one ever really sees me," or "It is *as though* I am losing my mind." This use of simile is one of the ways you can know that you are dealing with a dark feeling. But this kind of description is itself another story, never the actual feeling itself. These feelings can only be embraced by awareness—never by the thinking mind.

As stated earlier in the chapter, I call the darkest feelings *abysmal* because as you turn your awareness toward them, you never seem to be able to get to the bottom of them. They appear to have no beginning and no end, as if they are outside time. When you are besieged by the abysmal, it is as if you have always been this way and always will be.

These feelings seem bigger than you—as if you are being swallowed up in them, like Jonah in the belly of the whale. Your thoughts may try to tell you that the feeling will pass, which of course it will. But the experience itself is that the feeling seems, while you are in it, unrelenting and unending. Experiencing the abysmal feelings is more like an initiation or a rite of passage than a mere emotional experience. It has the potential to open big doors deep into the soul.

I also sometimes refer to these feelings as *untamed* to contrast them with emotions, which I refer to as *tamed*. Emotions like hate can be very destructive, so categorizing hate as a "tamed" emotion is intentionally provocative. I want you to realize that emotions, even those like hate, are tamed because no matter how unpleasant or destructive they may feel and be to you and others, they never actually threaten your ego. On the contrary, they *are* your ego.

Emotions such as self-loathing or hatred may humiliate your idealized self, which wants to come across as happy, fair-minded, or reasonable, but humiliation is still the emotional state of an intact ego. It still upholds a sense of identity. You may feel ashamed of your own emotionality, of how jealous or resentful you are being, but such shame is again just another emotional state of your ego.

In this sense, emotions are like domesticated animals in a farmer's barnyard: not always cooperative, couth, or flattering, but always ultimately under the farmer's—the ego's—control. They are never truly wild like a zebra, an animal so undomesticated that it can easily die of shock just by being transported from one area to another. As crazy as emotions can make you, it is a familiar, repetitive craziness that never brings you to something new. In comparison, untamed feelings are truly wild rides that confront you with the unknown depths of your being where it can seem as though who you are (as an ego) is being annihilated. But when you bring awareness to these feelings, you aren't annihilated; you are made more transparent to life and profoundly present.

A Word about Fear

Fear is a wall that every one of us hits again and again throughout our lives. Some people try to climb the wall by filling themselves with hope. Others try to ignore it, perhaps by keeping themselves very busy. Some try to go around it by taking care of everyone else, and there are those who put on blinders and let their world get smaller and smaller over time. But sooner or later, to fully live, we have to sit down in front of fear and let it teach us about ourselves. When we do, it becomes one of our greatest allies in the journey to wisdom and healing.

Fear is probably the most prevalent of the dark feelings. Yet the actual sensation we mean when we say *fear* is difficult or near-ly impossible to describe. Invariably, when we try to describe it, we use qualifiers: fear *of* spiders, fear *of* heights, fear *of* attack, and fear *of* crowds, for instance. Of course, probably the most basic of all fears is the fear *of* death.

But all of these attempts to describe or explain fear are actually stories, which create fearful emotions, not the actual sensation of fear. There are innumerable ways of rationalizing fear that give you the mistaken idea that you know what it is, when in reality you haven't engaged the feeling consciously. If you did, then you would clearly realize that at the level of sensation, all fear is the same.

When Franklin D. Roosevelt, in his first inaugural address, told the American people during the height of the Great Depression that "the only thing we have to fear is fear itself," he was speaking with exceptional wisdom. The stories that the mind generates around fear intensify it, causing more paralysis and despair than the ac-tual feeling itself. If you turn your awareness *toward* fear instead of thinking *about* it—and actually allow yourself to experience the sensation of fear while refusing to let that sensation carry you into stories—the stories will dissolve as fast as they form. Then, like all feelings, fear continues to transmute. It becomes energy—aliveness not frozen in contraction. No matter why it is there, almost as fast as you become aware of it you can stop the mind from thinking *about* it and turn awareness *toward* it. You become both focused on the fear and spacious at the same time.

If you are only focused on the fear, however, you will inevitably start telling yourself stories about it, and it will become emotional and much stronger. Telling yourself why you are afraid or what you are afraid of is the way in which your ego creates your identity around fear—in other words, the way it creates itself. It claims the feeling of fear as its own and starts feeding you stories: "This is fear *of* . . . ," and the list goes on. "*I* am afraid because . . . ," and the reasons are legion. "*I* have felt this fear before," "*I* am too weak to feel it," "*I* am ashamed of feeling it," "*I* have to get past it," and on and on. Story after story, your ego perpetually traps you in an identity built around fear.

If you interrupt these stories and come into the present moment, most fear subsides and you become more open and transparent to life. Whenever fear arises, it is an opportunity to witness what you are telling yourself—an invitation to inquire into the genuine nature of your experience. Ask yourself, "Who or what is afraid?" If the answer that comes is "*I* am afraid," then ask, "Who *is* this I?" Is it the one who says "I am afraid," or the one who is witnessing that statement? Just be quiet, still, and receptive.

If fearfulness lasts longer than a few moments, such as when you suddenly come upon a snake on a trail, this almost always signals the activity of ego. This gives you the clue to turn awareness toward the sensation itself and not the stories. As you begin to practice turning "fearward" and touching the fear with steady, soft attention while remaining spacious, you will soon stop running from the sensation of fear. Then you will have reached a whole new level of inner freedom.

In the course of evolution, fear was the essential sensation warning you of danger. Feeling it instantly brought about a state of high alertness and readiness, a good thing if you had to avoid or defend against a predator, or if you were a hunter or a warrior.

In this manner, fear was and, in some ways, remains your first teacher of survival (as it is for us all). But at least in the modern world, when so little of the experience of fear has to do with actual immediate danger, your primitive fear reaction has become much more problematic.

Now what we fear most often is not some actual life threat, but imagined threats to our identity, whether it is personal, financial, ideological, national, or religious identity. It is not fear for our lives, but fear for our egos. Fear has become mostly about psychological survival—it is mind-made fear. Ironically, our collective survival now depends on us learning to consciously turn our awareness *toward* the sensation of fear. Otherwise, if we continue trying to protect our egos, we will surely destroy ourselves.

How the Ego Co-opts Feeling

In an evolutionary sense, feeling is a much older mode of consciousness than thinking. The large brain and highly convoluted cortex that supports the thinking of modern human beings is a newer development than the midbrain and thalamus that govern most of your feelings. It is feeling that dominates a young child's experience because until the ego has developed, thinking is very limited.

Just watch babies, and you can see that they are constantly experiencing ever-changing feelings, from utter bliss and contentment to screaming distress and misery. A young child feels his own internal reality as well as the emotional environment around him. But he does not yet realize that some feelings arise from within himself and that others are being stimulated from outside.

Now try to imagine how a baby learns to deal with feelings as her ego develops, and she begins to see herself as a separate self: Gradually, feelings that seemed to come and go without cause become objects of consciousness that the ego interprets as self. The baby begins to identify with the feelings and to regard herself as happy or unhappy, good or bad, according to the nature of the feelings. Once the ego has claimed these feelings as self, her only defense against them is to try to turn the untamed into the tamed through thinking. In other words, the ego turns feelings into its emotions.

I think this is why the emotions of children change so quickly. A few weeks ago, for instance, I was with a friend and his five-year-old son. In the course of an hour or so, the little boy was smiling and happy, closed and complaining, angry and demanding, timid and clinging, crying and inconsolable . . . round and round. The father expressed concern because his son seemed more disturbed and emotional since starting kindergarten. Moreover, whenever his son expressed any unhappiness, the father wanted to immediately do something to take that emotion away; such a normal response for a parent who imagines that something is wrong.

But what I saw was completely normal and to be expected. I saw a young ego trying to come to grips with the flux of feelings (some of them agreeable, and others confusing and dark) that were arising in him because of so many things: having a new daily rhythm, being away from his family more, being in a new environment surrounded by new people (teachers and children with all their own behaviors and emotions), and even the changing of his own growing body.

I could just imagine his young ego bombarded by feelings and his mind racing with thoughts. And because a child has no way to meet feelings with focused-spacious awareness and no way to evaluate his thoughts, those feelings are instantly co-opted by the ego and invariably turned into emotions. For me, it was like looking at the history of humankind and how the thinking mind inevitably makes us all crazy once that which is not of the ego (feeling) has been appropriated by the ego.

How can you tell if your ego has appropriated a dark feeling? You find yourself compulsively *thinking.* Your mind will spin with story after story about what is wrong with you, what strategy to pursue, why your situation is hopeless, why your life is ruined or meaningless, or how you can save yourself. It will find every way it can to attack you, judge you, blame others, or even attack them. It will make you guilty, resentful, terrified, hopeless, impulsive, and aggressive . . . one after the other. It is frantically trying to create a known (albeit, terribly amplified) misery in a desperate attempt to be in control of an unknown and ultimately unknowable feeling that it doesn't even realize that it is reacting to.

But the ego can never control what comes from a deeper ground of consciousness. Even though thinking is a newer evolutionary development that has given human beings great power, it is the wrong mechanism for addressing feeling. The more your ego spins stories in the face of abysmal feeling, the more miserable you become. It is the thinking mind that drives a person to suicide or to abusing drugs and alcohol—*not* the actual feeling.

Until you understand what is happening to you and can stop your thoughts and instead turn your full awareness with focused-spacious attention directly toward the dark feeling, you might as well be in hell. Indeed, I believe this is the only hell that exists, and it is purely mind-made. The abysmal feelings in themselves are never as terrible as what the ego creates to try to control them.

Journey to the Underworld

In mythology, the domain of the abysmal feelings has been referred to as the underworld. It is the territory the hero or heroine must travel through in order to become cleansed of the ego's illusion, then to rise again empowered from the depths of spirit. Not only are the initiates taken down into the underworld, but they are also given clear instruction as to how to pass through and return once again to ordinary life.

A key aspect of this instruction is learning not to be distracted by your thoughts, especially by your memories and old patterns of response, such as automatically taking care of others or protecting them from what you are feeling. Also essential is learning how to be fully present without resistance to whatever you are feeling.

The mythic tales teach that when you return from this voyage into darkness, you are fundamentally changed. Meeting the abysmal feelings is life changing. After a siege in the Dark Night, when you go back to what can be called *normal* or *ordinary* consciousness (for lack of a better description), you find that your heart has broken open, fear has evaporated, love flows more spontaneously, and you have become much more compassionate and forgiving. You have entered previously unknown levels of your being, and it has made you a little more humble and a bit wiser.

The underworld is a gateway to the God within who is forever without a face or name. You cannot descend to the darkness without being carried up into the light, and you cannot realize the light without being called to descend into darkness. All feeling is mysterious, but in the lower realms in particular, some part of you knows that you are meeting what is and will always be beyond you as an ego or separate self. If you can meet the abysmal feelings with awareness instead of letting your ego take over, in that meeting you are reborn.

It is important to remember that it is because the abysmal feelings come from a deeper ground of being than the ego that they are so threatening to the ego. But your ego does not know that feeling itself comes from a deeper ground. From its earliest stages, the incipient ego begins to appropriate all feelings, to identify with them and tell itself stories that attempt to explain these feelings. But the abysmal feelings are so threatening to the ego that its only defense is to make them part of self-identity and then to bury them under emotion.

If one untamed feeling might be described as a sense of emptiness, for the ego it may gradually become the tamed (ego-sustaining) story "I am worthless, a nothing, nobody." If the abysmal feeling is a kind of inner pressure or restlessness, to the ego it might eventually become a compulsive drivenness: "I have to keep trying and keep on moving. I must keep on running, or I will be taken over." If the untamed feeling is stimulated in an infant when he sees or hears his parents fighting, later for the child that feeling might become the identity "I am unsafe." Or if the child feels helpless in the face of his mother's unhappiness, he might gradually start to believe that "Something is wrong with me."

Even though abysmal feelings (and all feelings) are not created by thought and do not have their origin in the ego, the ego must make you special either with depressive beliefs like "I am ugly"

or "I am unlovable," or with grandiose thoughts like "I am better than she is," or "You should do what I tell you." And throughout life, whenever the abysmal feelings are present, the ego explodes into its defensive emotional pattern, leading you into that same reactive process. The ego is a form of possession that nearly everyone considers normal.

The very presence of the abysmal feelings is a threat to the ego's sovereignty. But when the ego rejects these feelings and tries to convert them to known emotions, without realizing it, you are rejecting yourself, or at least a more complete part of you. By attacking these feelings, you are attacking yourself. Reviling how you feel, you are reviling yourself. This is the deepest form of suffering.

Working with the Dark Feelings

The abysmal feelings are part of the ingenious way in which our souls help us continue to evolve; therefore, experiencing them is ultimately intrinsic to deep healing. There could be no profound joy or love or gratitude without the existence of the abysmal side. There can be no real sense of freedom or abiding well-being until we have learned to make space for these feelings. But since they do not originate in the ego, we must learn to *feel* them without letting our ego take over control and throw us into thinking.

When you taste an orange, for instance, you do not think, you just taste. When you smell a rose, you do not think—you just smell its fragrance. When you feel a feeling, do not think, *just feel*. The essential teaching about working with abysmal feelings can be succinctly stated as: *Do not give to your ego that which is not of your ego.*

Not giving these feelings to the ego means staying present: focused and spacious, ready and relaxed. But it also means that you understand the ego's game—that is, your ego cannot bear these feelings and will instantly start telling you stories about the feeling itself, about you, the situation, how things used to be, and what might happen.

Once you let your ego hijack you, it will instantly lead your attention away from the feeling and into the stories. And these stories, like a deluge, will drown you in a frantic storm of emotionality. Make no mistake, the emotional reality created by your ego when it tries to encompass an abysmal feeling is far more miserable and inevitably more destructive to you and those around you than the actual feeling if you could just stay present with it.

In the previous chapters, the main instruction was to recognize the emotional suffering created by your own thinking. You learned how to use conscious self-inquiry to move into the Past, Future, Me, and You positions of the Mandala of Being and unpackage the stories underlying any situation in which you became emotionally muddy. You learned to feel the contrast between who you are when identified with your stories and who you are in the Now without those stories. In this way, you gained insight into how it is what you tell yourself that creates your own suffering and learned to free yourself from it.

But it is not your thinking that creates the dark feelings. They are a natural consequence of being alive. Therefore, it is not a question of unpackaging what you are telling yourself, but instead stopping yourself from creating stories that lead you away from the feelings and into emotions. It is knowing to stay rooted in the Now no matter how uncomfortable and destabilizing the feeling seems to be. It is teaching yourself to stop being afraid to *feel*.

Here again, the Mandala of Being can offer you a map so that you can make space to hold the dark feelings with awareness instead of collapsing into the ego's emotional defenses. To illustrate this, I have created an additional Mandala (see the following diagram) in which you will see that I have drawn stop signs between the center of the Mandala and each of the four positions. Stop signs are unequivocal; they mean *stop!* If you are driving a car and don't heed a stop sign, you are in danger of a serious fender bender, or worse.

In the case of untamed feelings, if you don't heed the signs that tell you *Do not enter* and instead allow your ego to carry you into Me, You, Past, or Future stories, you will end up in a real "mind bender" of emotional misery.

When the NOW Is Abysmal, STOP Your Stories

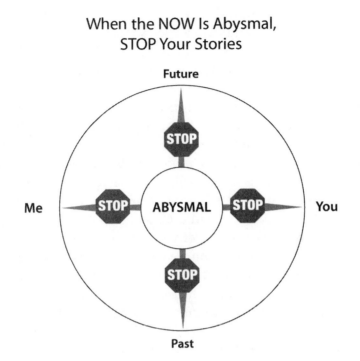

The essential difference between the work when you are emotionally muddy versus when you are with a dark feeling is that when you are muddy, you learn to recognize the stories that you are telling yourself and then return yourself to the Now. The work with the dark feelings is similar, but instead of looking to discover the stories you are telling yourself and then returning to the Now, you *stay* in the Now—with the feeling—and steadfastly refuse to give any credence to any story created by your ego. Once you can do this, you can also learn to channel the energy of these feelings in creative ways that can be very healing (a subject we shall discuss in the final chapter).

🔈🔈

If you have read this far, then you already recognize that for most of your life you have fled the dark feelings and been repeatedly carried into emotional suffering. Now you are ready to change. And what will really help you do so is to know ahead of time where your ego wants to lead you so that you do not follow it.

You will see that where your ego wants to lead you is obvious. The ego is the ego, so it wants to take you into Me stories, generally into depressive specialness or sometimes into explosive, aggressive grandiosity. And the way that it tricks you—which happens in a millisecond—is with the belief that you have felt this feeling, or something very similar to it, before.

Remember that for the ego, nothing is ever new or original; the present moment is always being compared to a previous moment, and the future that the ego can imagine is always a projection from the past. Recall the injunction stated earlier: Do not give to your ego that which is not of your ego. Well, as soon as there is an abysmal feeling and you believe or unconsciously assume that you have felt that feeling before, your ego has taken over. Then you will tend to think: *I remember the last time I felt this way. I've been here so many times before* [Past stories]. *It's back again* [You story]. *I thought I was beyond this. I thought that I had already healed this. I can't stand feeling this way* [Me stories]. *There's no hope for me* [Future story]. Down the slippery slope of specialness and suffering you plunge.

When you catch yourself saying that you have felt this abysmal feeling before, ask, "Who has felt this before?" If your answer is "me," or if you believe "I have felt this before," then you are back in the ego, *not* in awareness. Keep in mind that any thought about a feeling is ego.

But if you understand that nothing is new or original from the ego's point of view, you can recognize the belief "I have felt this before" as just a thought, a story. Instead of accepting this fiction as fact, you can turn toward the darkest feeling with focused attention while letting yourself remain spacious and your body relaxed. This undefended relationship to abysmal feelings is healing, not only for the soul, but also for the body. It allows new energy to flow that creates a healthier balance in the psyche and vitality within your physical self.

A New Experience Every Time

From the point of view of awareness, everything is always new, always original. You may still catch yourself thinking, *I've felt this before,* but instead of believing that story, you can begin an entirely new experiment: *Imagine that you have never before felt what you are feeling.* If you are comparing your experience to the past, instead try to actually experience the feeling as if for the first time. If your thinking mind is in the future awaiting an outcome, see if you can taste your present-moment experience just as it is, not as something leading to something else. Don't believe any story (simile or explanation) about the feeling.

Make it a practice to turn directly toward any disturbing feeling, whether it is just a kind of restlessness or a deep sense of threat, and clear your mind of any thoughts. Steadily "touch" the feeling with a soft inner gaze. Remain spacious, extending your senses far beyond your immediate location, and open your intuition into the limitless expanse of being. Keep relaxing without losing the sense of readiness.

This does not protect you from the abysmal feelings; you do *feel* them. You need to feel them because they are part of being human and can deepen your humanity. But not joining with any thought about them keeps you from letting your ego disguise the dark feelings by turning them into guilt, anger, terror, or self-loathing. Moreover, when you can make space for the dark feelings, you discover that they are never as terrible to experience as the psychological misery your ego creates with its stories about what is wrong with you.

Every day the collective misunderstanding of the importance of feeling and the inability of most people to remain aware rather than in ego result in untold misery. It is a repeating tragedy, the scourge of humankind.

When you stop treating these feelings as if you have felt them before and instead remain alert, relaxed, focused, and spacious, you will discover that the abysmal feelings are a window to your unknown self. And that self is not terrible. In the pure, naked experience of these abysmal feelings, they are never as terrible as the sense of despair, self-hatred, or rage—all emotional creations of the ego—that are truly terrible.

Darkness Becomes the Light

The underworld is dark and disturbing because it will not become familiar. It will not bend to your ego; it cannot be tamed. What lives there remains forever just beyond rational comprehension. It burns through you like a cleansing fire that brings you to greater humility. I believe that it is an essential process of psychological alchemy after which your senses are sharper than you have ever noticed before and your heart is filled with gratitude, love, joy, and compassion. By descending—and perhaps only by descending—you can then ascend and often heal.

Remaining undefended and transparent in the untamed feelings is an initiation each time. But you do not need to fear that you will drown. As long as you do not give these feelings to your ego, they always flow on, sometimes even transmuting into the sublime feelings. There is no way to be caught for very long in an untamed feeling if you remain inwardly silent and fully present. Invariably, the darkness becomes the light.

ᕼᕼ

We have been discussing the abysmal feelings, but it is also interesting to consider the ego's relationship to the expansive feelings (such as profound love or ecstatic joy), for even here, it creates suffering. Everyone experiences the expansive feelings from time to time, and sometimes we even have tastes of transcendent peace. But the main difference between the expansive feelings and the abysmal ones is that as sensations, the expansive feelings are not threatening to the ego. Initially, it can relax its vigilance and does not need to be in control because it likes these feelings and feels safe.

Inevitably, though, the ego cannot leave even the expansive feelings alone; it identifies with them and wants to maintain and prolong *its* pleasure. Of course, this intrusion of control immediately diminishes and soon eliminates any happiness that is there in the same way as consciously trying to control how you are surfing will almost instantly cause you to wipe out. Wanting joy or love to continue cancels those feelings, because *wanting* is itself a form of stress. In seeking to sustain or regain a positive feeling, you invite frustration, and dissatisfaction is never far behind.

But the ego has another problem with the expansive feelings: its identity rests on a platform of unconscious grandiosity or depressiveness, and expansive feelings threaten those identities. In the same way as the ego cannot be transparent to the dark feelings and just let them be, it also cannot be transparent to the higher feelings. Either it feels unworthy and flees into stories that quickly reestablish its depressive position ("I don't deserve this" or "This will pass, and then I'll feel even worse"), or it inflates itself by believing that feeling such magnificence is an indication of its exalted importance, its exceptional worthiness. Ego inflation of this kind sooner or later leads to a painful deflation, but even before that, the person is in an obvious state of imbalance.

The ego can achieve simple pleasures: momentary satisfaction with its achievements, happiness with its new car, for instance. But it cannot itself create any of the higher feelings. Take love, for example: the only love the ego knows is strategic, a manipulative transaction in which it gives to get. It gives kindness to be liked, praise to be praised, approval to be approved of, and love to be loved. This conditional love is shallow at best and usually turns into hurt or even hate when the transaction doesn't go as planned.

Similarly, the ego is not the source of compassion, joy, or forgiveness either. When these feelings come, all the ego can do is identify with them and start down the path of unworthiness or imagine that it has reached new spiritual heights. The ego is at most a voyeur when there is a positive feeling and at worst an impostor. Ultimately, the ego's inability to maintain any kind of positive feeling state results in a kind of low-level or background state of dissatisfaction that is the very note of the ego.

Why the Dark Feelings?

Abysmal feelings are intrinsic to being alive, and I believe they are in service to awakening to your deeper intelligence. Perhaps it can be said that when you are ready (even if you do not believe that you are), your soul calls you down into them as a process of spiritual initiation or for the purpose of healing.

Some religions explain the abysmal feelings as having a karmic origin: that they are the result of bad actions earlier in life or, as in the case of some belief systems, from previous lifetimes. The assumption is that experiencing this suffering now gives you a chance to balance the karmic scales.

Transpersonal psychology regards these feelings as both "pre-egoic" and "trans-egoic." Pre-egoic suggests that these are residual traumatic imprints from very early in life; and trans-egoic means that they are archetypal dynamics, part of the very structure of consciousness and never merely personal.

Personally, I do not ascribe to the notion of karma in the sense of punishment. It is too egocentric a philosophy for me. I don't believe abysmal feelings are ever a punishment, but they are a challenge and therefore also an opportunity. Once you accept this, instead of feeling cursed when the dark feelings appear, you can surrender and give yourself over to them and see where they lead you. This does not mean that you should seek out such feelings. Such egoistic ambition would pollute the intelligence that might otherwise be born in a genuine encounter with them.

In any case, there is no need to look for or provoke the dark feelings for purposes of spiritual growth; life inevitably brings them. As I said earlier, they are almost inevitable during an illness or whenever your ego feels threatened, such as in times of change or uncertainty.

Even taking a vacation can be notorious for stirring up the dark, as if something inside knows that the familiar daily busyness has been keeping you too distracted in ego-driven activity to attend to your soul's calling. For the sake of essential regeneration and rebirth, you must go down into the abyss for awhile.

Perhaps this is why few people, especially in the U.S., ever allow themselves a real time of letting go. Instead they have a "vacation" (often restricted to a week) with a tight, demanding travel schedule where they have to see all the sights, try out all the best restaurants, and shop until they drop. Unstructured open time is too dangerous: the "monsters" from the deep that have been held at bay by compulsive or near compulsive activity might rear their heads. The tragic truth of modern life is that it hardly leaves room for the necessary descent into the underworld that opens the heart, enriches humanity, and often rejuvenates the body.

One crucial support during the dark times is to pay close attention to your dreams. It is often through dreams that you are initiated into the dark feelings, or that their approach is announced. For example, dreams of tidal waves or earthquakes often signal that you are about to enter a very challenging time. But dreams can also help you understand what is happening and even instruct you about how to go forward.

I had such a dream many years ago at one of the darkest times of my life shortly after I had left medicine and begun my teaching work. In the dream, a werewolf was coming toward me, and I woke up in terror. I still remember exactly what my ego was telling me as I trembled in fear: "You are a phony. Your life is a mess. You are never going to survive this." But a few minutes later, as I rinsed my sweaty face in the bathroom and looked in the mirror, I suddenly saw my own reflection as that of the werewolf. And I growled. Then I growled even louder and louder still.

Suddenly I understood that the feeling I had been running from was a sense of power within me that I was deeply afraid of. But in that instant, I let myself become the werewolf and took on that power. I was filled with peace and a sense of strength. From that point onward, I was able to resume my teaching work with a new balance and strength.

A detailed discussion of dreams is beyond the scope of this book. Suffice it to say that often when you are touching the abysmal feelings and your ego starts telling you that something is terribly wrong, your dreams may give you an entirely different perspective that shows you another possibility.

As the biographies of saints and other people who have quested deeply attest, the spiritual path itself inevitably presents one with dark feelings. If this seems strange, consider for a moment that as soon as you desire to live God's will, or to awaken to your true self, you are inviting wholeness, and wholeness means making room for the full spectrum of your feeling intelligence. That means embracing the abysmal as well as the light.

The Hero's Journey

A big part of the challenge is that this particular aspect of healing is a journey you must take alone. It is in the nature of the abysmal feelings that the passage through them is always a solitary one. You are alone with these feelings in your hospital bed, or as you learn to live with a disability. You are alone with them during a divorce or in the dark hours of financial setbacks. They are yours in the solitary depths of grief.

Being able to speak about them with others is very helpful, and knowing that there is one person or a community that supports you at such times is also valuable. But ultimately, you have to make peace with the dark by yourself. Turning consciously toward these feelings and entering the "underworld": this is the heart of the hero's journey. It is also the path of liberation from ego.

Someone who has made the passage can accompany you to the threshold and instruct you—as I am now—that you do not need to fear the dark. But no one can carry you across. It is something that you must do alone, not once but many times. Each dive into the abysmal feelings is an original and private initiation into the mystery of being. These are the encounters that give you a unique and substantial depth of character.

You cannot borrow this rite of passage from anyone else. There is no group celebration, no "Rah! Rah! You can do it!" motivational pitchman who can prepare you. There is no spiritual transmission from even the greatest souls or healers that is a substitute for what you must do for and by yourself.

Perhaps this is why in our culture we continue to place such emphasis on the positive feelings and try to induce them with group ritual and celebration. But when it comes to the transformative descent into the underworld, there is no way to make the journey as a group, congregation, or community no matter how well intended the members may be. We each go alone.

No one knows when they will be called. But be assured that everyone is called again and again throughout their lives. Those who meet the call are the people whom we come to recognize as the wisest and most loving. A wise society would understand the inevitability of this journey and hold in special honor those who have been called down.

But such communities are rare. And the emphasis on the romantic combined with the materialistic orientation of modern societies does not recognize or know how to value the intangible nature of spiritual wealth. Any encounter with dark feelings is often regarded more as a stigma, something to be sorry for, than as something to welcome and even celebrate. But what you now know is that your aware self is always more than even the most troubling feeling. It is essential to respect the power of your own depths, but there is no reason to ever again fear the dark.

△ ✿ △

Part III

LIVING PRESENCE IN DAILY LIFE

If you are in the midst of a health challenge or a crisis of any kind, the chapters that follow will help you live each day with greater presence and peacefulness, even if you are in pain, facing tough decisions, or contemplating your own death.

With the support of what you find in these pages, you will be strengthening the muscle of attention that can keep you anchored in the haven of the present moment, regardless of your circumstances. You will develop a mind strong enough to let go of the need for control, because you will be able to remain present at a deeper level than thinking. You will begin to trust life as it is.

By exploring the possibility that there is nothing you can absolutely know for sure about death (except that we all die sooner or later) you have the opportunity to create a brand new relationship with death and dying. If you accept my invitation to question whatever you have been assuming about death, you may well be surprised to find a new sense of freedom in life.

Your relationships affect your well-being—for better or worse—so I encourage you to build the depth of rapport in as many of them as possible, and I offer some suggestions for meeting others more deeply in the Now.

Finally, as you grow in presence, the new energy living through you needs new vehicles of expression in order to flourish and fully exert its healing influence. Through spontaneous creativity and giving your heart a voice, I invite and guide you to let your new-found energy flow.

CHAPTER NINE

PAIN WITHOUT SUFFERING

Physical pain, whatever its cause, can be made much worse by your mind. Long experience has shown me that some degree of relief from nearly any kind of pain comes when you are able to let go of anxious stories that you are creating around the pain and bring yourself fully into the present. The following incident illustrates this observation.

Sometime ago, my friend Evelyn reached out to me in great pain, after she'd gone through a major surgical procedure. She was crying and spoke very candidly to me over the phone as she spilled out the raw, uncensored details of what she had been dealing with.

Although it had been several weeks since she had undergone colon surgery, she wasn't recovering as quickly as she expected. She was in constant pain that became extreme whenever she attempted to eliminate, and in addition to that, most attempts to do so had been futile.

As Evelyn sobbed, she said, "I have to squat like an animal over a paper plate on the bathroom floor because I can't make anything happen sitting on the toilet." She paused, perhaps afraid she had already divulged too much. "I'm sorry to sound so crude, Richard, but I'm just telling you what's really going on. The pain gets so bad that it's stopping me from being able to have a bowel movement, even when I'm squatting on the floor. It's so humiliating."

As she spoke about her situation, she became even more distressed: "Is this what I've been reduced to? This is no way for a human being to have to live. Am I ever going to be able to go to the bathroom like a normal person? What if I can't, and then I need another operation? I know I couldn't handle that. I've had so many surgeries already. This whole thing is already too much for me. Even just sitting here talking to you, I'm in so much pain."

My heart went out to her. Evelyn was a dignified woman, always fastidious in her habits, and I knew this must have been especially difficult for her. I also sensed that even worse than the pain was the shame and anxiety her thoughts were creating.

I suggested that she take a moment to become still and let her mind settle down. Then I asked her to notice her thoughts about her experience, the stories she had been telling herself about what it all meant and where it was leading.

She stopped crying and fell silent. One by one, as her distressing thoughts came into focus, we inquired into them together. Between stories, I kept inviting her back to the present: to the simple experience of letting each story go for a while, noticing her breath, and tuning in to how she was feeling in her body at that very moment.

Before long, Evelyn realized that she had been creating a self-demeaning emotional environment by comparing herself to an animal and telling herself that she might never again live like a human being. She saw that she was scaring herself with stories about more surgery, when in fact she didn't know whether or not that would ever be necessary. She realized that she had already decided she couldn't handle any more, without having any way of really knowing her own potential capacity.

She mentioned seeing her surgeon the day before and that he had not felt concerned that her symptoms were unusual at that stage of recovery. Considering that information, I shared with her my intuition about the pain she was in. "Evelyn, this probably isn't the kind of pain that will hurt you," I offered quietly.

"I'm not sure what you mean, Richard, but somehow what you said feels like it's true. I just felt myself relax, and suddenly right now for the first time in days, the pain is almost gone. . . . So what exactly do you mean by this isn't pain that will hurt me?"

I explained: "Certain kinds of pain are alarm signals from the body indicating serious problems, like the crushing chest pain of a heart attack. But my guess is that the kind of pain you are feeling—even though I hear how awful it is at moments—is probably just part of recovering from the surgery. Of course it hurts. The body has been unavoidably injured by the operation. It's saying *Be careful,* but not that anything has gone wrong, that you're in danger of getting worse, or that you won't eventually get better."

"You know, it never even occurred to me before," she replied, "that maybe the pain isn't necessarily a bad sign."

As I stayed with her on the other end of the line, it felt to me as if Evelyn's whole being was finally deeply relaxing after weeks of being held in a state of constant tension. She said that she felt peaceful and more confident about being able to cope with the recovery process, slow as it might be. She could even laugh at the image of this poor woman having to squat in the bathroom.

The pain Evelyn had been experiencing had been exacerbated by her stories. They had given her a deep sense of shame and created a future that looked like a life sentence. Note that all pain is made worse by fearful Future stories and by emotions like shame and guilt. But the painful sensations and disrupted processes in the body are not nearly as difficult to tolerate if you lift off the burden of your thoughts about them.

This doesn't mean that there might not still be intense pain at times or that disease and healing processes can't be tough even for the hardiest among us to endure. But by not overlaying the physical sensation with fearful imaginings and demeaning judgments, at the very least you won't be increasing or prolonging it.

Pain, like the dark feelings, opens a door to greater transparency when it's not resisted. You feel part of each moment, touched by the simple things of life, not exiled or separated. Pain, too, can open your heart. As soon as you let go of your stories and bring your attention fully back to the present—if only for a moment—you find there is a gentle space of stillness waiting to meet you right where you are.

In 1999 while I was traveling in South America, I became sick with a fever of over 105 degrees Fahrenheit and experienced by far the worst headache of my life. The fever and pain were unrelenting for several days, and there was little I could do to ameliorate it. Even so, I noticed that when my mind moved into despairing thoughts, the pain became worse, and when I came back to the present, it backed off slightly. But on about the third day, when I thought that I could no longer bear the pain, I made a far deeper discovery. I suddenly thought of how much suffering there is in the world: the millions with malaria and other diseases; the terrible misery we cause each other. My heart went out to all suffering people, and I spontaneously started to pray that their suffering would come to an end—that the fevers would drop and the pain would subside, and that people everywhere would truly care about each other and stop harming one another. As soon as I did this, my own pain diminished significantly.

Thanks to modern medicine, it is very rare that anyone has to stay in unrelenting pain. Once I was able to obtain antibiotics, my fever began to break and my headache quickly improved. But I discovered that day that when our own suffering is compared to something greater than ourselves, suddenly our own pain becomes more bearable.

I later learned that this understanding is very similar to the time-honored Buddhist practice called *tonglen,* which is a method for connecting with suffering—our own and that which is all around us—wherever we may be. It is a technique for overcoming the fear of suffering and relaxing the tightness of one's own heart. It is primarily used for awakening the compassion that is inherent in all of us by remembering that our personal reality is the microcosm of a larger one.

The practice involves synchronizing one's prayerful thoughts with the in-breath and out-breath. First, choose someone who is hurting and you wish to help. For instance, if you know of a sick child, breathe in the wish to take away all the pain and fear of that child. Then, as you breathe out, send the child happiness, joy, or whatever would relieve his or her pain. This is the core of the practice: breathing in the pain of others so that they can be well and have more space to relax and feel open; and then breathing out, sending them calmness and gentleness or whatever you believe would bring them relief and happiness.

In my case, I started from my own pain and then extended from my personal situation to a universal awareness of the pain that so many of us experience with a prayer that pain everywhere be diminished. Perhaps this sounds familiar: it is another way of practicing focused-spacious awareness. When I just focused on my own pain, it was nearly unbearable. But when I empathized with the pain that is in everyone, and even in the creatures that populate our planet, my pain became less personal and immediately more bearable.

Extreme pain can be so powerful that it wants to suck you in like a black hole, but if you do not amplify your suffering with stories—and instead let your whole being be a prayer for the lessening of suffering everywhere—your pain has become something more than just yourself. Life naturally brings us physical pain and sometimes extreme pain in the course of illness, injury, or normal events such as giving birth.

It is possible, if you so choose, to live these times as natural rituals of initiation. A woman can be in labor, bearing down in excruciating pain, and choose to remember the countless women who have given birth before her and the thousands all over the planet who are in labor at the same time as she is.

Whatever you pray for on your own behalf, you can pray for all others, too. You can be alone in a hospital room feeling the immediacy of your own suffering and make the choice to hold in your heart the millions of other people feeling alone as they face their own challenges.

You can never know whether shifting your focus from your own suffering to the alleviation of suffering everywhere will open you to the grace of peace and increased well-being. But this is not about success or some victory for your ego; it is about how pain can teach you to become humble and generous.

Expanding Your Capacity to Meet Pain

There is an age-old tradition in almost every society of using intentional suffering to create spiritual regeneration. One example is the Sun Dance ceremony of the Great Plains Indians of North America who dance, sing, pray, and drum around the clock for days at a time with very little rest. They also sometimes use piercing of the skin as part of a ritual that symbolizes the cycle of death and rebirth. The rite is dedicated to the spiritual rebirth of the tribe and of the living earth.

I, too, have explored rituals that involve the use of intentional suffering in my longer retreats, although at a far less extreme level than the Sun Dance. One ceremony in particular that I use when I sense a group is ready for a deeper experience of presence comes from an ancient Tibetan practice that I have renamed "The Heart of Compassion."[1] This is a valuable exercise that strengthens the capacity to stay present moment by moment, even when you are suffering.

In this exercise, each person stands facing a partner. Everyone lifts his or her arms straight out from the side and holds them up at shoulder height. The task is to keep one's arms in this position (without lowering or dropping them, or bending at the elbows) for a period of about one hour. This length of time is significant enough to push people beyond their initial limits—the protests of the ego—so that they can experience the shift to a deeper connection to themselves and to the present.

I ask that participants help each other as best they can, either by supporting their partner's arms with their own (while still holding their own arms out) or by resolving to do their own practice more impeccably whenever they see their partner flagging. This exercise is a clear demonstration that when any of us lets down our presence, we weaken those around us; and when we maintain presence, we can uplift and strengthen others.

Initially, almost no one can find his or her deeper center fast enough to keep up with the crescendo of discomfort. Thought after thought, the ego will not stop protesting, resisting, feeling sorry for itself, judging the experience as unnecessary or stupid, and so on. The discomfort intensifies so fast that it appears to be bigger than the mind that's aware of it. Of course it never is and never can be, but until one finds one's deeper center, the pain will convincingly appear to be bigger than the person.

Almost all of the participants in this exercise drop their arms or bend over to relieve the discomfort for a few moments. Some sink to the floor temporarily daunted, but with a little encouragement, those who get past the first ten minutes generally complete the exercise.

Those who stay with the process for the entire time discover many things about themselves. Some find that they have to finally embrace humility when they cannot do the exercise as well as they imagined they could. Others are delighted when they discover that they can move through fear and weakness into a sense of strength and joy.

Undertaken in the appropriate spirit, this ancient exercise has great transformational potential. Participants can find a type of strength they don't normally know they have. It requires that they use all of their will to hold their arms up, and simultaneously shows them that their will alone is not enough. What is nearly universally experienced is that when someone begins to care for another, and is even willing to accept a greater burden for his or her sake, that person's suffering diminishes significantly.

I have seen many individuals who have truly embraced this exercise reach a state in which it is effortless to maintain the position, and they are radiant with presence and love. People have told me years later that what they realized in this ceremony translated into a greater capacity to meet challenges and stay fully present at the most difficult moments. Some continue to use the practice to help center themselves and access energy at such times.

In my group retreats, the exercise ends with an hour-long period of "letting go." Everyone lies down comfortably and is asked to stay present and not just drift away or fall asleep. In some ways, it can be just as challenging to let go for an hour while still remaining alert as it is to stand with one's arms out for an hour.

Restlessness can easily set in, and before members of the group know it, they are once again caught up in their thoughts.

Trying It Yourself

If you feel moved to explore The Heart of Compassion at home, I recommend that you begin with 10 to 15 minutes, since you won't have the support of group energy. As you become familiar with the kind of opening and energy this practice can call forth, you can then extend the time. This practice will help you center and build your capacity for presence, but it can also make you more vulnerable later on that day, so go slowly. The important thing is that you focus on something more than endurance, and don't forget to allow yourself to "let go" for an equivalent period. Offer the practice as a means of centering yourself and learning to stay expansive. Dedicate yourself to bringing more presence into your life and into the world.

When I am coaching the group, here is what I often say to help people, and perhaps it will be of value to you: "Slow your breath down. Turn your attention totally toward every instant of your breath. Don't let the discomfort pull you away from that focus. Single-pointed focus leads to vastness."

When someone is struggling, I might say, "Let yourself be helped. Don't try to resist the pain. Let the fire of your effort connect you to something greater, in whatever way you imagine that." Other times I will point out that, "your being doesn't stop at your skin. Find a bigger body."

The Heart of Compassion exercise is a practice you can use whenever you get caught up in emotional turbulence or feel overwhelmed. Stand in the arms-up position long enough so that the intensity of your focus displaces the thinking that is causing your emotional agitation. Then, having come back to center, you can examine your situation and, with greater clarity and poise, address whatever needs to be done.

This kind of exercise helps you build the muscle of attention that supports you in remaining present at a deeper level than thinking. The importance of building this muscle is not that you can keep pushing harder and harder to find a place of stillness, but that your capacity for focus and attention grows strong enough to be gentle.

A strong mind can touch pain or abysmal feelings softly because it is also spacious. It can make a space for dark feelings or pain and be gently present without collapsing into thinking and emotion. A strong mind is strong not because it can stay in control but because it doesn't need to.

You can let life be . . . let life flow. Regardless of the circumstances or the kind of pain you are dealing with, your state of consciousness transforms your experience—for better or worse—constantly.

CHAPTER TEN

DECISIONS AND CHOICES

When my mother developed a rare form of uterine cancer for which there was no known treatment, she asked me what I thought she should do. An oncologist had offered her the option of chemotherapy, although he made it quite clear that there was no medical evidence that it would affect her type of cancer. It would be an experiment, a gamble. From his point of view, it was the only hope he could offer.

My suggestion was to boost her immune system with good nutrition and supplements and see what happened. Certainly that was unlikely to cure my mom, but it seemed to me that the vital thing was for her to choose the best quality of life. My concern was that the chemotherapy had no track record for her cancer and would most likely make her feel more unwell. It could even shorten her life. All it offered her was hope, and while I knew how significant that can be, I also knew that my mother was a realist. As we discussed her choices, I urged her, "Don't gamble on a long shot; enjoy the time you have left. You've had 80 good years of life. The important thing is to enjoy each day as much as possible."

"You're asking me to give up hope," she responded.

"No, Mom, not to give up. I'm suggesting that you live one day at a time."

"Wouldn't I be doing the same thing taking the chemotherapy?"

"Yes," I agreed. "I just don't want you to suffer unnecessarily when the chances of the chemotherapy helping are so slim."

My mother decided to take that chance and went ahead with the treatment. She felt awful at times and lost her hair, but she found a wig she liked and made jokes about her new look. And almost immediately, her cancer blood-test markers went down—a positive sign. She told me with excitement, "See, it's working!"

But five weeks later, the same markers came back fiftyfold higher than they had originally been: the cancer was growing even faster. From the time my mom began chemotherapy, she lived eight months. During that period, she made nearly 60 trips either to her doctor or to the lab for tests. Because she didn't drive, she had to take a taxi or ask my brother or one of her friends to give her a ride, and she hated inconveniencing others. She spent hundreds of hours in travel and sitting in waiting rooms, sometimes engulfed in a cloud of nausea and fatigue, always waiting for hopeful signs. True to the spirit with which she had lived her whole life, Mom never complained.

Powerlessness is one of the most difficult things for us to face. Even though we are all ultimately powerless before death, facing it with no strategy for prolonging life, even briefly, is very difficult.

The friend I mentioned earlier in the book who had pancreatic cancer was told that his case was hopeless and was offered only palliative care. But being a doctor himself, he talked an oncologist into giving him chemotherapy in the very remote chance that it would shrink the tumor enough so that the whole pancreas, tumor and all, could be removed. He would then use insulin as if he were a diabetic, and compensate for the absence of a pancreas by modifying his diet and taking digestive enzymes. It was a plan, and as he himself admitted, there was maybe a 1 or 2 percent chance it would work.

Unfortunately, it didn't work. But as soon as he began implementing that strategy, he was able to let go into whatever life brought. He admitted that the only time he felt distress from the moment he learned of the cancer was when he had no plan of action. It was taking a chance that mattered, not whether it worked. In our last e-mail exchange, eight days before his death, my friend wrote: "I am at the nadir of physical presence and at what feels like an apex of realization, floating along in a state of wonderment." Amen.

A Healthy Relationship to Modern Medicine

As a man trained in science and medicine, I have learned that a great deal of what we physicians believe and practice is eventually proven wrong. We don't know which specific concepts or treatments are wrong until we see the consequences of our actions and our knowledge grows. Then we halt mistaken efforts, propose new theories, develop new treatments . . . and the cycle continues. This is the experimental nature of science and the practice of medicine. At its very best, we can hope that the data is examined impartially and that we, following the urging of Hippocrates, do our best to do no harm.

So what is an intelligent relationship to modern medicine and health care in general? Do we bow before science and passively accept whatever is offered to us? Do we eschew it because it is *not spiritual,* as some people believe? Do we run to alternative treatments that promise so much but also often do so without any substantiation through controlled studies? Do we accept that we are all part of a great experiment, all guinea pigs in a noble but imperfect project of discovery?

The latter is my own position. I respect modern medicine and know that it is a work in progress—a work that will forever be in progress. I also respect much of what continues to emerge through complementary modalities. When I have needed help, I have done my own research and listened to my own intuition about which regimen or procedure to follow and with which doctor(s). Once I have made my decision, I am willing to trust the doctors I choose. But I also know that while they can care for my body and have more information than I do about their area of specialization, I am responsible for my consciousness. Said in another way, I am responsible for remaining present and accepting what *is,* yet I am also responsible for listening to what I am sensing, being prepared to ask questions and seek new information, and even radically changing course if that seems appropriate.

Moreover, I am responsible for eating healthily (as all of us are), and I have learned that there are many detoxification and immune-system-boosting practices that can be extremely valu-able. Through these ways, I have eliminated a troubling problem with heart arrhythmia and brought my blood pressure—a signifi-cant problem in my family—down to benign levels.

A Personal Journey with My Stories

For some years, I had mild sciatic pain in my right hip, but one day I moved some heavy furniture and the pain got much worse. I could barely walk 50 yards before I had to lie down and wait for the pain to subside. I couldn't even stand long enough to brush my teeth.

In thoroughly researching what to do, it came down to two op-tions: laser surgery or a procedure called microdiscectomy, which is a minimally invasive form of surgery (and the option two pain specialists recommended). I decided on the laser surgery because it seemed even less invasive, and the rates of recurrence and in-fection were lower. Although I had to travel to New York instead of remaining in California, all things considered, I believed I was making the wiser choice.

Initially, everything went well. After the operation, I was im-mediately able to walk again, and after two days of rest, I took a flight home. But then things didn't go as well as I had antici-pated. A week or so after returning home, I carried a few logs into the house for the fireplace, and within minutes, I began to feel a strong, sickening ache in the area just above my tailbone.

When it didn't get better by the next day, I called the doctor in New York. His recommendation was: "Go back to bed and rest. And, by the way, you shouldn't lift more than about 15 pounds. It takes at least a year for the disk to heal and even then you shouldn't overly stress it again."

After that I became more careful about my activity. Thinking that it would be beneficial, I also soaked in a hot tub every morn-ing, but the ache only kept getting worse. About five weeks after the laser surgery, I returned to the two pain specialists to get their opinion and advice about this new pain. They worried that the laser had caused severe inflammation in the disks, and they took some blood tests to investigate.

One of them remarked, "I'd never let anyone put a laser into my disks." That wasn't great to hear, but then the other made a seemingly offhand observation: "Our patients who have the microdiscectomy are usually back playing tennis or surfing by now." My heart sank.

I drove home from that consultation feeling very anxious. But I also knew that it was my thinking, not my actual situation, that was the real problem.

As soon as I got home, I went to my study and laid the Mandala out on the floor just as I teach others to do. I began noting my stories: "The disks are now dangerously inflamed." Immediately, I recognized this thought as a You story, a belief about the disks themselves. I could not really know that was true. Then I saw a few Future stories: "I am going to have bone-on-bone degeneration in my lower spine. I'm going to have chronic pain and disability. I may never be able to mountain climb or backpack again. I won't be able to exercise in the ways I love to anymore." There is no way to believe any of those thoughts without fear and despair.

Me stories flooded into my mind: "I can't trust my own intuition. I don't want to live as a partial invalid. I've ruined my own back. I am arrogant because I disregarded the advice of the pain specialists I sought out for advice." Each thought created a sense of anguish.

Then more You stories arose: "The doctor who did the laser surgery should have informed me more about the potential complications of recovery, such as serious inflammation. He didn't adequately prepare me for how to take care of myself afterward. He didn't tell me that the disk would be chronically weakened." I felt angry at him, and at myself for relying on him to be thorough.

And all of this played against the background of my fond memories of hiking, climbing, and backpacking—things I have enjoyed all of my adult life. I told myself Past stories: "I've always been an active man. Backpacking is where I've nourished my soul." And this created even more Me stories: "I need to be active in order to enjoy life." Round and round it went.

I stepped into the center of the Mandala and consciously brought myself back to the present moment. As quickly as I recognized the stories, I knew they were just thoughts about who I had been, what I had lived, and what I might live. Some stories were judgments of the doctor in New York and of myself. I knew that I couldn't possibly know the future, and that who I had been did not need to determine who I was.

In my mind and heart, I set down all of the stories and just stayed quietly present, listening in my body and sensing my awareness extending everywhere into time and space. I asked myself, "Even if I can never mountain climb, backpack, or run again, does that mean my life is diminished?" I knew that it did not. It would be changed, yes, but not diminished. I could feel the truth of that right in the moment. I was fine. As that feeling of being fine, of being whole as I was, gently grew, I knew that there were many new ways I could find to enjoy being out in nature. Beyond that, I knew that I would keep learning more about being a loving person, even with degenerative spinal disease. I was also aware that I had no way of knowing whether that would ever develop.

It took only a short time to see clearly that my sense of happiness or well-being wasn't dependent on backpacking, mountain climbing, or hiking. It was available all the time in any moment when I was present and not fighting against my life. Within minutes, I landed back in a familiar state of freedom: *No matter what happens, I'm already okay. My wholeness isn't determined by my level of activity or adventure, or by whether or not I'm somewhat handicapped.* I became completely at peace even though I was still in pain. And from that moment on, I never felt distress about my choice to do the laser procedure or what might come because of it.

As it happened, a few days later I ran into a friend who is a physical therapist. I mentioned what was happening in my back and how I was trying to help the inflammation by extensive soaking in the hot tub. He looked at me in horror and explained that using heat for this kind of inflammation had been a big mistake; instead, he instructed me to use ice packs several times a day.

Apparently my own misguided efforts, more than anything else, had delayed my healing. The blood-test results came back and confirmed that there wasn't severe inflammation. I followed my friend's advice and quickly improved. Today, I can do almost anything I want: hiking, backpacking, running, bicycling, and even careful weight training.

Having engaged the Mandala practice countless times now, as soon as I become aware of what I am telling myself, I immediately know whether it is factual or a story that will lead me into some emotional reaction. And if it is the latter, I already see how it will make me feel. I am also aware that the deeper presence may be temporarily overshadowed by my thinking but ultimately will be undiminished by any external circumstance. There is a freedom in this knowing—something that I know all of us can experience.

Choosing from a Place of Peace and Clarity

Once you start working with the Mandala yourself, you will see that it becomes a very efficient way for you to understand and work through anything that is disturbing or confusing you. It helps you to observe and gain distance from your thoughts, and will guide you to decisions with greater clarity and efficacy. The more embodied, spacious, and still you are as you contemplate a decision, the more your awareness participates with a larger intelligence. In this state, you make far better decisions than if you are agitated and your focus is narrowed.

As you approach an important decision, weigh the pros and cons of different options, solicit the opinions of others, and make a practice of working with the Mandala; it will help you make decisions with a more peaceful heart. You will find that once you have identified a story, you can move swiftly through the steps to see what it creates and will then be able release it. This is a tool for establishing yourself in presence in any situation and acting in accord with a deeper sense of flow, liberated from so much mind-made unhappiness.

When you feel confused or uncertain about a decision, take out the Mandala and ask yourself, "What am I telling myself (and believing) about this decision that is causing me to feel confused and uncertain?" Are you subconsciously telling yourself, "I have to make the right decision"? How can you really know that you are making the right decision? Putting such pressure on yourself only makes it difficult to hear your own intuitive wisdom because the noise of the anxiety that your belief and your other stories create drowns it out. The simple truth is that you are making a decision. That is all.

Are you telling yourself, "I should know (or I need to know) what is best for me"? Again, that belief creates tension, which masks the subtlety of your intuitive wisdom. Consider the opposite story: "I don't need to know what is best for me." You are going to make a decision anyway; the one you believe is best. Does setting yourself free from thinking you *should know* relax you more? And then perhaps you can take a deeper step and let both stories go. After all, knowing or not knowing what is best for you is not really the issue. No choice, no matter how well considered, leads to what is best for you. What is best is who you already are in the Now.

Decisions scare most of us when it comes to health concerns because we are afraid of making a bad choice, losing something that cannot be retrieved, or burning our bridges and finding that certain options are no longer available to us. Often we postpone making decisions until the last minute or evade them by letting someone else make choices for us. At times we default to simply making the same decisions we've made before.

But if you allow yourself to become present and quiet enough, the decision that is a good one for you often becomes clear. At that moment, it is no longer a decision; it is simply taking the next step in life, like taking the next breath.

Once a decision is made, doubting and dividing yourself by second-guessing will only drain your energy. Whenever you believe that you should have done something differently, that's a Past story, and it generates regret or self-attack. Second-guessing your own decisions is just ego; it is not a process that arises from presence. It is the ego keeping you unhappy. Emotional contraction is never helpful on a healing journey.

In the context of a health issue or any challenging situation, bringing yourself into the present—alert yet relaxed, attentive yet spacious—is always the optimal state of well-being possible in that moment. By doing so, you are able to dance with any story and then come back into the Now and begin anew, in harmony with your life.

ร่ร

CHAPTER ELEVEN

THE FACTS
ABOUT DEATH

Beyond what we can observe regarding what happens to the physical body when we die, is there anything we know about death or the afterlife that isn't really just a story inherited from our family, culture, or religion? What do we *really* know about death?

Some years ago, I was interviewed about my work by a respected journalist in Argentina. He asked thoughtful questions, and our conversation was stimulating. Just as the interview was coming to an end, he suddenly tossed out one last question as if it were an afterthought: "Dr. Moss, what are your beliefs about life after death?"

The question took me by surprise because it was out of context with what we had been discussing, and it was a *big* question. I thought for a moment and replied, "I really don't have any."

"Nonsense," he brusquely responded. "Everyone has some kind of beliefs about an afterlife." He then told me that in the course of his career, he had interviewed Mother Teresa, the Dalai Lama, Pope John Paul II, Deepak Chopra, and other religious and spiritual leaders, all of whom had something to say about this. The journalist's tone made it sound like I wasn't being serious and giving his question the consideration it deserved.

"I've thought about this carefully," I said, "and the only thing I know about life after death is how the various ideas and descriptions that I've heard or read about the subject make me feel."

I explained further: "I have no personal experience that would lead me to believe that life or consciousness as I know it continues after death. If it does, I will find out when the time comes. For now, I have noticed that when I try to accept some of those beliefs,

I feel less vital. Accepting that I don't know means living with a sense of unknowing. As I live with that uncertainty, that vulnerability, I feel more vital. This moment, this day . . . none of it can be taken for granted. Life becomes more immediate.

"It is the ego that needs a story about life after death to protect its sense of identity. Death is the ultimate humiliation for the ego even though it is inevitable. Believing that I will be with my loved ones after death or that I have lifetimes in which to evolve takes my ego off the hook; that is, the unknown and the importance of each moment is minimized. When I have tried to take on any belief about life after death, I have also immediately felt a subtle loss of presence. So for the time being, unless or until something comes along to change my experience, I am content not to hold any belief."

"So you believe that life just ends at death?" the journalist queried.

"No, that's not what I said. I don't know that either, but . . . why not?"

He looked at me quizzically for a moment and then said, "That is the most original response I've ever heard to the question."

My Own Inquiry into Death

One day I discovered an enlarged lymph node in my neck, in the space just above the clavicle. As a doctor, I knew that when any of those nodes enlarge, it can mean nothing . . . or it can be a harbinger of serious illness. Instead of immediately getting the node biopsied and learning one way or the other, I decided to live with the apprehension I was feeling for a while and work with it.

Since the issue was my fear of having cancer and perhaps dying, I purposely inquired into that fear using the Mandala of Being: "What do I really know about death that I am afraid of?" I started in the You position and began with obvious statements: "The heart stops. The brain stops due to lack of oxygen. The body dies." I immediately recognized that the basis of these thoughts was observations from the past. As a physician, I had seen many patients in the hospital die. "Okay, the body dies." It seemed factual —no argument.

"But what does that mean about death itself?" I asked myself. "Does it mean that there is or isn't some kind of consciousness after death?" To the thought *There is consciousness after death,* I realized that my response was "I don't know." To the opposite *There isn't consciousness after death,* I again realized, "I don't know." And finally to the thought *Death is something to fear* (or variations of it, such as *Death is a tragedy* or *Death is unfair*), I immediately recognized that this depended on what stories I told myself about death. But about death itself, I knew nothing.

I looked at my Future stories about having cancer ("I may die sooner than I expected," "I am going to need chemotherapy," "I won't be able to work," and "I won't bring my work to full maturity") and saw that those stories created fear. But as soon as I stepped into the Now position and imagined myself facing cancer and death *without* those stories, I felt myself relaxing. Life would be as it would be. I would dance with fear when my stories gained the upper hand, but that no longer felt very threatening.

One after another, I examined each of my beliefs. Suddenly it dawned on me that *I knew absolutely nothing about death.* Instantly, I felt an oppressive weight lift off of me and dissolve. All of my fear vanished. As it turned out, I later had a biopsy, and the node was benign. This was certainly happy news, but the real freedom was already present.

What Kind of Death Do You Want?

The moment you realize that there is nothing you know for sure about death, you will also see that there is no point in polluting the present with stories about it. And if you, like many people, believe in an afterlife, and it gives you a sense of peace, then that is your choice and your path. In either case, it is wise to consider what kind of death you would like.

What I am suggesting is that you have a conversation with yourself in which you decide how you would like to die. It is not a question of whether you will get your wish—it is about taking the time to choose how you want to be present for your death. Do you want to be alert or pass quietly in your sleep, for example? Would you like certain people to be with you? Do you want to be able to look into their eyes? Is there anything specific you would like to say? Would you prefer to be alone? If you are taken by surprise and there is no one you know with you, how do you want to experience those last hours or moments?

A friend of mine who was a spiritual teacher in Europe had been sick for many years and knew that his death was getting close. Then in a dream, he saw the number three. Because his mind was clear and he could still walk and function a little, he interpreted it to mean that he had three more months to live. Even so, he immediately tied up the last details of his affairs; he also got a haircut, had his beard trimmed, and treated himself to a manicure and pedicure.

As it turned out, it was three days. On what became his final night, while he and his wife were talking in bed, he turned to her and said, "Now I am going to die." She asked him if he wanted her to call the doctor, and he declined. She asked if he wanted his teenage children present, and he said to wait until after he had passed and then let them sit with him. What he wanted was to lie next to his wife with his head on her shoulder. Lying that way, in a few minutes, he passed away peacefully.

There is no way to know how much time we have left, so it is never premature to consider how you want to die. In thinking about it, you will get a chance to see some of what you believe about death. You will be able to notice how empowered or disempowered you believe yourself to be when it comes to the proposition of dying. Do you believe that it is "bad luck" to think about your death? Who do you imagine you are speaking to, or who or what do you imagine is listening to you, when you have this conversation with yourself?

Death may be a final event for the body, but in our minds it is a recurring event, something that most of us think about off and on throughout our lives. Yet rarely do we give that much thought to how we want to die. Psychologically, death is a problem because when we cannot actually know what will happen, we try to imagine something to make us feel better, such as the belief in an afterlife. Or we may try to block it out completely and refuse to give any effort to considering our deaths.

In the Mahabharata, a Hindu sacred text, one of life's great mysteries is said to be how ordinary mortals go through their lives surrounded by death, yet they don't believe they will die. The meaning of this observation is that although we know intellectually that we are going to die, we do not live as if that were a reality; we do not consciously let the real certainty of death guide us in how we choose to live day by day. A joke shows how common this denial is: Two men are commenting on the death of a very wealthy man. The first man says in an awed tone, "Did you hear how much he left behind?!" "Yes," the second answers. "He left everything behind."

I once was counseling a friend who was in despair about a relationship. I asked him, "If you knew that you only had a few seconds to live, could you let go of your fear of aloneness and your resentment of your partner?" When he said yes, I then asked if he could do so knowing that he had an hour to live. Again he answered yes. "What if you had a month to live?" I continued. This time he said, "I see where you're going."

But seeing wasn't sufficient for my friend to let go then and there. Yet, as his first answers suggest, it is likely that seriously considering how one wants to die may make many aspects of living easier and bring what really matters in life into focus.

Seeing Life in the Face of Death

Much has been written about near-death experiences. In my study of these accounts, it seems that they are similar in some aspects to states of spontaneous realization or very deep meditation in which individuals enter into a profound sense of presence that transcends ego. These events are often inexplicably transformative.

As my friend Charlotte tells it, one morning as she lay motionless in a hospital bed, she reached her breaking point: she could no longer tolerate the deep, incessant pain burning through her. After almost three months, acute peritonitis, a widespread bacterial infection caused by a burst pelvic abscess, was rapidly taking its toll. Surgeons had performed three emergency operations during that time, but she was deathly sick and sinking fast.

So ill and weak that she could only move her eyes, my friend stared blankly toward the bare wall at the foot of her bed and finally gave up, asking God to let her die.

"I'm sorry," she said silently, "but I just can't take any more. Please let me go." She was only 21 years old.

Charlotte does not know how much time passed, but suddenly something caught her attention. In the center of the bare white wall beyond her bed, a hint of color appeared out of nowhere. As she watched, that hint turned into pastel pink, yellow, green, and blue—and then they slowly turned brighter and became an abstract pattern painted on the whole wall. Then the surface was no longer flat; it steadily became more and more textured with contours and shadows.

Eventually a three-dimensional scene that was alive with movement came into view, and Charlotte scanned the verdant depths of a tropical rain forest. It was exquisite; everything was thriving. Trees, plants, bushes, flowers, fruit, butterflies, and birds: each element was idyllic, reminiscent of Shangri-la or the Garden of Eden. Different elements kept advancing to the forefront, drawing her attention.

Then a large tree appeared in the center of the scene. As it sharpened into focus, Charlotte realized that what had at first looked like a tree was actually a very large cross made of thick, gnarled branches. Then it all became clear: attached to the cross by his wrists and feet was a man she recognized at once. She was looking straight at the figure of Jesus.

His head hung limply to one side, and his eyes were cast slightly downward, looking toward her. Charlotte knew immediately that he was in extreme pain, yet he was not suffering. He was clearly at peace despite the pain. The depth of surrender in his eyes was more profound than anything she had ever witnessed.

As she continued to stare at him, she heard a voice from somewhere not clearly inside nor outside herself. It seemed to be a male voice and was benevolent, direct, and clear. The voice asked her in a tone that was purely neutral, each word receiving equal emphasis: "You think you have suffered?"

For Charlotte, time stopped. As if the barriers that normally held in place everything she understood about life had suddenly all collapsed, she found herself in a new and entirely unfamiliar reality. She was inundated with a barrage of emotions tumbling in upon one another: she felt guilty and ashamed for giving up, foolish for not seeing more clearly, humbled by the beauty and strength she was witnessing, astonished, and grateful . . . all in one simultaneous rush.

Immediately, she knew without doubt that if she answered the question affirmatively ("Yes, I have suffered"), she would be allowed to die. The pain would vanish, and she would be fine in every way. And she was certain that if she answered no, she would continue to live. But in that case, she would be right back to playing the hand she had been dealt: excruciating pain and all. At that instant, the pain was temporarily suspended, but she understood clearly within herself that it would return at once with full force depending on her answer.

She also knew that whether she chose to live or die, there would be neither praise nor retribution. It was as if whomever or whatever she was communicating with wordlessly made it clear that God, or life itself, was entirely neutral regarding her choice; she would receive no honor or reward for staying, and could expect no judgment or punishment if she decided to go.

All at once a kaleidoscope of images filled Charlotte's field of vision, like an intricately woven tapestry or detailed mosaic. She was being shown a montage of various scenes from her life like short movies on dozens of tiny screens. At first, it all seemed random and confusing. She didn't understand why she was seeing so many minor events and interactions that she had forgotten or considered inconsequential in her life.

As she became curious about any particular event, her attention automatically zoomed in on that scenario, and she could watch it in more detail. One by one, she came to recognize the significance of each event; she saw exactly why it had to happen in order for everything else in her life to fall into place. She also understood for the first time the effects of her own words and actions on others who were involved.

As Charlotte observed, it dawned on her—as though she'd always known but curiously had forgotten—that everything that had seemed to happen at different stages in her life had, in fact, occurred simultaneously. The whole notion of time, of past and future, was apparently an illusion. And each seemingly separate scenario revealed itself to be not only interconnected with all the rest, but also holographic in nature, containing each of the others within it.

Charlotte realized that she was not located anywhere in particular: in a way that was paradoxically both personal and highly impersonal, she was viewing all events at the same time and from every possible point of view. Focusing her attention on different aspects only made them *appear* to be linear and discrete. And the revelations all felt more like recollections: she had an overriding sense that it was profoundly peculiar to have been so blind to all this, because she clearly understood that everything she was now seeing had been right before her eyes all along.

She saw that she had often been wrong about what mattered and what didn't, and that she had completely misjudged numerous incidents in terms of which were beneficial and which were harmful. She now realized that even a violent assault several years earlier, which she had regarded as the worst thing that ever happened to her, had its necessary and therefore precisely perfect place in the grand scheme of things. With total clarity, she suddenly comprehended that everything was happening exactly as it should, and couldn't possibly be otherwise. For Charlotte, there was no longer any such thing as a mistake, an accident, a missed opportunity, or a tragedy; nothing had ever gone wrong.

Through all she was seeing, she also knew that she had a definite and unique purpose to serve and that she had barely begun to scratch the surface. For perhaps a fraction of a minute, all the details of that purpose were clear, but they were obscured very quickly. She was left with only the unmistakable knowledge that there was *something* specific she was meant to do, and that it involved directly helping others younger than her.

Above all, she knew that she had greatly underestimated her own capacity: she had given up far too soon. Charlotte understood now that she was capable of bearing much, much more pain than she had ever imagined possible. From deep inside herself, she answered with absolute conviction: "No. I have not suffered."

There was no medical explanation for Charlotte's sudden turnaround. Just 24 hours earlier, a doctor had reluctantly informed her father that her chance of survival was estimated at 10 to 15 percent. Despite the medical team's best efforts, each week she had been sliding further downhill, and everyone was quietly preparing to lose her. Experimenting with a new antibiotic had been their last hope, but so far it had appeared to have no effect. Now all of a sudden her vital signs were remarkably better, and her blood tests were showing a significant improvement.

Charlotte became lucid and explained in vivid detail all that she recalled about the vision she had seen and the voice she had heard, and how she knew that she had to go on living. Despite her gaunt and pallid face, everyone who entered her room remarked that she looked radiant. There was something about her, they said, that nobody could quite put a finger on. Each day after that, she regained a little strength, and the infection continued to subside. A few weeks later, Charlotte was allowed to go home for Christmas; she had been in the hospital since Labor Day weekend. A long period of rest and rehabilitation lay ahead of her, but she was on her way to a full recovery.

᠔ ᠔

Of course, it is impossible to say for sure what caused the sudden reversal in Charlotte's condition. Some doctors concluded that the new antibiotic needed a little time to have an effect, and that it probably saved her life. Other people who heard about what happened felt that Charlotte's inner experience was clearly the reason for the turnaround. Perhaps her healing was a combination of the two; ultimately, it remains a mystery.

One thing is certain: the story my friend was telling herself about her situation changed radically through that experience. She went from utter despair—believing that she had reached her limit and couldn't survive another minute of pain—to knowing beyond the shadow of a doubt that she could handle far more than she ever imagined. In that change, Charlotte gained access to inner resources that provided the strength she needed to rally and heal at a time when she had given up.

It could be said that this young woman had lost the will to live. But maybe when that happens, it can serve a deeper potential: in Charlotte's case, it was as if a *greater* will was waiting to inhabit her. For a while, the pain remained as severe as it had been before the vision, but her level of suffering was drastically reduced right away. What she saw in her vision of Jesus, and especially in his eyes, she somehow recognized as a possibility not only for herself, but also for *everyone.*

Charlotte resumed her life very differently as she continued to recover her health. As soon as she was well enough to work, she took a position as a child-care worker in a group home for emotionally disturbed adolescents.

My friend also lost her fear of death. There was something so inexplicably welcoming and benevolent about the state in which she was held while she made her choice whether to live or die, that she just knew there was nothing to fear. She doesn't recall seeing a white light or the long tunnel reported by many of those who have had a near-death experience. She had no distinct sense of a heavenlike place or deceased loved ones in a spirit world waiting to greet her. But Charlotte emerged from her experience—whatever it could be called—irrevocably changed and unafraid of dying.

The Final Moments

Many years ago, as I was driving on a highway at night, a car up ahead suddenly swerved, flipped over, and skidded off into the desert brush. I pulled over as fast as I could and ran to see what had happened. I saw something by the side of the road—at first, it looked as if the car had hit a large dog, maybe a collie. But as I approached, I realized that it was a woman with thick, long reddish-blonde hair, lying there on the shoulder of the highway where she had been thrown from her car.

When I got closer, I could hear her moaning, and then I saw that one side of her head was caved in. I knew immediately that she was dying. I noticed that her moaning sounded more like anguish than pain, so I knelt down very close to her and whispered in her ear: "You have had an accident and were thrown from your car. Don't be afraid. You are loved. You can let go and relax. Everything in your life is forgiven."

Right away, the woman stopped moaning and began making soft, peaceful, sighing sounds; within seconds, she slipped into a coma. Eventually, an ambulance arrived, and I rode in it with her to the nearest emergency room. While the doctors and staff tried to resuscitate her, I just stood nearby quietly. When they pronounced her dead and then left the room, I talked to her, continuing to tell her that she was loved and forgiven. I held her hand for about 15 minutes, and then I left.

Why did I tell this stranger that all was forgiven? I spontaneously wanted to ease her suffering, and those are the words that came. And I believe that they are true. In the Now, each of us is continuously renewed in wholeness. I said those few words to her not knowing if she could hear me, but caring that she have a chance to let go into freedom. Why not live a final moment, a final Now, that isn't one of ego-based struggle?

Resolving Old Pain Even to the Very End

Dr. François Blanchard, a friend and highly respected professor of gerontology in France, sent me a beautiful letter shortly after my mother died. I had discussed with him how in the final few months of her life, Mom would sometimes bring up unhappy memories of conflicts that she and I had had from much earlier in our relationship. She did it in a way that re-created the old recriminations and hurts instead of resolving them. It saddened me, and it could have led to renewed conflict if I had let myself be defensive.

Dr. Blanchard wrote me about his observations that the elderly and even those with severe dementia appear to try to resolve old wounds, right until the very end of their lives. He cited an example of an old woman on his ward who was near the end of her life and kept ranting in a way that neither he nor the other clinicians could make any sense of. The medical professionals chalked it up to her age and mental state—until a childhood friend visited the woman and recognized that she was calling out the name of a beloved cat, who her father had abruptly taken away from her when she was five years old. With that piece of her history, Dr. Blanchard surmised that the woman was still attempting to resolve that pain.

In his letter, he speculated that my mother was bringing up old conflicts because she was trying to ease old hurts, albeit not very effectively. His observation made sense to me and helped bring much closure to the unhappiness that my mother and I both wanted to resolve, but had not really managed to do so.

I believe that the main reason Mom and I failed to resolve the past conflicts (and why, I suspect, so many of us similarly struggle) was that she couldn't release the past. Certainly, I had been insensitive and self-involved in my early 20s, but I had changed and genuinely apologized many times over the years. Yet none of that was enough to help her have a new relationship with me—or more truly with herself—in the present. She did this same thing with other relationships. Living in the past was such a profound habit that she was imprisoned and didn't know it.

Deep down I believe that my mother was trying to resolve the old pains, but how could that happen if she couldn't bring herself into the present where forgiveness arises spontaneously and new connections build new love? Like most of us, she did not realize that as an aware being, she was always and already more than anything she had lived and more than all of the emotions that her Past stories re-created.

What if the urge to resolve conflict that Dr. Blanchard was describing is one aspect of an innate potential to grow toward ever-greater wholeness that lives within each of us? Awareness by its very nature makes us more than whatever we are aware of. Therefore, as aware beings, we are always on a path of self-transcendence.

Said in another way, your soul continuously tries to help you forgive and become ever-more transparent to life. Of course, if you cannot get past your ego, you can die bitter and closed. But, despite even the most terrible of wounds or injustices, if you give your soul half a chance, it will lead you to reconciliation and forgiveness. In this sense, you are being invited to die (to your ego) before you die physically so that you are reborn.

Surrendering to change is always a leap of faith. For something new to enter your life, you have to let go of the past and join your immediate experience right now. The key is less in *what* you do than how connected you are in yourself as you do it. In life there is no predetermined path you should or have to walk; you lay down the path by how you take each step. This is one of life's great truths.

Whether you live in stories or awareness is the essence of creativity and the heart of free will. In the Now, it is the quality of your attention that determines how you experience each moment. Presence builds presence. You build a relationship right now by how you relate right now. You build love by being loving. Ask yourself, "How would I live right now if all I wanted is for love to grow?"

The path of healing is the same. Rather than asking, "What should I change in order to heal myself?" the question might be: "What would my life look like right now if I chose to honor and value this feeling, this touch, this conversation, this day as sacred?"

Living Without a Destination

If your primary focus is to get over your health problems or get past a relationship crisis so that you can return to your former life and old patterns—that is, get back to *business as usual*—you are not really living. The distinction is paradoxical and sometimes subtle. It's the difference between walking *through* your life on your way to somewhere, and walking *as* your life. Even if you believe that where you want to get to is extremely important, that destination is secondary. Your immediate experience is what really matters. It is your life.

In the Now, there really is no destination. Each moment is lived for its own sake, even as you move toward whatever you may choose to pursue. When you are focused on some outcome or achievement—or are always looking forward to the day when you are able to live in conditions that you imagine will be superior to whatever currently exists—your life right now becomes just an interval on the way to the next event.

The egoic mind lives in time and, unless consciously checked, will compulsively create intervals and events depending on whatever anticipated activity grabs its focus. If catching a plane this evening is paramount, that becomes the event, and most of what you live as you pack and travel to the airport is just an interval. If an upcoming family wedding is the event, then the weeks and months preceding it can become largely just a passageway, not vivid life itself. If retirement is the event, you will not be wholeheartedly present at work. If you are ill and getting well is the event, you won't let yourself be surprised by life in all the simple, exquisite ways it offers all the time.

Now it's your turn: make a list of everything that you regard in this sense as an "event" today: for example, picking up groceries, calling your doctor's office, or going to the bank. As you flow through the day, connect to where you actually are and to what you are genuinely experiencing in each moment. If you are driving home from work, feel how softly you can hold the steering wheel and listen to every sound. Pay attention to your breathing.

Try to become present until there is less of a sense of intervals and events. The resistance or discomfort you feel in making this effort is the pressure of egoic conditioning.

You might go further and jot down a list of everything that is an event (in your mind) for the upcoming week: the ski trip next weekend, the dental appointment on Wednesday, the presentation you're making to your boss on Friday. Now as you flow through the week, connect all the more immediately to where you are right now, to what is actually happening. Try to relax so that each moment is rich with presence.

Death is the final event, at least for our bodies. Of course, the belief that there is some kind of existence after death is, psychologically, a very powerful concept that can bring consolation or fear. But the lure of heaven or the threat of hell robs life of its profound mystery and unplumbed depths, because as long as there is an imagined future more important than this moment, the present remains relatively shallow.

The facts about death are that there are none.

CHAPTER TWELVE

INVITING PRESENCE INTO YOUR RELATIONSHIPS

The two greatest sources of life-force energy that you can directly access come through how present you are, moment by moment, and through how deeply you meet other people in the Now.

We have all experienced feeling enlivened after spending time with someone as well as feeling drained after being with someone else. A relationship that depletes you can undermine your health and healing capacity, but a relationship that enlivens you can very much support your health *and* healing. For this reason, taking responsibility for how you offer yourself and invite relationships becomes important, especially where healing is concerned.

Some people, even if they mean well, can be so self-involved or threatened by your illness or situation that they do not know how to be real with you; these relationships are usually draining. Individuals who live in the past can also be depleting. Similarly, those who are always looking ahead to what is coming next aren't really available for a meaningful connection. There are so many ways in which people miss the opportunity for deeply enriching relationships primarily because they tend to live in their Past, Future, Me, and You stories and continually try to avoid uncomfortable feelings.

On the other hand, relationships become nourishing and even augment your energy when you can engage each other in the present with honesty. People who are more available—perhaps because they have lived through big challenges of their own or have discovered the blessing of living in the present—are the ones you want to be around when your own health is precarious. They can actually lift your energy. They know how to be empathetic and lead you away from your own self-limiting thoughts. You find yourselves laughing or crying together or sinking into a rich silence that brings both of you to a sense of heightened presence and aliveness.

This is why support groups are vital: the participants are generally able to understand the challenges of your situation without minimizing or exaggerating them. And because fellow members are less likely to deceive themselves or you, together you can access more life force through your energetic connection.

Listening and Being Listened To

When I am counseling people who are grieving or those who have received a diagnosis of a grave or terminal illness, I consider them my teachers. My commitment is to be fully present, attentive, and spacious. Although I deeply empathize, I know that in the moment, I am not truly in their shoes. I don't presume to really know what they are feeling. I often don't know enough of their history to fully appreciate the depths of what they have lived. And I cannot know how their soul is guiding them. Trusting this state of unknowing is essential to the authenticity and spontaneity of how our connection will unfold. I want to be the servant of whatever supports an individual's potential for clearer seeing and self-acceptance.

All relationships, especially these kinds of deeply vulnerable meetings, are an invitation to practice the art of listening. For me, listening takes place on many levels, but the essential aspect is leaving behind my own stories and becoming fully present. I visualize myself stepping to the center of the Mandala and experiencing the other person as someone completely unique. I intentionally suspend my own thinking and remain attentive and receptive. It is as if I am taking all of my being and journeying to another world.

In doing so, it is important not to automatically plug the other person's experience into my way of seeing or interpreting the situation. As I listen, I give careful attention to what is being said, but I also stay alert to what thoughts or images spontaneously come into my mind, as well as whatever sensations or feelings arise in me.

All of this provides me with clues as to what is happening in that individual and to the quality of our connection. But since I can never be sure what is mine or the other person's, I let this information sit for a while without trying to organize it or make sense of it right away. Eventually, though, it gives me a direction for any questions I might decide to ask or any of my own thoughts I might choose to share.

There is an inductive process to listening deeply. In fact, I have found that being fully present tends to create a field that gradually short-circuits the egoic mind in the individuals I am with. They begin to hear what they are saying and spontaneously become more self-reflective. Sometimes we fall into silence.

Often it is silence that speaks more than the words. But these quiet spaces can sometimes feel awkward, and I have learned to resist the tendency to fill them with small talk. There is a place for creating a sense of social ease and safety through casual conversation, but there is also a place for acknowledging that you are together at a time or in a situation that in many ways is beyond words. I cannot tell you how many times I have been thanked by people for those silent spaces.

Unconsciously Avoiding Relationships

In many relationships, there is an unconscious conspiracy for self-deception: some people don't want to tell you what they are really thinking and feeling about your situation for fear of appearing judgmental or of frightening or depressing you, and you don't want to make them uncomfortable by telling them how you really are or what you really want. Words are exchanged, but nothing that cuts to the heart of what is real is ever broached.

What you say to others and what others say to you is inevitably shaped by the stories you each are telling yourselves. If, for example, you are ill, some of your friends will feel sorry for you but may not say so. Instead, they will make small talk. Others will be afraid to really engage you because they will not want to imagine themselves in a similar place. And some will actually tell themselves stories that make them feel guilty for being well when you are sick; then they will pretend to be relaxed and open. Still others will automatically put a positive spin on your situation because they want you (and themselves) to feel better.

Often your loved ones believe that they are protecting you. But all of this hiding and disingenuousness are actually the ways in which people avoid connection in relationships. Sometimes consciously being sensitive to another's needs may mean withholding your own difficult feelings. You have to weigh the needs of the moment. But in general, the energy created when you avoid being genuine—or disguise your own vulnerability so that there is no real connection taking place—is tiring to you and others as well.

If you recognize that this is the case, your first decision is to stop hiding yourself. This means being more open and vulnerable about how you are and being willing to ask for what you need. Of course, you cannot control the behavior of others, but once you have decided not to play it safe, you have several choices: You can consciously allow others to remain in their unconscious, self-protective stance and let the situation follow its own course. You also don't have to be closed or reactive; you can practice moving into the Now and really listening.

You can silently observe that the attitudes and comments of your friends often differ from the way you are choosing to understand and deal with your own situation, but not speak about this with them. Alternatively, you may wish to take the risk of inviting them into the present moment with you. For instance, when a loved one says something like, "Oh well, don't worry; things will probably be better tomorrow," you can invite him or her into your world by gently saying, "I know you love me and you're trying to be encouraging, but what matters more to me is this moment and being here with you."

Your closest relationships are often the ones that have the most effect on you, but they are frequently the ones most difficult to change. These relationships are complex and have long histories. Lifetime habits of avoiding being really present with each other may exist in many of them. Family members, for instance, might want to support you, but will not necessarily know how to genuinely listen or be present with you in a way that is enlivening. As in the case of my mother, even with the best intentions, it can be very difficult to get beyond the past and into the Now.

Speaking Your Truth

The choice then is to find a way to speak what is true for you or to set boundaries on how much time you wish to spend even with those who are closest to you. It can be very painful to accept that some of your family members may also be the most depleting to be with. You will have to decide what is best for you. But at least be clear that what you owe yourself when you are trying to heal, whether it is your body or your spirit, is to respect the truth that presence is your best ally.

It may seem ironic that at a time when you need the most energy, you have to take the risk of challenging some of the oldest relationships in your life. But this is often an essential part of the healing process. It will take courage, but every time you overcome an inhibition to be yourself and take a risk to speak your heart or set an appropriate limit, you gain energy. So don't be afraid to take care of yourself, particularly if you are feeling very tired or drained from a steady stream of well-wishing visitors.

Consider asking a visitor to come back another time or saying, "Let's just be quiet together for a few minutes, okay? I want your company, but I'm feeling quite tired, so it's better for us to connect in silence right now."

Being Present in the Supporting Role

In the previous remarks, I have been writing to you, the reader, as if you are an individual who is ill or has experienced an emotional shock. I have been offering advice on how you can invite relationships that are supportive and energizing for you. But it is just as likely that you could be in the supporting role. Understanding the healing power of presence will be just as important to you in how you offer yourself to someone who could benefit from your energy.

Synchronistically, as I was writing the above paragraph, my phone rang. It was Tom, a young man whose ailing father had recently taken a turn for the worse but seemed stable at the moment. Tom was trying to decide whether to take an important trip he had already committed to and risk leaving town for a week. He knew that his father was in good hands, but he feared being gone if "the worst" were to occur. I suggested that he talk to his father and tell him his plans and concerns.

"But Dad isn't really coherent, and right now he has a tube in his mouth, so he can't talk," Tom countered.

"Things may be scrambled when they come out of him, but that doesn't mean they are scrambled as he listens," I replied. "Why don't you ask him if he is okay with your leaving? If you are worried that he might pass on while you are away, tell him that this is your fear. And take time to share whatever you want him to know about how you feel toward him."

Tom was silent for a while, so I continued: "Are you afraid that if you talk about his death, you will frighten him? We all know that we're going to die, and by pretending that it isn't going to happen—especially at a time when it appears imminent—we miss the opportunity to connect with each other. You'll not only miss connecting with your father but also to your own deeper feelings."

"But if he can't answer me . . ." Tom wondered.

"True—he can't talk right now, but he can communicate in other ways," I assured him. "He can look you in the eyes or nod his head. He can reach out with his good arm. There are many ways he can show you that he is or isn't okay with your going ahead with the trip."

"But what if he's just trying to make me feel okay?"

"You mean if your father won't tell you what he really wants?"

"Yes."

"Isn't that his right?" I asked. "Can't he want for you what you want for yourself? Maybe he wants that even more than whatever he wants for himself. Would you feel guilty if you accepted that gift?"

"I'm not sure."

"Hold his hand or touch his shoulder as you talk to him. Get quiet in yourself, and listen to the space that is created between the two of you. Speak from your heart. Deep down no one wants to be patronized about his or her death, and it will be especially good to share with your dad how important he is to you. That communication isn't just for him; it's for you, too.

"Open your heart, and as you do, you will discover your own feelings more clearly. You'll also communicate a presence that is more than just your words. That presence will be good for you, and in my experience, people who were even in a coma—and your father isn't in a coma—can recognize that kind of subtle energy. You will know if he is hearing you, and I think that as you share yourself, you will know what the right thing to do is."

Tom thanked me as we got off the phone. I learned later that he had subsequently engaged in a wonderful connection with his father. He was able to make the trip, and when he came back, he still had several more months to visit with his dad before he passed away. By that time, Tom had a real sense of completion because he had shared deeply with his father, and there was no unfinished business between them.

The Magic of Conscious Breathing

One of the easiest ways to enrich the field of presence in a relationship is to breathe together. More precisely, it is a matter of synchronizing your inhalations and exhalations with the other person while at the same time keeping your mind from drifting away into thoughts and fantasies. It can help if you maintain eye contact through the process, hold hands, or otherwise touch in some way.

Of course, if it is a situation in which you are visiting someone, perhaps a friend who is ill at home or in a hospital, you can initiate this process yourself even if this person has his or her eyes closed or is asleep. Carefully observe your friend's breathing and begin to match the depth and pace of your own breathing to it as best you can.

As you do so, you may be able to sense a field of presence building. Once you feel this presence, it becomes easier to remain silent and focused, as if the field itself is joining with and supporting your breathing. But even if you don't feel anything unusual, you will notice that you become calmer and more peaceful.

∽∽

In 1985 I published my book *How Shall I Live?* which is about using a health challenge as an opportunity for awakening to deeper consciousness. That book addressed certain themes that I have touched on again in these pages. In particular, as we have discussed briefly in this chapter, there is a tremendous potential to amplify life-force energy when two or more people are gathered with the intent to be fully present together.

Presence, specifically collective energy, is a source of aliveness that is not well understood in contemporary society but is well known in spiritual communities of all persuasions. It is an energy that I am very aware of cultivating in my retreats. A powerful field is created by groups who meditate and worship together, or who create a space of deep listening to themselves and each other.

You can tap into this energy by practicing the synchronized-breathing exercise with a group of people. Since you may not be able to see each other breathing, one person can start by making some kind of visible motion to indicate when to breathe in and when to breathe out. The others can then synchronize to that motion as if they were watching a metronome.

If you are the leader, the motion can be something simple like nodding your head slightly forward as you exhale and bringing it upright as you inhale. Or you can move your hand up and down indicating the same thing. Be sure to keep the speed constant, neither too slow nor too fast, so that everyone present can easily match their breathing to yours. This can become a kind of group prayer in which no words are used, and it can create a strong field of presence.

Whether individually or in a group, you can create this field of presence to share with someone for healing or just as a way of silently offering love. In either case, you may want to lightly touch the person to whom you are sending love.

Breathing together is a wonderful way to create a deeper state of connection in a relationship. Words can take you so far, but by synchronizing your breathing, something happens that causes the energy fields to align very powerfully and simply. For this reason, it can be a highly effective and enjoyable way to rebuild a connection when words have failed—assuming, of course, that both parties are willing.

Deepening Your Connection with Health-Care Providers

Some of the potential to increase life-force energy resides in your ability to invite an energetic connection with the medical professionals or alternative practitioners who may be part of your healing journey. Your doctors, therapists, and other health-care providers carry special knowledge and skills; but, first and foremost, they are fellow human beings. It is important not to let the doctor-patient or therapist-client relationship remain too solid a boundary.

It is essential for you to feel free to ask questions and speak openly about whatever you believe would be respectful of your healing journey. If you are unsure about a treatment that your doctor is recommending for you, one of the best ways to cut through the impersonal tone that pervades professional relationships is to ask if she would also recommend the treatment for herself or for someone else in her family.

Creating a deeper rapport that will bring greater aliveness takes conscious effort and intention. Before I spend time counseling my patients, I sit with them in silence, hold their hands, and bring myself as fully into the Now as I can. I wait for our energies to join, refine, and deepen.

It is unlikely that most professionals you will deal with will make the effort or take the time to create that kind of space with you, but you can still sense the quality of connection you are having with them. If you do not feel that you are making contact at a level that is deeper than just the professional relationship, do not force yourself to work with someone whom you do not feel some kind of rapport with.

In his book *It's Not About the Bike: My Journey Back to Life,* Lance Armstrong discusses the process he went through to find the doctors and treatment center that felt right for him as he faced having metastatic testicular cancer. He could have chosen a very competent doctor and respected medical institution near his home, but when he met the doctor and visited the facility, something felt wrong to him. So he traveled to another facility, and as soon as he walked through the main doors, he had a feeling that told him that he was in the right place. Armstrong underwent an arduous treatment, recovered, and went on to win seven consecutive Tour de France bicycle races.

It is crucial to listen to yourself and trust how you feel. Never underestimate the extra value of feeling a natural or deep rapport with those you choose to help you on your healing journey. Professional competence is important, but the energetic quality or chemistry of your relationship also counts for a lot.

Of course, in our contemporary health-care system, you don't always have a choice. But you have more choice than you may realize. You can choose to seek another doctor, not just for a second opinion, but because you are sensing for the quality difficult to name that tells you that you are in the right place. Even if you are not quite sure that you have found a good match, remember that you are dealing with a human being, not just someone in a white coat with diplomas on the wall.

Just staying in the Now and not being caught in your stories will give you deeper discernment in regards to how the connection is going with your professional health-care givers.

I know of an instance in which one of my students was so present during a hospital stay that followed emergency surgery for a leaking aneurysm that her doctor started checking in on her much more often than seemed necessary. Finally, he admitted that he just liked spending time with her. He wasn't flirting; it was her energy. Needless to say she recovered quickly and, just as important, her time in the hospital was something she truly enjoyed.

CHAPTER THIRTEEN

NEW WINESKINS

You are now on a path that leads you to embody greater aliveness and presence. But as you awaken on this journey, it is essential to use your new energy in creative ways that keep your life force flowing. As Jesus counseled, you must put new wine into fresh wineskins.[1]

There is a generative cycle to the healing journey: as you free yourself from story-created contraction and no longer close down against expansive or dark feelings, you have much more energy. Then as you discover new ways to express and give life to that liberated energy, that creative process in turn frees even more energy. Round and round the cycle goes, and you become more alive and radiant with presence.

Keep in mind that the ego's old habits are never completely overcome, and if the new energy isn't channeled into life-affirming attitudes and activities, the ego will co-opt it and may then intensify its negative and destructive habits of grandiose or depressive specialness. As a result, the emotional and physical healing process will be interrupted.

Speaking to this very issue, the poet Robert Bly told me some years ago that the first thing he did each day upon waking up was write poetry. By doing so, he said, "Then the shadow won't get me." What I think he meant is that the creative process of writing allowed him to channel his subtle and expansive vision as well as the abysmal feelings that he, like anyone, is prone to. Composing poetry is his way to hold both the light and the dark and build a bridge between them. It is not something that he does occasionally; it is a practice he engages every day. Bly was acknowledging that if he didn't make space for this means

221

of expression, the darker feelings could overwhelm him, and his creative vision would become morbid or simply wither.

Bly is one of the founding fathers of the contemporary men's movement, which is an attempt to reintegrate traditional forms of masculinity that have been displaced or eschewed by modernity, particularly over the past few centuries. He is also the author of *Iron John,* one of the seminal books of that movement, which describes the inner journey that allows a man to dissolve his psychological armor by getting in touch with his vulnerable and darker feelings. By doing so, he is restored to his essential masculinity and can also begin to integrate more of his inner feminine nature, thereby achieving a new rapport with women.

In my conversations with Bly, he expressed frustration with a lot of what has become popular in the men's movement, particularly the emphasis on enthusiastically drumming for hours around a fire and getting intoxicated by the group energy. My understanding of his criticism is that he believed the ego had found a way to take the experiences of expansiveness and presence created by such rituals and turn that into an addiction to intensity instead of relaxing its hold on the men's psychology. He felt that many men were willing to get high on, or enjoy the intimacy of, the personal sharing in a group; but most were not really willing to do the laborious, solitary, and very vulnerable work of making their shadow conscious in healthy ways.

How the Shadow Originates

Bly uses the term *shadow* in the way it was originally coined and defined by the psychologist Carl Jung. In Jungian psychology, the shadow is the repository of certain feelings, perceptions, impulses, and urges that are too disruptive to a child's developing ego, and therefore needs to be repressed and buried in the unconscious mind.

This process of repression begins in early life, and every child goes through it. Whatever aspects of the child's self-expression—particularly the more intense displays of moodiness, reactivity, and self-assertion—that cannot be accommodated during the socialization stages of development must be repressed.

Perhaps we can sense our parents' disapproval or even their fears in response to certain behaviors or moods that we have, so we unconsciously bury those parts of ourselves because we dare not risk losing parental acceptance and support. Of course, some of the ways our parents may inhibit us aren't necessarily bad; much is for our own good.

But beyond parental influences, repression—and the resulting formation of the shadow—is necessary so that the incipient ego can achieve a stable foundation. Picture yourself trying to build a sand castle at the edge of the ocean: you need something to protect your structure from the waves, or it will keep being washed away. Repression is the protective shield that keeps the developing ego from being drowned by waves from the unconscious mind. The shadow is virtually everything that is barred from entering the castle (the ego). Because Jung found evidence that the shadow occurs in all people and in all cultures, he called it an *archetype*—a universal symbol and dynamic within the unconscious mind.

In each of us, the basic ego structure that we eventually manifest is as much the result of what has been repressed as it is the expression of what has been allowed to emerge. For instance, feelings of powerlessness or insignificance are particularly likely to be repressed in men whose ego develops more in the direction of appearing strong or powerful—that is, grandiose specialness. In contrast, someone tending toward a more depressive character would have, early in life, unconsciously repressed most aggressive or dominating tendencies. However, in adulthood, these repressed qualities ultimately need to be integrated in order for an individual to mature psychologically and spiritually. This is when the shadow begins to erupt into consciousness, and when it does, it can wreak havoc with a person's ego.

The Shadow in Daily Life

Imagine, for example, that you are talking to your boss, and suddenly he or she says something in a particularly critical tone. Before you know it, you are intensely anxious and your voice seems paralyzed, even though ordinarily you are quick with words and feel confident in most situations. This is the shadow rising up in you.

The shadow interrupts your usual ego patterns. When it surfaces from the unconscious into the conscious mind, it disrupts or, at times, even drowns the ego. It doesn't always make you scared and mute; it can make you fly into a rage and use abusive language. Whoever you thought you were—whatever idealized aspect of your ego you believe yourself to be—is suddenly replaced by a powerfully aggressive alter ego. The shadow can make minor appearances that create brief, embarrassing situations, which cause you to wonder what happened to you—how you became so *unhinged,* or so *not yourself.* These appearances by the shadow might take the form of a petulant outburst, a spontaneous inflammatory comment, or sudden rudeness.

But the shadow can also, at times, break through in fuller force, and when it does, it can be like a tsunami that sweeps away the conscious structures propping up the ego's familiar sense of security and identity. You become flooded with very confusing, troubling feelings and potentially overwhelming images from deep in your unconsciousness. It is often this intense emergence of the shadow that is a crucial step in what, if properly integrated, can become spiritual awakening.

It's important to realize that the shadow is not intrinsically negative. It can contain some of your highest, most unconditionally loving qualities. It can be where your deepest sense of justice and rightness has been hiding. So when the shadow reveals itself, it does not always make you paralyzed or aggressive. It can also bring a conversion experience, such as what happened to John Newton, a British sailor who was captain of a merchant ship that transported slaves. One day at sea during a severe storm, he prayed to God for salvation and was overwhelmed by a sense of amazing grace, the name of the very song he composed some years later after abandoning all involvement with the slave trade.

But whether the energies of the shadow appear to be positive or negative, you cannot awaken and embody your higher self without being able to integrate those energies. I have seen much evidence in my work that leads me to believe that it is the ongoing, unconscious defense against allowing the emergence of the shadow energies (at a point in life when they are needed for psychological and spiritual maturing) that lies at the root of much illness.

Whatever mood or quality the shadow may introduce, you must find a way to make room for it. As we have discussed, the primary skill is to use your focused-spacious awareness to grow large enough to face and hold both your sublime and abysmal feelings. But often this is not enough—or rather, it is only the first step. The next step is to find a way to channel the shadow energies in positive, creative ways that support their integration, just as Robert Bly did by writing poetry each morning.

Channeling the New Aliveness

Poetry is just one way in which your newfound energy can be channeled, thereby enriching your life. Yet anything you do that brings your body into the Now is also a means of building your focused-spacious awareness.

Movement (I am referring to unstructured and untrained dancing) can be a way of expressing aspects of yourself that can come to life in no other manner. As you first learn to explore this mode of expression, you might want to play with visualizing yourself moving like a tiger through the forest or like seaweed drifting to and fro in a listless ocean current. Eventually, you may find that as you let go into movement, the movement itself spontaneously invites images and carries you into states of power and presence. There is a kind of grace when you—the dancer— become the dance.

Of course, if you are dancing with a group of people, how you connect your movements with another can become very playful and creative, erotic, or dramatic. You can explore imitating how another person moves, and by doing so lead yourself into a whole new sense of your own body and being. You can use music or not—sometimes you can move to your own sounds. Once this exploration of movement becomes unselfconscious and spontaneously creative, it can bring so much aliveness and joy. To me, this is when movement has become a kind of prayer.

Singing is another way in which you can give birth to a deeper aliveness, such as when you let go into your own rendition of your favorite songs and lose all sense of self-consciousness (perhaps when you sing karaoke with friends). To initiate such playfulness, you may need to make an effort at first in order to get past any sense of inhibition, but after a while, you may find yourself noticing that your voice seems to be coming both from within *and* around you. You may be surprised by the notes you can hit or how softly you can sing and still maintain a clear tone. And if you take this exploration a step further and relax into spontaneously making up your own lyrics along with your own tunes, the state in which that creativity happens can feel like magic.

Walking can also be a way of letting the deeper aliveness shine forth in you. Being alert and consciously absorbing as many impressions as you can as you walk in nature or through the streets of a city is a way of connecting with the environment and falling deeper into yourself as well. It is a form of active meditation that can immediately increase your endurance, not to mention your pleasure.

In the past when I led people on wilderness retreats, I would teach them to match their breathing to their walking pace. When the slope got steep, I would demonstrate how to maintain the same pace and rate of breathing while shortening our strides. And when my group and I were going downhill, we would keep the same pace and rate of breathing but lengthen our strides. After some practice, walking became being, and being became being at one with the environment: the inner and outer worlds would merge into a unified state of consciousness.

Through this walking practice, individuals who were not particularly well conditioned could hike for a whole day during which they would ascend moderately challenging mountains. Again, at least for me, this is walking that has become a kind of prayer.

Many ordinary activities, such as gardening, can become doorways to higher energy and ways of letting your larger self live through you. Other than willingness—which is the essential element—it is not necessary for you to have special training to explore new ways to let your energy flow. The truest expressions, the ones that liberate the greatest aliveness, often begin spontaneously.

Maybe one day you feel motivated and excited about finally trying something that you have always said you wanted to do, but have never gotten around to actually doing. For example, perhaps a friend invites you to a pottery class or a local amateur theater group and that opens new creative opportunities. If you pay attention to things you hear or see, or that pop unbidden into your mind, sometimes it is life synchronistically pointing you toward the very thing that will open a new door for you.

This happened to me about a year ago. I was out for a run one morning, and a woman I didn't know called out to me and said, "I see that you run and don't just ride your bike." I realized immediately that she had me confused with someone else because I hadn't ridden a bike for years. But a few days later when I prepared to go out for my regular run, I heard her voice in my head. Coincidentally, some months earlier my son had put new tires and tubes on my long-unused bicycle as a Christmas present for me. So instead of running that day, I pumped up the tires and went for a bike ride for the first time in nearly ten years. Since then, bicycling has become a true passion for me, and I find it much easier on my body than running.

The Three Keys to Higher Energy

There are, in my experience, three keys that open the door to moments and even hours of higher energy during which your soul soars and your body is filled with aliveness. The first is **spontaneous creativity:** acting in accordance with your natural feeling without premeditation. It is "letting go and letting flow" in any way that is in harmony with your disposition and uses your natural talents. The second key is **unself-conscious and wholehearted participation:** whatever you do, you do it without holding back; you are totally engaged, fully present, completely authentic. The last key is **grace.** Grace isn't something you do, but something that may unexpectedly join you and carry you beyond yourself once you make your own effort.

There is a direct relationship between effort and grace: first you must make a sincere effort, put forth energy, and let go spontaneously and wholeheartedly into whatever you are doing. That enthusiastic self-expression seems—in the moments of unself-conscious activity—to invite the grace of deeper aliveness that joins you and carries you beyond yourself into new spaces. Suddenly you are effortlessly flowing in your movements or your sounds. You can feel as though your body does not stop at your skin—that you are part of a larger space, a larger being.

In my earlier books, I have written about incidences in my retreats when people became so alive while dancing, singing, or walking that afterward they were filled with silence and love. One woman even experienced complete remission of advanced metastatic cancer when she became completely overcome with love while singing a hymn from her childhood.

There are many therapeutic approaches that use musical resonance and vocal toning to create vibrational states that have been shown to help alleviate pain and produce feelings of well-being.[2] But you do not have to make this a therapy; you can make this kind of exploration a form of play, a way of honoring and shining forth your inner light.

Drawing, painting, or sculpting can also become ways to channel the energy that is awakening in you as you stop letting your stories create your identity. The creative process itself is a birthing of new possibilities from within you and a means of awakening to new dimensions of yourself. There is no specific discipline that you have to follow unless you enjoy taking lessons or having formal instruction. The most important part is not technical skill, but to enjoy yourself and let your ego get out of the way.

Contemplative communities have always known that the energy liberated by prayer, solitude, and silence needs to be given tangible forms of expression. That is why monastic life always sets aside time for chanting, writing, craft work, and other creative endeavors, along with the hard work, community service, and scholarly and research studies expected of the ascetics. Gregor Mendel, the father of modern genetics, was an Augustinian priest and abbot of St. Thomas Abbey, where among his other duties, he experimented on plant and bee breeding. Moreover, in the East, the skill of calligraphy is practiced over and over until the artist's brushstroke is so embodied in the art that a single stroke can symbolize a timeless truth.

The Zen Buddhist tradition emphasizes the development of expressive arts and activities that provide ways to embody the energy that is accessed through the practice of meditation. Archery, crafts, flower arranging, and other forms of creativity are the means to give new "wineskins" to the new wine of awakening consciousness. Still other monastic orders channel their spiritual practice into martial arts. Your own choices are limitless.

If you do explore some form of artistic expression, what you paint, draw, or sculpt does not have to make sense to anyone— not even to you. All that matters is giving yourself over to the process of flow. You let go of control and allow whatever you are sensing or feeling, as well as whatever may come to you as visions and images, take some creative form. Eventually, you may discover that what at first seemed to be random or meaningless becomes a doorway to your inner genius.

᎓᎓

Embarking on new forms of self-expression can be scary, and making the effort can test your willingness to trust yourself and can even lead you right up to some of your abysmal feelings. But if that happens, it becomes an opportunity to take the energy of those feelings and release them through your voice (or through movement, drawing, or writing) instead of letting them fester in you.

All of these ways of giving expression to your life force are a means of having a relationship with yourself but also potentially with others. You don't have to have an audience, but I have found it valuable to imagine that you are sharing with others. It can be your children, grandchildren, friends, or just people in general whom you want to offer something to. It can even be to a higher force: you can sing, dance, draw, or write as a way of conversing with God. All that matters is that you are enabling yourself to express, and not suppress, your aliveness. Remember that it is the doing that is important and the energy it sets free in you—not what you actually create.

This is a primal act of self-invention. Once you let go into the creative process, you cannot know where it will guide you. Unlike the ego, which always leads you to what it already knows, this is a way to lead yourself to a new appreciation of yourself and the world. The energy you set free can open your heart and fill you with strength, love, and compassion. It *can* heal you.

Taking the Risk of Yourself

To know yourself, you have to show yourself. You must risk expressing your authentic self, whether with words, sounds, movements, or drawings. If you are going to support your own healing, you cannot bottle up your energy.

This is a path that has been central in my life and teaching. When I was still practicing medicine, but sensing a call to move on to something else, I had a life-changing dream. In it, I was with one of my patients who, in real life, had been instrumental in opening my eyes to acupuncture and alternative medicine. She and I were at a dinner club in the dream, and a trio of musicians was performing. Suddenly I was onstage singing popular songs that I had memorized, with the three musicians backing me up. Then there was a shift, and I was singing songs that I had composed sometime in the past, and only the pianist was accompanying me. The dream shifted again, and this time I was alone on the stage singing a cappella and improvising completely new songs, spontaneously composing the melody and lyrics. When I stopped singing, there was only silence and a powerful presence. My whole body was charged with energy. I returned to the woman, who handed me an apple and said, "Welcome."

Awakening from the dream, I realized that practicing medicine was singing the songs I had learned from others. I understood, too, that I often lived from my past, sharing ideas over and over again that I had formulated long before. Because of the dream, I understood that there was another step to be taken: to discover my own original voice; to build my life from the inside out, moment by moment.

Essential to that, I would gradually learn, was to integrate the light and dark within me—in biblical metaphor, to eat of the tree of knowledge of good and evil. Shortly after having that dream, I resigned from my medical practice to see where life would lead me. It was not long before some of my old patients found their way to my door, which eventually led to my work as a teacher.

Letting Your Essence Shine Through

When you are no longer the doer, that is when something deeper within you begins to live through you. This is a state of remarkable aliveness. This is what every athlete, artist, and writer has discovered at some time in his or her career. For me, it was during the many extemporaneous talks I have had since becoming a teacher: I have heard myself saying things that I had never consciously formulated or even thought of before. I came to recognize the truth in many of the things I heard myself say, and those new understandings became additional guidelines for my life and teaching.

When you become a vehicle for your inner wisdom, you are witness to an inner creator, and that experience gives you faith in yourself and a sense of marvel about what is hidden within you that, given a chance, can live through you. It also offers you profound appreciation for all those who have let their deeper aliveness and inner genius be born through them.

When we are urged to express ourselves in these ways, some of us may understandably become quite afraid. Chances are, we were criticized at vulnerable times in our lives and lost trust in expressing our natural creativity. But if we are on a journey of healing, we can find within ourselves the energy of the playful child or the wise muse and let them guide us. This does not have to be serious business—it requires that we take a risk, but it is a risk that pays tremendous dividends.

When you *stop* taking the risk of giving expression to your deeper energy, that is when the trouble starts, for you obstruct a fundamental way of discovering who you are. When your ego tells you that you have no talent or skill or nothing to say, or that what you do is not good enough or is a waste of time, and you buy into its fear, criticism, and cynicism, you shut down your life force. And then that energy, with no way to be healthily channeled, can become negative and even turn against you.

I suspect that many forms of illness—in particular, autoimmune diseases—originate in the ego's self-inhibiting habits that obstruct the healthy flow of life force. Without good pathways for self-expression, repressed energy becomes disease. I suspect this is why, in my retreats, as the participants discover how to set their deeper energy free, so many of them noticeably improve their health.

Since I know that many people have a deep fear of risking embarrassment or humiliation and, rarely, if ever, allow themselves to be spontaneously creative, part of the work during my retreats is about inviting each person to learn how to channel the new energy that is awakening in them. One way that is particularly useful—especially during the rest days when everyone has lots of time to relax and self-reflect—is to explore writing, including writing poetry.

Spontaneous Creativity Through Writing

Writing, of course, is a powerful way to creatively channel emotion and feeling, or to give life to your perceptions and ideas. If you allow yourself to pursue writing, what matters is that you are willing to risk the creative process—that you are willing to make the effort to challenge yourself. What doesn't matter is whether what you write is "good" by anyone's standards, including your own.

Here is what I suggest to the participants in my retreats and seminars, and you can explore it for yourself if you wish (note that you will need a notebook or journal of some kind): Spend some time sitting in one place, outside in nature if possible, and notice as much as you can about that tiny piece of the world. Next, write a poem, drawing inspiration from what you observe in your environment and giving written voice to your inner state.

You may want to start by composing a haiku, a form of Japanese poetry that uses 17 *morae* or sound phrases (what we would call syllables, although it is not quite identical) organized in three lines of 5-7-5 syllables. Here is an example of a haiku, using one of my own creations:

> *The bird's darting flight*
> *Insects caught for hungry mouths*
> *Death renewing life*

Poetry in general and haiku in particular are ways of reaching to the core of your seeing, both outwardly and inwardly, and then translating that into a mode that uses words. It is a way of conveying through language precise images while sensing a larger theme that unites those particular images.

In this book, you have seen how often it is words, and stories in particular, that get you into trouble. In the writing that I propose you explore, words can also be redeeming. You can practice using haiku, or some form of metaphorical expression, to learn to channel your inner world—to express creatively whatever feelings or states of being you may spontaneously find yourself in—instead of letting the ego take it over.

If you are feeling lonely, instead of writing "I am lonely," or trying to write *about* being lonely and thereby identifying more with it, you can let loneliness initiate a poem. You can choose images from the world around you that help you write about loneliness metaphorically.

You might observe a solitary tree and start with that as a symbol for loneliness. Then perhaps you can see that the tree isn't really alone and maybe write: "A solitary tree / never refusing the sun's warmth / uncomplaining in the wind / in solemn dignity stands / a lone sentinel beneath the ever-changing sky." This is a poetic way to let your inner world and outer world begin to unite in creative collaboration. It is a kind of intimate dance of impressions and feelings translated into words that allows new associations and movements of feeling and appreciation for life and for yourself. Not only have you prevented yourself from plunging into loneliness, but you have also creatively channeled that feeling and allowed it to lead you to a new space.

This is something you can do anywhere: you can stay present and take even the most vulnerable feelings and let them become the inspiration for a poem, drawing, or song. One of the most powerful things is to speak or sing out loud and hear your own voice giving expression to a feeling without collapsing into that feeling.

This is what songwriters do: they start from their own passion or angst or outrage. The best songs speak of feelings that we all understand and put them into some kind of context we recognize. You can learn to write your own poems or sing your own songs and hear your voice discovering the words you didn't know you would say or sing until they started flowing forth from you.

One simple guideline is very important: avoid using the words *I* or *me*. This means that you do not refer to yourself in the first person. By not using the first person, there is less identification with what is written or said. If you want to write about yourself, refer to yourself as "he" or "she," "him" or "her," or use your name. This gives you distance, as if you are looking *at* yourself instead of caught up *in* yourself.

Becoming Radically Alive

In essence, all that has been said here about using new forms of expression—new wineskins for the new wine of your awakening energy—has been a way of inviting and encouraging you to engage in creative play. Children play constantly; they run, tumble, and dive through the air, all along delighting in some self-invented reality. They add sound effects and sing with little if any inhibition about using their voices. A child's play is a form of prayer, an unself-conscious way of celebrating being alive. When children stop playing, they stop thriving.

The majority of adults have for the most part lost the ability to play for fun or to play innocently. Hopefully, as you have been reading, you have taken in the injunctions to not be self-critical, to not have to prove anything, and to accept that whatever you create does not have to make sense. Throw away the scorecard, and enjoy developing your natural gifts. But don't let whatever you begin to enjoy become the basis for a new identity. Writing doesn't have to make you a writer, nor dancing a dancer, nor singing a singer. They are just ways you can relearn how to play and be alive.

Prayer, too, can be a form of spontaneous creativity that allows you to access new energy. Prayer doesn't have to be traditional, supplicative, or even religious. How many ways can you find to say *Thank you* or *Yes*? How many ways can you find to talk to Life or God or your deeper self about the heartache, love, and power of some of your own experiences and feelings?

One of the most moving of all spiritual practices is learning to let your heart speak or sing spontaneously: to praise life, your family, your friends, yourself, and even your enemies. You can praise God or even argue with God. Once, while I was in Egypt, I was able to witness a Sufi sect that used a form of worship where a group of men sat in a room simultaneously speaking aloud their questions, heartache, anger, and gratitude to God. The presence in that room was palpable.

When your voice and heart are united in deeply felt speech or song, there are few prayers more powerful. The gates of heaven can open to you. Perhaps you don't believe you can do this; maybe you think you don't know how. But as a teacher who has been opening these doors to people for more than 30 years, I can assure you that indeed you can. You just have to be willing to take the risk of yourself.

This is really what it comes down to: risking to let yourself become radically alive. It will help you heal. At the very least, it may soothe your body and take away pain. Being that alive, even if only for a matter of moments, may actually cure you of illness. But even if that doesn't happen, your heart will be overflowing with gratitude. And there is no medicine more powerful than the energy of your own grateful heart.

AFTERWORD

I have spent nearly 35 years listening to men and women speak candidly about their deepest life questions, from their heart-wrenching struggles to their greatest hopes. I have accompanied many people through difficult separations, assisted numerous others in rebuilding their lives, and helped still others prepare for death.

Together, we have laughed and cried about ourselves and reflected on the human condition and what we are collectively doing to the planet. In one way or another, what each of these individuals lived and suffered represented and spoke for a part of myself. And the experiences I invited them into, and the path I offered by which they found their own answers, was the path that I myself have walked. It is what this book has been about.

You and I, dear reader, will be gone soon; our lifetimes are hardly the blink of an eye in cosmic time. But the earth and our descendants will be here after us. Honoring that fact, one question worth each of us asking ourselves is, "What has been the legacy of my life?"

I believe that the legacy we all leave is the quality of the presence we have lived. In this book, I have offered a path by which to live an emotionally intelligent life—a way of understanding how to forgive the past, transmute destructive emotions, and embrace a new life in each new moment.

You have seen that freedom is how you accept your own un-knowing and pain. It is how you step back from your judgments of yourself and others and allow life to deeply touch you in each moment. It is how you grow spacious enough to hold your darkest feelings instead of running from them.

For each of us, the legacy of our presence is an emanation that can influence the lives of others. It is a field of intelligence in which others find breathing room to realize themselves and life more completely. Our field can be a space for greater well-being, compassion, and wisdom that others can bathe in without ever necessarily realizing the source. Even after we are gone, what we have helped awaken in them continues to live through them and becomes part of their field and ultimately their legacy.

✿✿

Years ago, I did an experiment involving partial sensory deprivation. On several occasions I asked groups of people, sometimes as many as 60, to lie down on individual mattresses in a big room. All of the participants put on blindfolds and wore earplugs. This particular experiment lasted for two days and nights. During that time, there was no talking. There were no meals, but water was always available. Occasionally, a few ripe grapes or raspberries were left in a small bowl near each person's mattress. The participants could do whatever they wished, provided they stayed on their mattresses. People stretched; did yoga; meditated; drifted in reverie; and, of course, slept. The only time anyone left their mattress was to go—still blindfolded and with earplugs—to the bathroom.

A team of people assisted me around the clock, taking four-hour shifts in the room and then four hours of rest. The team members silently delivered the bowls of fruit, refilled the water bottles, and were always present in case anyone had a particular need. They were watchful whenever one of the participants went to the bathroom, but did not assist unless there was some danger. All of the participants knew that they were being cared for and were safe.

Afterward, the individuals who underwent this exploration described becoming deeply still within themselves. Many remarked that the fruit exploded with flavor in their mouths, a vividness of taste they had never experienced before. Some spoke of how refined and intensified their senses of smell and touch became; and others described a sensation like swirling clouds of gentle turbulence moving through them, which they presumed were caused by people crawling or walking past them.

But something the participants could not see, which became very evident to me, was how sensitive they became to even the slightest disturbance in the energy field within the room. For example, at one point a man got up from his mattress, seemed a little restless, and then carefully began to make his way along the rope lying on the floor that led to the bathroom. A few moments after he sat up on his mattress, his ex-wife, who was on a mattress quite far from him, began to stir. As he quietly made his way on hands and knees to the bathroom, she sat up, seemed strangely agitated, and then she too began to crawl to the bathroom. Because he had much farther to go to reach the door into the hallway that led to the bathroom and she was coming from much closer, they ran into each other at the door.

Immediately, they both realized who it was they had bumped into even though they could not see or hear each other. I could see their recognition and amazement. To me, it seemed more than an unusual coincidence. In fact, I had been observing something equally as fascinating: From the evening of the first day and then throughout the whole rest of the time, no matter how quiet and centered the team members were as they traded shifts, the participants sensed something and became restless. Whereas midshift, only an occasional individual would get up to go to the bathroom, the moment the rested team arrived to relieve the on-duty team, as many as 15 participants would suddenly become restless and start crawling to the facilities.

Try to picture the comedic procession of a dozen or more adults rousing themselves all at once, crawling from their different places, and converging en masse on the hallway, thereby resulting in a full-blown traffic jam. The team members had to guide the participants one at a time to the bathroom and then lead them back around the others who were still awaiting their turn. Accommodating everyone easily took half an hour, and during that time, both teams were needed. The only thing I could determine that provoked this mass restlessness was the slight change in the field as the teams traded places.

This did not happen on only some of the shift changes; it happened every time without fail. Each of the six or so occasions when I offered this exercise during a retreat, the same phenomenon occurred.

I describe this observation to point out just how deeply interconnected we actually are and do not realize it. Your experience right now—how you feel in your body, aspects of your state of mind or your mood, probably even your health—is emerging out of a collective field of consciousness. Said in another way, your presence matters a lot. You are your brother's keeper, whether you choose to be or not.

Perhaps this is more responsibility than you want. On the other hand, it means that maybe the greatest gift, or certainly service, you can share—and this, I believe, is your true legacy—is the quality of your presence.

Throughout this book, you have learned that you can take responsibility for your emotional state by stepping back from your stories and returning to the Now. You have seen that there is nothing to fear but your reaction to fear. You have gained strength and understand that you no longer need to be afraid of any feeling. You have learned to let your emotional mud settle and return to clear, spacious awareness.

I am not claiming that we can become completely clear of our emotions. I know that I still become angry about the folly and injustice in the world. I still feel distressed about the correctable forms of human ignorance that go on, generation after generation, uncorrected. And at times, my ego commandeers my emotions, although nowadays such times are very brief.

What is the way through? We each need to take a stand and do our best to stop identifying with our thoughts, especially those that close our hearts. We each need to make a space for all of our feelings. These are forms of correctable ignorance that must change if we are to mature spiritually as a species. And while we may not always live in complete joy and peace, our field can become much more spacious, and we can emanate a catalytic presence that supports the transformation of others. It is a worthwhile legacy, a testament to a life well lived.

At the end of the Introduction to this book, I said that presence is contagious and it is the epidemic we need. Now that you know how to deepen your individual presence, let us go out together and infect as many as we can.

I am deeply grateful to have been able to share this work with you.

APPENDIX:
THE MUDDY ME WORKSHEET

Name the issue: As succinctly as possible (like giving a title to a book or a short story), name the issue.

Briefly describe the issue: In a short paragraph, describe what the issue involves.

Frame the issue for inquiry: To frame an issue for inquiry using the power of awareness presupposes that you are willing to accept that it is your own thinking about the issue that is the source of your distress. Using the Mandala of Being™ as a map for understanding how you leave the Now and lose connection to your aware self, ask yourself, "What am I telling myself about myself, others, the past, and the future that makes me so muddy?"

Gently turn your attention inward and become receptive to what this question helps you see. Then, to further assist you in your inquiry, fill in the following sections for each of the four directions of the Mandala of Being. Use a separate sheet of paper if necessary. (*Note:* the following examples are just suggestions to catalyze the investigation. Your own stories may have many other formulations.)

Me stories: What thoughts/beliefs/judgments am I telling myself about myself regarding this issue?

I should be _____

_____

_____ .

I shouldn't be _____

_____

_____ .

I need to have _____

_____

_____ in order to feel good about myself.

I need to do _____

_____

_____ in order to feel good about myself.

I always _____

_____

_____ .

I never _____

_____

_____ .

(Use this space to write other Me stories about this issue.)

In the space below, describe what feelings/emotions/images these Me stories create. Hint: try to answer with one word or very short phrases (for example, *small, furious, tired,* or *as if I am nothing*). Avoid creating new stories.

You stories: What thoughts/beliefs/judgments am I telling myself about the specific person or situation (job, money, fatigue, health issue, and so on)?

I believe _____

_____ should be _____

_____

_____ .

I believe _____

_____ shouldn't be _____

_____

_____ .

I need _____

_____ to be/not to be _____

_____

_____ .

(Use this space to write additional You stories about this issue.)

In the space below, write what feelings/emotions/images these You stories create. (Remember to try to answer in one word or short phrases.)

Past stories: What thoughts/beliefs/judgments about the past am I telling myself regarding this issue?

If only I had/hadn't done/said/avoided _____

_____

_____

_____ , then this would not be an issue for me.

If only (he/she/they) _____

_____ had/hadn't done/said/avoided _____

_____

_____ ,then this would not be an issue for me.

I remember _____

_____ , and my thoughts about that memory are that

_____

_____ .

(Use this space to write additional Past stories about this issue.)

In the space below, write what feelings/emotions/images these Past stories create.

Future stories: What am I telling myself about the future regarding this issue?

I am hopeful that _____

_____

_____

_____ .

I am afraid that _____

_____

_____

_____ .

I believe (I/he/she/they) will/won't_____

_____

_____

_____ .

(Use this space to write additional Future stories about this issue.)

In the space below, write what feelings/emotions/images these Future stories create.

ENDNOTES

Chapter 1

1. It has also been documented that patients with multiple personalities will have allergic responses in one personality and not in another. An even more dramatic example is that of a woman, admitted to a hospital for diabetes, who "baffled her physicians by showing no symptoms of the disorder at times when one personality, who was not diabetic, was dominant" (Goleman, 1985).

   D. Goleman, "New Focus on Multiple Personality," *The New York Times,* May 21, 1985.

   FW Putnam et al., "Multiple Personality Disorder in a Hospital Setting," *Journal of Clinical Psychiatry,* 45:4, April 1984.

Chapter 2

1. It is beyond the scope of this discussion to examine the many complex circumstances that affect how a child develops his or her own sense of specialness. There are so many influences, tangible and intangible, that affect the amount and quality of attention a child receives, such as the number of siblings parents must divide their energies among to mention just one. I have discussed how children develop their sense of self and their ego defenses in my book *The Mandala of Being* (Novato, CA: New World Library, 2007).

Chapter 3

1. In fact, this is true. When you are present, not looking out at life through the filter of the ego, every moment is always completely new and original. In contrast, your ego cannot imagine a new experience; therefore, it can never imagine a new future. It can only project some form of what it already knows. Ego converts everything that you are living, including your sense of yourself,

into something old and familiar and doesn't free you to have a new relationship with your actual and immediate experience.

2. Studies made on the relationship between language and health, for instance, indicate a connection between physical health, sense of control, and "symptom labeling." That is, a patient's sense of control affected the way he or she experienced and labeled bodily sensations as symptoms relevant to health or illness. Specifically, people who have less of a sense of control are more apt to label a physical sensation as a "symptom" of illness. Likewise, the label given to a particular physical sensation will affect the degree of control a person feels about it. For example, a patient with a stomachache can either say, "My stomach hurts" (a bodily sensation), or "I am getting the flu" (a symptom of an illness). This type of labeling determines a great deal about how the person approaches dealing with his or her situation.

    J. Rodin, "Aging and Health: Effects of the Sense of Control," *Science*, vol. 233, September 19, 1986, pp.1271–1276.

Chapter 4

1. I have written about this in my books *The Black Butterfly* (Berkeley, CA: Celestial Arts, 1987) and *The Second Miracle* (Berkeley, CA: Celestial Arts, 1995).

Chapter 5

1. In the instructions for working with the Mandala of Being, you will notice that I say, "When you stand in the Now position," "Step to the You position," or "Take a step back to the Now position." The instructions to *stand, step,* or *step back* actually refer to physically moving to a specific position on the Mandala. I have always taught the Mandala work as a combination of mental contemplation and positional changes because by moving the body, you appreciate the distinctions between the states of consciousness at each position.

    There is much evidence in children that learning is facilitated by movement and that children need to physically experience concepts in order to learn them. For more information, I suggest that readers search "Movement and Learning" on the Internet.

    In an article published in *Psychological Science,* authors Koch, Holland, Hengstler, and Knippenberg report that cognitive control is improved by literally taking a step back. See also: **http://scienceblogs.com/developingintelligence/2009/05/cognitive_control_improves_by.php.**

2. In the Mandala of Being, the Me and You positions are a continuum of subject-object consciousness, which we have already discussed briefly. In a continuum, neither side exists independent of its complement: there can be no *me* without *you* and vice versa. In meditative traditions, deep sleep is referred to as "objectless" awareness. This means that in deep sleep, you lose all consciousness of being a separate self—the egoic *me*. Therefore, there are no images, sensations, or thoughts, either—just the blankness of deep sleep.

   Sometimes the state of fundamental realization or enlightenment is described as consciousness-without-an-object and as well, consciousness-without-a-subject, although in this case the individual is not asleep but in a super-aware state.

   For a more complete discussion of subject-object consciousness, take a look at my previous books *The Second Miracle* (Berkeley, CA: Celestial Arts, 1995) and *The Mandala of Being* (Novato, CA: New World Library, 2007).

   Also, for a discussion of consciousness-without-an-object, see: Franklin Merrell-Wolff, *Experience and Philosophy: A Personal Record of Transformation and a Discussion of Transcendental Consciousness* (Albany, NY: SUNY Press, 1994).

Chapter 7

1. Many readers are familiar with the use of positive affirmations. My consideration of this technique is pragmatic: if you are drowning in negative thoughts about yourself, using positive affirmations such as *I am completely healthy* or *I am a beautiful, desirable woman [or man]* can be an important and effective way to temporarily balance the scales and pull you out of the negative posture. However, this does not address the deeper issue, which is that you are still at the level of the ego's stories about you. Even if you are reversing the negative to the positive or asserting a deeper truth—for example, that you are, indeed, in your essence, completely healthy—you are doing this with thought, and invariably, thought is an instrument of the ego.

   I believe there are two basic kinds of "positive" affirmations. First, there is a spontaneous emergence of self-recognition, such as realizing "I am completely healthy" that arises unbidden without any conscious intent. Immediately, you *know* that you are completely healthy. You could be on your deathbed or have an incurable illness, and this inner knowing instantly brings you to a state of well-being and wholeness. It may or may not change your health, but such recognition is not really about physical health; it is about the intrinsic health of who you always and actually are as an aware being.

In contrast, when you intentionally employ a positive affirmation, it is always inferior in its healing power to what arises spontaneously. Why would you—other than to restore a temporary balance as mentioned above—need to affirm something positive about yourself, except that a part of you believes the opposite and is frightened of your own self-judgments and the emotions they create? Even though you can temporarily restore a feeling of well-being by using positive affirmations, you are nonetheless subconsciously affirming the negative judgments, too. As soon as the effect of the positive affirmation wears off, the negative will be there once again, at least until you truly know it is false. Then, of course, you no longer need a positive affirmation.

The deeper work is to see that you are neither the negative nor positive affirmation—these are just thoughts—and as in the work already described, you can learn to let them both go and taste your true state of uncontaminated awareness in the Now.

Chapter 8

1. Richard Moss, *The I That Is We* (Berkeley, CA: Celestial Arts, 1981); *The Black Butterfly; The Second Miracle; The Mandala of Being.*

Chapter 9

1. The translation of the Tibetan name for this exercise is "The Cross of Gold." I changed the name because I did not want the confusion of associating this practice with the image of Jesus on the cross.

Chapter 13

1. Matthew 9:17 (American Standard Version Bible). The whole quote is: "Neither do men put new wine into old wineskins: else the skins burst, and the wine is spilled, and the skins perish: but they put new wine into fresh wineskins, and both are preserved."

2. I invite the reader to search the following topics online: "Resonance Healing" and "Resonance Therapy." There are numerous websites that describe the various forms this can take.

ACKNOWLEDGMENTS

I am very grateful to Susan Jane Griffin. Through hours of recorded discussions and using material from my earlier book *How Shall I Live?* she created the first rough draft of this book. Without that beginning, this project would have been much more challenging. Later, she gave the manuscript many careful edits and made many improvements in its readability before it went to the publisher.

I am especially thankful for the many hours my wife, Ariel, spent reading and editing. She was the voice that kept reminding me of how vulnerable people are when they are ill or struggling in a life crisis, and that a book like this needs deep sensitivity as well as clarity. Her thoughtfulness and sensibility have significantly enriched the tone of love and compassion we together strived to bring to this work.

I am also very grateful to Three Mountain Foundation and its donors for their generous support of this project.

I want to thank my business manager, Randy Collett, for his friendship and helpfulness with my work and this book. Also special thanks to James Twyman for introducing me to Reid Tracy, the president of Hay House. It has been a pleasure working with Reid and with Jill Kramer and Lisa Mitchell, my editors at Hay House. Thanks, too, to Ann Hillman, Annalisa Mather, Lisa Luckenbach, and Tom Pike for reading the manuscript and giving me helpful feedback. Finally, kudos to Matt Dale for help in formatting the diagrams.

To all the people who have participated in my seminars and mentoring programs, you were always present in me as I wrote. There are elements of your lives and stories on nearly every page of this book. I can think of few greater privileges than to have been able to share this work with you and learn with and from you.

෴ ෴ ෴

ABOUT THE AUTHOR

Richard Moss received his doctorate of medicine in 1972, but eventually left that career after a life-changing realization led him to his true calling: the exploration of consciousness and the integration of self-realization in daily life. For more than 30 years, he has been a guide to people from diverse backgrounds and disciplines in living a path of love and wisdom. He is the author of six seminal books about consciousness transformation, self-healing, and presence. He lives in Ojai, California, with his wife, Ariel.

For a calendar of future seminars and talks by the author, and for further information about his CDs, DVDs, and other available material, please visit **www.richardmoss.com** or contact **info@ richardmoss.com**.

To visit his European website, which is in French, please go to: **www.richardmosseurope.com** or e-mail: **r.moss.europe@live.com**.

⌘ ⌘ ⌘

NOTES

NOTES

HAY HOUSE TITLES OF RELATED INTEREST

YOU CAN HEAL YOUR LIFE, the movie,
starring Louise L. Hay & Friends
(available as a 1-DVD program and an expanded 2-DVD set)
Watch the trailer at: **www.LouiseHayMovie.com**

THE SHIFT, the movie, starring Dr. Wayne W. Dyer
(available as a 1-DVD program and an expanded 2-DVD set)
Watch the trailer at: **www.DyerMovie.com**

ॐ ॐ

DEFY GRAVITY: Healing Beyond the Bounds of Reason,
by Caroline Myss

*EXCUSES BEGONE! How to Change Lifelong, Self-Defeating Thinking
Habits,* by Dr. Wayne W. Dyer

HOW YOUR MIND CAN HEAL YOUR BODY,
by David R. Hamilton, Ph.D.

*INSPIRATION DEFICIT DISORDER: The No-Pill Prescription to End
High Stress, Low Energy, and Bad Habits,* by Jonathan H. Ellerby, Ph.D.

*THE MAP: Finding the Magic and Meaning
in the Story of Your Life,* by Colette Baron-Reid

THE POWER IS WITHIN YOU, by Louise L. Hay

*THIS IS THE MOMENT! How One Man's Yearlong Journey
Captured the Power of Extraordinary Gratitude,* by Walter Green

All of the above are available at your local bookstore,
or may be ordered by contacting Hay House (see next page).

ॐ ॐ

We hope you enjoyed this Hay House book. If you'd like to receive our online catalog featuring additional information on Hay House books and products, or if you'd like to find out more about the Hay Foundation, please contact:

Hay House, Inc., P.O. Box 5100, Carlsbad, CA 92018-5100
(760) 431-7695 or (800) 654-5126
(760) 431-6948 (fax) or (800) 650-5115 (fax)
www.hayhouse.com® • **www.hayfoundation.org**

ぷぷ

Published and distributed in Australia by: Hay House Australia Pty. Ltd., 18/36 Ralph St., Alexandria NSW 2015 • *Phone:* 612-9669-4299 *Fax:* 612-9669-4144 • www.hayhouse.com.au

Published and distributed in the United Kingdom by: Hay House UK, Ltd., 292B Kensal Rd., London W10 5BE • *Phone:* 44-20-8962-1230 *Fax:* 44-20-8962-1239 • www.hayhouse.co.uk

Published and distributed in the Republic of South Africa by: Hay House SA (Pty), Ltd., P.O. Box 990, Witkoppen 2068 • *Phone/Fax:* 27-11-467-8904 info@hayhouse.co.za • www.hayhouse.co.za

Published in India by: Hay House Publishers India, Muskaan Complex, Plot No. 3, B-2, Vasant Kunj, New Delhi 110 070 • *Phone:* 91-11-4176-1620 *Fax:* 91-11-4176-1630 • www.hayhouse.co.in

Distributed in Canada by: Raincoast, 9050 Shaughnessy St., Vancouver, B.C. V6P 6E5 • *Phone:* (604) 323-7100 *Fax:* (604) 323-2600 • www.raincoast.com

ぷぷ

Take Your Soul on a Vacation

Visit **www.HealYourLife.com®** to regroup, recharge, and reconnect with your own magnificence. Featuring blogs, mind-body-spirit news, and life-changing wisdom from Louise Hay and friends.

Visit **www.HealYourLife.com** today!

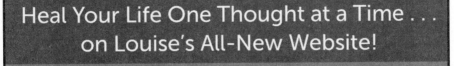